I WISH I HADN'T WRITTEN THIS

*An Archive of Being Too Online in
the Culture Wars, 2016-2019*

Sam White

CONTENTS

INTRODUCTION

From the middle of 2016 to around the end of 2019, I became very online, and very politically outspoken. I started a blog, fired off polemics to well known publications, a few of which were accepted, and spent hour after hour on Twitter. My opinions went against mainstream, progressive orthodoxy, I was combative and sarcastic, and something unexpected happened: I gained traction, and watched my follower count rise. It was far from stratospheric, no big deal, but also not bad for someone with no relevant qualifications and no media appearances, basically just mouthing off on the internet.

Gradually, though, it all came to seem pointless. The positions I'd staked were overcooked. Anti-tribalists (of whom I'd considered myself one, when I wasn't following conservatives lines) were an increasingly obnoxious tribe in themselves, and it was as obvious as a cricket bat to the ribs that arguing online was deleterious to one's mental well-being and personal development.

I started to feel like I was brain damaged, and shackled to a screen, while only a fraction of what I said online represented who I was in real life. Deleting all my tweets, which I did regularly, was the most satisfying aspect of the routine by this stage.

The jokes were all hackneyed, the arguments circular, the passive aggressive sarcasm grinding. The same back and forths, about the same subjects, over and over again. And even after I deleted tweets, I'd only go and rack up some more, knowing they too were soon to be flushed.

And now there were new voices, not known for politics, but famous for acting or comedy, and backed by fuck-you money, coming along and making all the same worn-out points and tired jokes as had already been made for years by anonymous online malcontents, while being heartily slapped on the back for it by the very people the lines were stolen from.

Well, good, I suppose. I should have been glad, because they were echoing us now, so that means we won, doesn't it?

Now let's never speak of it again.

Except that then, you look on Twitter, and nothing has changed, other than a ramping up of intensity and aggression. It's somehow just a little darker now, as if no-one has won anything, or ever can, but everyone has been pushed to further extremes.

The professional culture warriors are biased and hypocritical, morally bankrupt, and behave mechanically: every statement, reaction and counter-reaction is predictable.

And you realise, this isn't what you supported, this wasn't it at all. The online rotation never ends, so you finally get it: you just have to step off.

But what of all that writing I'd done, over weeks and months, turning into years? I don't want it hanging around without explanation, misrepresenting who I am and what I believe to anyone who might look. But I also don't want to delete it forever, and anyway, much of it also exists on domains over which I have no control.

So I decided the best thing is to package it all up in a book—compartmentalised, if you like—and then it can be put away on the shelf for good.

Don't get me wrong, the writing itself is not bad. I wouldn't want to preserve it if it were. Over-the-top? Too many adjectives? Partisan and misguided? Sure, after all, it was a war or something. But occasionally correct. And even when wrong, still, certainly, a reflection of how things were, and of how social media can warp its users, and drag a person away from their own centre.

So, yeah, not bad, but at the same time... looking back at what I wrote... I hate it. I mean, it's worth keeping. But I hate it. What a way to introduce a book, hey? *Here's a platter of compositions I'm revolted by and want shot of. Bon appetit.*

A contradiction fitting for the digital derangement from which it all came. None of it was worth the effort. But it was, at the time, what got written.

So here is an archive, of things not to remember. Of three and a half years of being far too online.

PART ONE

2016: INTRODUCTION

B rexit happened. For me, that's how this all began. Or rather, Brexit and the reaction to it. I'm not even kidding. If Remain had won, or if Leave had won and the left-wing media had accepted the result and moved on, I might still be reading the Guardian every day. Or maybe not. But either way, it was amazement at the overwrought reaction to the result that yanked me out of the left-wing rabbit hole and plunged me down any right-wing burrow you might care to mention.

Freshly *red-pilled*, as they used to say, which really means nothing more than suddenly right-wing. Obsessed with reason. But on the road to losing all reason.

There is nothing like the zeal of an apostate, and I was convinced that the entire left wing had gone from being a good thing that I identified with, to being—at best—demonically infuriating. And here's something else: the right wing is waiting, to let you know that your *new* instincts are correct. Because if you're not one thing, then you must be the other, right? *Right?*

There are people who enjoy zeal as much as they profess to hate it, as long as it's *their kind of zeal*, and zeal against the zealous is no exception. So there I was. Zealously anti-zealous, all my biases shot through, but being efficiently replaced with a full set of brand new ones, to be reinforced daily in the bearish online trench into which I'd tripped.

The political writing that went up on my blog starts in October of 2016. How pissed off I must have been, to have then consistently hammered out that much opinion, although I'm honestly not sure where I found the time, what with all the snarking on Twitter.

And though I found it out by accident rather than design, that's how you get attention on social media. Attacks, spats, outrage, output. And it helps if everyone else is fired up, fractured and spoiling for a fight too.

That would be another tip, actually, if I were offering cynical advice on how to build your follower count: you can keep your powder dry sometimes if you like, but don't hesitate when there is a huge blow-up in the news. Tragedy, terror, celebrity handbags, whatever, at moments when it's all kicking off, just dive in with extreme partisanship, and start hammering away at your counterparts on the other side. Such times, in the online frenzy, are when people have no emotional control, pound the likes and retweets, and follow anyone who looks to be voicing or amplifying the viewpoints with which they agree.

If I were offering sincerely felt advice though, on how not to waste your time, it would be this: don't even log in.

CORBYN'S LABOUR: A PROTEIN SHAKE OR A SHIT SANDWICH?

12th October 2016

In the Labour Party today there are three distinct factions. This is taking into account not just the Parliamentary Labour Party, but also party membership, whose numbers have ballooned to make it the largest in Europe, in precise correlation with plunging its polling levels down to a dark point just a few inches above the bottom of the Mariana Trench.

On one side is the dwindling New Labour faithful- a dispassionate collection of breezily ruthless clean shirts. They look like glib senior managers, and behave like them too. While they could be dismissed as insincere careerists, their careers depend on winning elections, so perhaps realistic would be a fairer tag. Roundly dismissed by their detractors as narcissistic Blairites, they aren't slow to point out that Blair nailed three elections.

Opposing them is the Corbyn accumulation. This in itself is a varied cluster, but can be broadly broken down into two groups.

First is what we might call the New Left. These people are young, judgmental and prone to tantrums. They almost certainly follow Owen Jones on Twitter, voted Remain, and think climate change is racist.

They admire true socialists like Tony Benn, but fail to recognise that their identity-driven, self-absorbed interpretation of left-wing ideology is something else entirely. Having chosen to shackle themselves to cumbersome PC moralizing, they are critically restricted in their ability to reason or debate, but can subsist solely on wi-fi in times of hardship.

Then there is the Hard Left. These guys are not politically correct. Oh Christ, no. On no account must they be let near a microphone. At their fringes are some hard-line bits and pieces who are more than likely to say something deeply sexist, issue a physical threat, suggest burning down Tory HQ and then exchange texts with Corbyn.

En masse though, the Hard Left are the keepers of the socialist flame, and they like nothing more than a long, shouty march, about anything- doesn't matter.

The ideal Labour Party then, would be one whose leadership took all the best elements of these three factions and whipped them together into a restorative, left-of-centre protein shake, while ditching the noxious, dreggy aspects of each group.

From New Labour: Keep the suits, the haircuts and the media training, remembering that they're right to think everyone judges on appearance.

Throw away the dishonesty, the lack of a moral compass, and the impression of being open to the idea of premeditated homicide.

From the New Left: Keep the laptops. Ditch the defeated obsession with the EU. Do away with the misconception that it's normal to despise your own country because you went to Berlin one weekend and the clubs were good. Dispose urgently of the undergraduate virtue signalling- really, no-one gives a fuck about sombreros.

And from the Hard Left: Keep the collective fortitude, the understanding of Brexit, and above all, keep the love of a good buffet well stocked with pork pies.

Casket up and bury deep in the cold, hard Earth like nuclear fallout: the threats, sexism, antisemitism, block headed inflexibility, pettiness, spite, regressive anti-Western rhetoric, and paranoid conspiracy theories.

Successfully merge this protean, diverse crop and you're on to a winner, Labour, just like when you had Tony Bl... No, sorry, nothing like him. Just really good.

On the other hand, such experiments are unstable, and we mustn't forget that the Labour Party is now led, precisely as it was before the pointless, no-contest, leadership pantomime, by a man who wants to ban "early evening socialisation" and is stalked by a mob of knife sharpening malcontents.

Be prepared that what you might end up with in attempting to unite the disparate cliques will be a spliced together, dysfunctional atrocity: promoting feminism while refusing to address the abuses of radical Islam; marching for workers' rights and higher pay while calling all poor people stupid and campaigning for open borders; aware of the need to work the media, while also refusing to speak to the media.

Realistically, get ready for the possibility that your protein shake is a shit sandwich, and don't even think about after work drinks.

WELCOME TO DYSTOPIA UNIVERSITY

17ᵗʰ October 2016

I didn't go to university to have my preconceptions challenged, or to open myself to weird knowledge and dangerous ideas. I wasn't seeking to push my personal boundaries or take intellectual risks. It's not that I don't think those are valuable experiences, it's just that such things can be done by anyone, anywhere, without the empty validation of a reading list and a final exam.

University life wasn't that far removed from not-university life anyway—sure, there were a few misanthropic left-radicals who were angry and judgmental, but they were an avoidable fringe. Not many people were trying to force your worldview, show off about correcting social justice or, even worse, blame you for social injustice. If there were people like that, they were easily ignored from the depths of the SU bar.

Which is why the current state of politically correct academic culture is so troubling. Ideological fanatics, with the backing of fully complicit college authorities, are fostering a campus environment that looks far removed from the norms of everyday life. In this sealed-off, Lord of the Flies echo chamber irrational ideas are being allowed to exert control, and it's all been officially signed off at the top.

The historical left-liberal bias of academia has allowed the new regressive left to claim authority. Administrators bow to the petulant demands of student unions not fit for purpose, and lecturers are carried fearfully down the river. While some staff might resist, it's difficult not to think that the soft liberal consensus many of them have slavishly adhered to for their entire careers is what enabled this takeover in the first place. Here's your petard. Now get hoisted.

When the campus Overton Window lets in light from all-out Marxism to the centre-left but nothing beyond that, you need to call an Overton glazer. Either fix the imbalance or buckle yourself in to a rattling, lunatic feedback loop, in which dissent and debate happen only within the biased ideological spectrum defined by the prevalent orthodoxy.

If I were 18 now, would I like to go to university? It would be hard to escape the feeling that I'd be stepping into a dystopian science fiction novel. Spiteful blowhards who'd be told to sit down and shut up in any normal environment have appropriated control, and I wouldn't look forward to spending three years trapped in a power struggle with such self-serving, morally dysfunctional creeps.

In a recent online conversation between Jordan Peterson, a University of Toronto professor fighting back against the social justice autocrats, and Gad Saad, the well known scientist and academic, Saad mischievously slips in the 'sneaky fucker' strategy' from zoology with reference to male social justice warriors.

Basically, they're disingenuous geeks who've slipped in the backdoor and joined the social justice crowd in search of sexual opportunity. This looks believable, but I'd extend it further—the entire PC/SJW mob movement is a conglomeration of sneaky fuckers. Disguising themselves as progressives campaigning for equality, they have corrupted and undermined the entire concept of social justice. Not looking for sex, but searching for power, or in the case of the more deranged individuals at the top of the SJW power structures, motivated perhaps by other questionable motives.

Where those who instinctively understand the checks, balances and clarity inherent to real justice have straightforward, consistent ideals, in the far left we now have a shifting, self-contradictory mess in which relativist nonsense, crass identity judgments, and belligerent, immature rhetoric have sabotaged the very concept of social justice, whatever that once meant.

Review the infamous Yale University video from one year ago, in which a mob of cry-bullies intimidate their professor on the campus grounds. When not yelling expletives at him (their professor!) they would burst into tears.

Why did they do this? Because they got a gentle email from his wife, also a professor, telling them politely that it wasn't the university's business to proscribe what students should and shouldn't wear at Halloween. Quite simply, they read an innocuous mail, it didn't compute with their rigidly simplistic groupthink, and the sole response they could manage was to meltdown in anger.

Taking a further look at the Yale video, the students' behaviour is still appalling, but the professor's response is also frustrating. It must have been an overwhelming situation and his intentions were good, but he indulged the students' group hysteria. Engaging earnestly with an angry mob gives the impression that it's acceptable to form angry mobs. Offering partial apologies for hurt feelings to hyper-sensitive neurotics legitimizes the notion that their own out-of-control emotional inconsistencies trump all other considerations.

Years ago, 'PC gone mad' sentiments were associated with Basil Fawlty-esque Little Englanders, upset that they could no longer use bigotry-loaded racial epithets while lamenting the retreat of Empire.

Cut to 2016 and you'd be forgiven for thinking that the blazer-at-breakfast B&B owners were in fact stunningly prescient, as political correctness has, actually, gone mad. That's mad as in pathological, while the ideologies it's coupled with have become skilled at cult-like indoctrination, and at acquiring formidable amounts of real power.

Political correctness is used to shield regressive left politics from criticism, and has allowed our society to be altered in non-consensual, corrosive ways. The next time you hear a public figure being shouted down and discredited for bigotry, racism, or any of the other slurs employed without restraint by PC enforcers, be sure to check just what exactly it is that the silenced party wanted to say, and why those shutting them down might not have wanted it to be heard.

One way to navigate an argument you can't win legitimately is to pull the mic on your opponent. That's a little conspicuous though, so here's another way. You let it be known that certain topics are beyond discussion, and that by extension certain ideas are unconscionable. You don't have to make your opponent believe it at all—as long as the audience buys in, then you can't lose. It will take time and deceit to achieve a consensus—you'll need to be a very sneaky fucker indeed—but once that consensus has been established, then who will be able to withstand the heat, face down the mob, and break the spell?

EMOTIONALISM GOES IN STUDS UP ON THE TRUTH

25th October 2016

An enormous shitstorm has engulfed the UK over the past week or so, and it's all about immigration. Here's how events unfolded.

1.   *A celebrity goes to Calais to make a video illustrating the situation in the migrant 'Jungle'.*

Pop squelcher Lily Allen went to Calais and emoted painfully, providing little background or context and not enough useful information.

When confronted with a blameless teenage migrant, who had the right to enter the UK and has now done so, she began sobbing. Prior to that she croaked out an apology "on behalf of my country".

Simply by front-loading the report with her London-lubed

feelings, crying a bit, and being literally incapable of discussing any of the hard details of the crisis, she managed to lather up a salty tide of knee-jerk emotion among the kind of viewer swayed by a baffled looking boy being not-helped by a choking luvvie.

At the same time, Allen infuriated and embarrassed a different section of the audience, who watched through their fingers as this born-rich moralizer had the gauche conceit to apologise on behalf of a nation she doesn't represent on matters she didn't demonstrate any proper, balanced understanding of.

Her video, far from bringing Britain together in purposeful compassion (or whatever it was she intended), either yoked out useless, weepy emotions, or infuriated more pragmatic watchers.

She strongly enhanced the feeling that Britain is divided and tetchy, and demonstrated exactly why employing right-on celebrities for anything other than supermarket openings is counter productive. Well done Lily. On to the next phase.

2.   *Child migrants arrive in the UK from Calais to be given asylum.*

The UK was to give refuge to unaccompanied, vulnerable children, an idea that has wide support. This is just the kind of immigration that most people are happy to get behind.

But then, among the migrants who stepped off the buses in Croydon were a number of adult men who had, bewilderingly, managed to pass themselves off as children. One man was identified as looking late thirties, and from the photos that seems a reasonable estimate.

As the bizarre scenes in Croydon took over the media, the Daily Mail reported a British volunteer working in the Calais camp as saying:

> "I know there are vulnerable kids, kids with epilepsy, who are still here that have family in the UK they could be with right now. It's a shambles. Children are not being told what they are queuing up for, they are not being given information, there is complete confusion."

However, such considerations didn't factor in to the thinking of the rabid social justice warriors scrambling to make it known that not only was nothing unseemly happening, but that there was something dreadfully wrong with anyone who said there was.

3.   *Reaction unfolds to the migrants' arrival.*

Imagine for a moment if Britain's plans—for vulnerable children to be brought in to the country and given the opportunity of a new life—had actually proceeded as anticipated.

We can only speculate, but it would be churlish to assume that there'd have been anything other than goodwill and a sense that we were finally getting something right with regard to immigration.

In reality though, social media fired up rapidly with clear sighted observers who'd spotted, without difficulty, that a fast one was being pulled. They pointed out in no uncertain terms that blatant lies were being sold, clearly evidenced in the pictures of the men among the boys in Croydon.

The I'm-alright-Jack celebrity emotionalists, however, didn't like that. Here's what holier-than-though multi-millionaire Gary Lineker tweeted:

> "The treatment by some towards these young refugees is hideously racist and utterly heartless. What's happening to our country?"

Notice the glaring disconnect here. There's no mention of the crucial substance of the dispute: that some of the children are adults. And when this was put to him by another Twitter user, here was the response:

> "Idiot"

This is the wealthy, metro-leftist worldview encapsulated in a single insult. If you dissent from the official narrative and tell the truth, if you work honestly with the crystal clear evidence which is right in front of you then you are, in this case, "hideously racist and utterly heartless", and ultimately, an "idiot".

The Mirror ran this headline:

> "Gary Lineker Faces Torrent Of Abuse After Defending Child Refugees Arriving In England"

The untruth which had caused the story to *be* a story—that some of the 'child refugees' *weren't children*—is actually used here to attack those who pointed out that untruth.

Quickly and with a ruthless disregard for basic decency, criticism of being obviously lied to was coldly misrepresented as criticism of the plan to take in child refugees. As the car crash unfolded, outright lies have been defended with crude personal slurs.

Where does this leave us?

One side of the immigration debate—those proclaiming that we mustn't discuss the age of the migrants—has rendered facts and truth as at best optional and at worst, by some strange twisting of reason, as emotionally debasing.

In a brick wall denial of reality, those who'd like to dismiss the age issue entirely have told stone cold lies in the face of contradictory evidence, and have deliberately slurred those who disagree with them.

They've also placed an unhealthy emphasis on subjective emotional reaction over clearheaded, objective analysis. And if you happen to have the 'wrong' emotional response, then prepare for a whipping.

One of the tragedies of this mishandled fiasco is that it could have been a genuinely unifying story. After all, helping desperate children is hardly a difficult sell.

Instead, it's divided the country still further, and starkly demonstrated the regressive left's zealous contempt for truth, honest reporting, and plurality of opinion.

YOU CAN'T BUILD WALLS AROUND A CULTURE

2ⁿᵈ November 2016

Cultural appropriation fanatics are operating under a fatal error — that culture belongs to anyone. Here's the reality: it doesn't. Just to be absolutely clear about that, your culture isn't yours, and mine isn't mine.

You can't build walls around culture, because once an idea has been transmitted, whether willingly or not, it can no longer be restrained. It's beyond ownership. It will be bounced around, split, mutate, crossbreed and reconfigure.

It will be appropriated, reappropriated, misappropriated, changed and then changed back, but different. After being cooked, flipped and reformed, it will unexpectedly give birth to something entirely new, to which the same process will occur, over and over again.

This is a part of the evolutionary process. It's progress. It's the constantly expanding intellectual and social capacity that has led human civilization to every single one of its most mind-blowing achievements.

The best music, the best literature, the greatest scientific, technological and political advancements — none have been achieved in a vacuum, all have been reached through a process of cross-pollination, co-operation and mixing. And also through disagreement — through challenge, rigorous debate, and mercilessly bruised and battered feelings.

All culture is accessible now. All knowledge is within reach. Everything we have is available to be remixed, rebooted, and reimagined.

Sometimes that might result in something bad, something worse than the original. Well, that's just the way it goes, not every experiment works. But in order to achieve anything new, we have to be able to perform those experiments in the first place, and we must be able to do so whenever we want, spontaneously, and without anyone's permission.

As in science, the cultural path, though littered with cast-off ideas and full of kinks, ascends inevitably toward new and exciting things.

Protesters against 'cultural appropriation' are wasting everyone's time in an unwinnable battle: they're attempting to deny nature, chill history, and shackle the basic components of what it is to be human.

They may as well lecture the trees not to grow because they're stealing the sunlight.

The social justice luddites wish to freeze us in time, at this exact moment, apparently unaware of how artificial and arbitrary that would be. Why now? Our civilisations have spent thousands of years mutating and inter-breeding, what on Earth leads them to think that this is the moment of cultural purity at which we must all stop following our social instincts and instead reside forever in splendid (disastrous) cultural isolation? Why, for example, designate dreadlocks as black? Shouldn't we assign them to the Ancient Egyptians or the Scandinavians, who wore them thousands of years ago? And who is to take charge of assigning everything in existence to a specific ethnic category? Nineteen year old gender studies students?

Taking offense on other people's behalf is staggeringly patronizing. To arrogantly declare, for example, that non-Japanese mustn't wear kimono for fear of causing offense, forces Japanese people into an unwanted victim role, attempts to rope off a beautiful culture, and implies that they lack emotional robustness and require protection.

The self-appointed, jobsworth offense-seekers treat those they've unthinkingly labeled as 'oppressed' like children, forcing them into the psychopathic nanny's smothering bosom in an act of control masquerading as comfort.

And it *is* a way of controlling people. Assign them an identity, and make sure they stay within its bounds. The idea that this is for their own protection is a profound dishonesty. The snotty, tearful snowflakes might be weak and easily offended, incapable of dealing with hurt feelings or harsh words, but most people aren't, and don't need such fake protection. A word in your ear, SJWs: you're not society's mentally deranged, over-protective mum.

Living in Tokyo, I've appropriated some knowledge. Anyone who lives in an earthquake zone and has wondered which buildings would survive a big quake probably knows this too: strength comes through flexibility. Rigidity is weak. As with architecture, the same is true of ideas. It's the cultures which are adaptable, generous, and open to the exchange of ideas that thrive. Those that define themselves by exclusivity and self-imposed blockades are likely to end up left behind. Japan, as it happens, has tried both ways.

Seven years ago, the BNP — a far right wing party in the UK —

had a surge in popularity. This came to an end soon after its leader appeared on the BBC's political discussion programme Question Time. His toxic extremism was exposed. His fixation on ethnic origin was sinister and without value.

The race obsessed new segregationists of the millennial social justice movement are strongly reminiscent of that former leader of the BNP.

And perhaps that indicates why they're opposed to free speech and constantly push for the censorship of their opponents. Their leaders seem aware that if exposed to the cleansing light of open discussion, their ideologies would be revealed as regressive, irrational, and potentially dangerous.

YOU ARE THE 48%

6th November 2016

So you want to block Brexit?

Well that makes sense. Democracy can be applied selectively to ensure favourable outcomes. You'll put the in-group's preferences first, because their decisions are well-informed.

There's no moral impasse because the out-group are uneducated and selfish. You're not selfish because the in-group's wants are called *progressive*, while the out-group's are not.

Your opinions are more valuable than the out-group's. You don't read the same news as they do, you read the right news. You're not a low information voter. You believe in facts, data and expert opinion. You know, for example, that 48%, or 16.1 million, is equal to or greater than 52%, or 17.4 million.

That might be because each Remain voter is one person, but each Leave voter has a value slightly lower than one, due to their fecklessness and lack of information.

Maybe you should be paid more than any Leave voting colleagues. After all, your vote carries more weight and you're more valuable than they are, so why shouldn't you be remunerated accordingly?

You're not indoctrinated like the credulous out-group. There's no pro-EU bias in the education system–teachers all have the same opinions because they're all educated, and they educated you too.

And you're not anti-democratic, you're upholding democracy. You acquiesce to the political class because that's how it works. Why rock the boat? You're in the smart group. Smart enough to let your betters call the shots. You know your place.

You're the tolerant one, you're liberal. This is clear because the values you want to see compulsorily enforced by the state are tolerant, liberal values. The ends justify the means. And you have plenty of self awareness—there's a group consensus on that.

You don't look down on people who have a different opinion, you want to help them. It's not good to let people with opinions like theirs decide on important matters. They don't know what's good for them.

You think working class people are romantic and witty like in those wonderful Ken Loach films. But they shouldn't be allowed to influence politics because they're thick racists too. There must be some way to help them. You help by voting Labour or Green.

You're glad that there are so many unbiased comedians unpacking this whole EU disaster. They really cut through the bigotry and lies, and they all agree with you. And the actors and pop stars too. All the rogues and the rebels, you love their anti-establishment radicalism, and it's great that they know to toe the line right now.

Post-truth Brexit Britain is shot through and psychotic, it can't survive. You're glad you were right about the pound falling, and now we all have to pull together to talk the economy down. It hasn't worked yet but it will—somebody has to show the out-group how much they've screwed things up.

Maybe Scotland will sort things out, or Jeremy Corbyn, or some lawyers.

You don't feel British anymore, but what will happen if you're not European either?

You are the 48%.

TRUMP: LET THE MEDIA HISTRIONICS BEGIN

9th November 2016

An enormously costly mistake was made this week, and it is this: Toblerone chose the wrong day to announce that they were shrinking their weirdly shaped chocolate bars.

That calamitous information could have been buried without a trace if they'd timed its release to coincide with the growing certainty that Donald Trump's path to the White House was opening up.

Hopefully you're sanguine about the Donald's unlikely ascent to nuclear arsenal commanding power. Maybe you're even cracking open the Trump brand vodka you've had in storage in preparation for this moment (to be had with a cryogenically preserved Trump Steak, perhaps.)

So long as you're not *#LiterallyShaking*—having piled all your furniture against the front door lest Trump's stormtroopers should already be on their way—then something you'll be looking forward to is soaking in the broiling furnace of catastrophe-laden opinion pieces to be unleashed by the more panicky sections of the media, while also following the resultant vomiting up of despair on Twitter.

Having endured almost five months of Brexit-triggered snow-flake histrionics we have a solid idea of what to expect. In the light of some desperate post-referendum fear mongering, it's surprising that the Earth still orbits the sun—predictions were that the planet should've crashed by now—but here we are, so these are my predictions as to the kinds of headlines we can expect to be brutally pummeled around the head with soon.

I'm Ashamed of my American Passport

This is on its way. The author will be painfully aware that America is to blame for everything bad that has ever happened in the world up to now, including the crucifixion of Jesus, but has learned to carry the burden. Trump, however, is a bridge too far. What the writer's mawkishness will actually mean is that they hate themselves and they always have, and now they've a good chance to let it be known just how deep their pathological self-loathing runs by projecting it revealingly onto their inanimate passport.

We Must Ask Why So Many Voted For Trump

We don't understand these people, who are they, what do they want? Why don't they know anything, do they live underground? Maybe they live in old mines or something? Do they have guns? We made a celebrity video, didn't they watch it? Maybe they don't have TVs so they couldn't watch it. But they watch Fox, how can they watch Fox without TVs? Why don't they like Hillary? She's speaks for everyone, she called them deplorable, why don't they like her? Why don't they have exactly the same ideas about everything as we do? Maybe they're racists, are they racists? How can we ever know?

Trump Voters Are People Too

This comes later, after a period of loathing, fury, pity-hate, and confusion. Eventually, a not entirely hysterical commentator will venture into 'Trump territory'. Perhaps they're originally from some non-Metropolitan area, and have vague ancestral memories of vast plains, in which can be found nomadic Anglo-Saxon hunter-gatherers who don't like Michael Moore documentaries. The crux of this piece will be, basically, "my God, they didn't shoot me and you know what, they're not actual racists!" This will come as an enormous shock to the writer, but will ultimately change nothing of the mainstream narrative.

All the while, no matter what Trump does, good or bad, and no matter what information is published about who voted for him and what their reasons were, one side of the story will remain unchanging. Trump and his supporters stand for racism, misogyny, and even, some will insist, fascism.

This is the *Never Trump* camp's truth, they're set on it, and no matter what happens, they won't let any other peskily true bits of truth stand in the way of their own, morally virtuous brand of truth.

HOW THE LEFT TRICKED YOU

11ᵗʰ November 2016

Opponents of the radical left's excesses have for a long time warned that over-bearing, often nonsensical levels of fervent political correctness are having a deleterious effect on public discourse.

The censoriousness, anti-democracy, and plain nastiness of the regressive left is not only wrong on a moral and a civil level, but is counter-productive to its own aims.

When normal disagreement on issues such as immigration and the threat of radical Islam is rendered impossible by vacuous, anti-intellectual social justice cackhands, what can be expected to happen? Did they really think that people would accept their all-encompassing new definitions of 'racism' or 'bigotry'? Their definitions are cheaply self-serving, allowing any and all dissenters to be silenced through fear of slander, while undermining real concerns about discrimination.

Perhaps you can, for a very short while, police people's words, but certainly not their thoughts. While you might be able to twist perceptions of the truth among the feeble-minded— that is, those confused and credulous enough to be indoctrinated by the PC fanatics' corrupt algorithms—you can't hinder a free population's ability to recognise when a lie is being sold.

There is a remarkable level of ignorance involved in the radical left's belief that it can win an argument *in the long-term* simply by spewing abuse and falsely sullying the reputations of its opponents.

Safe spaces, trigger warnings, no-platforming—all are symptoms of a self-indulgent, infantile approach to public discourse, whereby retreat, fragility, and conformity take the place of exchange, evidence, and debate.

Then there is the noxious rot of identity politics. Who on the radical left thought that it would be a good idea to categorise people according to the colour of their skin, their gender, or their sexual preferences? Who wants to box us in like this without considering for a moment the resentment that such inhumane dogma would call forth? Who has the audacity to declare that some opinions are more valid than others based on—what?–family tree? Whose bed you slept in last night? Which church you might visit?

This is bigotry, pure and simple, and speaks to a move among the regressive left toward the arrogant, unnatural cruelty of social segregation.

When you read opinion pieces by liberal left wing commentators questioning how it is that Donald Trump has been allowed to claim the presidency, you should already know the answer—he has been propelled to the White House by, among others, the writers of those columns themselves.

The regressive left can tell people how to vote, and declare in crude terms that the electorate are despicable fascists if they don't comply. It can threaten to root people out and have them sacked, or call them racist, stupid, and beyond redemption. It can leave no option other than to get in line and support the authorised candidate. And with the full, bullying force of the liberal media against them, many people will publicly fall into step with the agenda, and agree that the bad candidate is, indeed, unconscionable, while the leftist agenda is pristine.

On 9th November in the United States the illiberal left forgot that their wretched dominion ends at the entrance to the voting booth.

The identity politics corrupters have been roundly beaten at their own game, and the outcome they were warned about for so long has come to pass, as a huge number of reasonable people felt that they had no choice but to opt for the only non-PC alternative on offer.

This should be a wake-up call for the left—an invitation to reflect, self-analyse, and dissect how badly they've been led astray by ideological extremists.

Some are doing this, but unfortunately there are a great number who refuse, or are simply unable to snap the Mobius Loop to which they're bound. Instead, they continue to whirr endlessly round like a piece of unwanted, stale sushi.

Incredibly, recklessly, they are now doubling down on the identity politics, going all in on political correctness, and utterly denying the possibility that they view events through a distorting ideological veil.

Having confused politics with morality, the PC leftists have the impression that all who take a different view are contemptible low-lives. They've isolated themselves on an illusory, desolately sterile moral high ground.

Any attempts to compromise with them are seen as unclean and ethically compromised. They'd rather just keep belching rhetoric, self-reinforcing, and upping the ante—the same accusations, the same untruths, the same tiresome, muddled gloop, over and over until the doctors arrive.

AS A PANSEXUAL, GENDER FLUID MUSLIM I CAN'T BE WRONG ABOUT ANYTHING

13th November 2016

I read a tweet under a piece I wrote on cultural appropriation, and it said, paraphrasing, that my race and gender devalued the worth of the ideas I'd presented.

I'd like to point out that I don't usually roam Twitter looking for critical tweets to dissect, but this one succinctly encapsulates a particular mindset, which is often used to discredit arguments against political correctness. It holds, in less than 140 characters, the core essence of identity politics.

The poster couldn't objectively assess the ideas contained in my article simply by reading it and thinking about its content. He needed to know my race and my gender, and I presume that all those other virtue markers so perversely fetishized in SJW circles, such as sexual preference and religion, would've been of use to him too. His assessment of my work would change depending on these things. A strange extension of this is that in a world ruled by identity politics, all texts would need to carry not just the author's name, but also a list of their personal characteristics.

Measure for Measure, by William Shakespeare
(straight/white/cismale/Protestant)

According to PC/SJW ideology, an obscenely privileged hack like me is at the bottom of the hierarchy. I have zero chips to cash in, and no cards to throw down, because I am white, male, straight, gender normative, and non-Muslim.

I am consigned to roam unloved at the base of the regressive left's mercilessly rigid caste system. Of course I don't say that with any actual sense of self-pity—their algorithm is deranged and they're insufferable puritans, so no-one in their right mind would seek their approval.

But to the SJW contingent people like me are low value, with nothing of merit to offer except self-flagellation and rote mantras expressing our unending guilt.

For the social justice bigots it isn't out of the ordinary to think that the opinions of a very large number of people carry no weight. And just think about that: some opinions are more likely to be dismissed, regardless of their content, on the grounds of (among other things) race. What kinds of people would think like that? What kinds of people *have* thought like that, throughout history?

This is the kind of anti-humanist, identity political garbage that is being propagated by the far-left, and disseminated throughout academia.

The absurdity of such a mindset can be illustrated. If I wanted to play their peculiar game, how could I earn myself some credits, and hike myself up the rankings a little? I can't change my race, but what's to stop me publicly identifying as a pansexual, transgender Muslim?

According to the PC left, sexual desire is a social construct, and gender is mutable. There's nothing in their rules to prevent me shifting from straight to Miley Cyrus-inspired pansexual, and from 'cisgender' to, well, take your pick—gender fluid, a-gender, bi-gender... I can be a different gender every day if I like, with my own made-up pronouns to match. And furthermore, I don't have to do anything to prove it—it's all based entirely on my own subjective feelings.

If I'm a straight, white male, then my opinion is morally unclean, but if I use my new identity—a pansexual, gender fluid Muslim—then my opinion is of greater purity and carries significantly more weight.

Well that's great, who knew that their game is so easy? Strengthened by my freshly reconstructed, ideologically spotless identity, my newly acquired victimhood supplies an all-powerful shield and mace, and anything I write on political correctness from here on in will be *righter* than it was before. In addition, I'll be joining the worthy cause of the righteous oppressed, making me an essentially good person. It's a win-win.

STOP FUNDING HATE, START FUNDING CENSORSHIP

14th November 2016

Under pressure from campaign group Stop Funding Hate, the Danish toy company Lego has publicly announced that it will no longer be working with the Daily Mail, a newspaper the campaign group alleges promotes "hatred, discrimination and demonisation."

Stop Funding Hate is claiming this as an emphatic victory, and continues to self-aggrandize and attack the profit mechanisms of other media establishments.

If you're unfamiliar with the organization, Stop Funding Hate is a 21st Century hive mind version of Mary Whitehouse in her free speech crushing prime, hacked and rewired into the online politics of Millennial leftists.

From their Facebook page:

"Help us take on the divisive hate campaigns of the Sun, Daily Mail and Daily Express by persuading advertisers to pull their support."

Their campaigns aim to have crucial advertising revenue cut off from the blacklisted media groups they've decreed to be politically incorrect, and in doing so force them to either revise their politics or endanger their business model.

They make no bones about their intention to make editors think twice before running content which dissents from Stop Funding Hate's own political preferences, and they explicitly target only right-of-centre organisations.

Judging from their recent moves, they oppose robust debate around immigration policy, and would force journalists to step very carefully around the judiciary. Journalism which is strongly critical of the EU, while at the same time promoting Brexit, also appears to be in their sights.

Regardless of left/right allegiances, tolerating tabloid broadsides, particularly those which go beyond the pale, is a sign of a well adjusted, free society. The holier-than-though moralizing of Stop Funding Hate is itself a perfect example of the kind of authoritarian pomposity that needs deflating with a good old-fashioned tabloid kicking.

These censorious do-gooders have learned precisely zero from Donald Trump's success in the US election. The clearest lesson from America is that if you drive popular points of view underground they won't magically disappear. We have social media now. Forbidden opinions will circulate, self-reinforce and sometimes become powerfully distorted in the potent echo chamber of illicit caucus. Having memed their way to readiness, they'll triumphantly yank the rug out from under your feet and piss liberally all over your politically correct strawberries, and get a round of applause for doing so.

There's no way of making social progress which has been shown to work better than free and open debate, with all the rhetorical excesses, bruised egos, and occasional hurt feelings that are involved. It might rub you up the wrong way sometimes, but it works magnificently.

Should Stop Funding Hate come up with an alternative means of doing politics, then they must be sure to let us know, but de facto censorship is off the cards.

HOW TO AVOID LEFT-WING BIGOTRY

November 17th 2016

There's an overwhelming groupthink among left-wing liberals right now which pretty much invalidates their being called 'liberals' at all.
It's not the jackbooted conformity of the far-right, it's a rigid intellectual purism, and a supreme sense of cocooned arrogance. It resembles not socialist principle, but rather the hubristic conceit of French aristocrats.

When I present a dissenting point of view among left-of-centre, usually nice people it's as if the aging family dog has released a noxious fart on Grandma's birthday. There's a wrinkling of noses, sideways glances, and pitying, polite smiles. Just ignore it, the poor thing.

My disagreeable opinion will be brushed aside as an unfortunate mistake and the conversation hurriedly re-routed to something which I might find easier to understand. Mental notes are taken all round. He might be a bit right wing. Keep an eye on him and no more wine, he could do something weird.

At the same time, I've heard friends who regard themselves as liberal progressives say, after Brexit and the US election, that democracy doesn't work and should be replaced with something else. They're half joking. But they're half not.

And that thinking is just fine. No stink, no awkwardness—screw democracy because chavs don't understand it and they keep voting wrong. Great. Pints all round.

It can feel beyond the pale to challenge the liberal consensus in supposedly polite company. Even standing up for freedom of expression, which requires, for example, *not* thinking that the Daily Mail should be censored, is a little infra-dig at the moment.
Whatever faults modern conservatism might have, it understands the necessity of heterodox opinion, respects freedom of expression, and tends not to sulk when it loses.

And then there's the problem of the modern left's unthinking embrace of identity politics, moral relativism, and all the anti-Enlightenment vandalism of political correctness, which can do nothing but undermine the more workable, potentially popular aspects of leftist thinking. Criticise any of this and you'll be shunned by 'progressives' who ask few questions, and have almost no understanding of just how ideologically contorted PC thinking has become. But there's simply no way of challenging their orthodoxy on this—it's like a religious devotion.

So in light of the social leprosy attached to being anything other than left-wing among metropolitan 'liberals', I'm thinking about using a new political identifier.
It's very right-on to be campaigning for trans rights at the moment. Proclaim that you're furious about mis-gendering, go off on one about restrooms, and you'll immediately gain clout among the identity politicking liberal set.

With that in mind, when discussing politics with the regressive progressives, I'm not right-wing, I'm trans-conservative. I was raised to be a Labour voter but then became aware that I'd been mis-winged. In fact, I'm wing-fluid, and today I'm feeling a bit Ukip with a dash of Rousseau.

So respect my trans-opinions, you wretched bigots: no, you can't shut down the right-wing press for disagreeing with Gary Lineker.

TRIGGERED LIBERALS ARE BAN-HAPPY

November 19th 2016

Have you heard the news? Liberal progressives (yeah, right) have just woken up to the fact that identity politics is divisive and counter productive. That is, a form of politics that *divides* people according to race, gender and sexual preference turns out to be *divisive*. It appears that people prefer to be judged on the content of their character rather than on superficial identity categories. Well, well, who would've thought it?

Political correctness isn't going down quite so well now either, because, much to the chagrin of its enforcers, it's apparent that we're capable of treating one another fairly and being polite without having our language and thoughts scrutinized from above. And you know what, it wasn't really about those things anyway, that whole line is a distraction. PC's less thoughtful adherents are just now making the connection that *political* correctness is, let's see... *political.*

So please, spare us the whole *"what's wrong with being nice to people anyway?"* fallacy. Modern political correctness is a means of coercion, a way of leading people down policy paths they haven't consented to by preventing them from expressing legitimate concerns. It isn't racist to question immigration policy. There's nothing bigoted about criticizing Islam.

And then there's the current, wearisome trend for unrestrained catastrophizing. Constantly. About every decision that doesn't go the 'progressive' way. But the gasping hyperbole isn't working anymore, if it ever did. It's to be hoped that the frantically jabbering oracles of doom are noticing, finally, that there's a majority of voters who prefer to base their political decisions on logical reflection, rather then hyper-ventilated, unformed emotion.

Breaking down in tears because the UK is going to leave an undemocratic, federally-dreaming EU is ridiculous behaviour. Across the Atlantic, burning flags, throwing insults and tantrums, and holding campus cry-ins because you don't like the new president appears unhinged. These cloying, snotty-nosed attention seekers have finally lost the plot, and you know what? Nobody cares, snowflakes: your sickly, overwrought feelings are irrelevant.

At City University London, home of one of the best journalism schools in the country, the student union has just voted to ban three of the most popular newspapers in Britain—the Sun, the Daily Mail, and the Daily Express—because they disagree with their editorial lines.

Ordinary citizens up and down the land now line the streets in celebration at this brave stand, as huge bonfires of tabloid filth burn triumphantly in the Autumn... oh no, hang on a minute. No, it actually seems that most people are stunned by the utter, shit-for-brains ludicrousness of banning newspapers from a journalism school.

You might think, though, that we'd have got used to such

jaw-dropping campus childishness, what with Oxford University law students being given trigger warnings during parts of their studies, so that the delicate *future lawyers* won't collapse like fainting Victorian ladies during lectures. In case you didn't know, studying law involves READING ABOUT CRIMES, and crimes aren't very nice.

Presumably, legal chambers across the land have been stocking up on colouring books and Um Bongo to soothe the fragile nerves of their future new employees. Courts are to be redecorated with Peppa Pig wallpaper, and the Thomas the Tank Engine theme music will be piped gently through the air to take the edge off harrowing witness statements.

Don't be alarmed if you look up in court and your brief has their fingers in their ears and their eyes screwed shut—they've been triggered, that's all, a quick back rub and a little lie down and they'll soon be back in business.

But of course, mentioning these things reveals my callousness, because the liberal progressives hold a permanent monopoly on kindness. Anyone who doesn't subscribe to their politics is beyond hope—amoral at best, sadistically cruel in most cases. Such dissenters from the Guardian line are poised, salivating and giggling, in anticipation at ripping up the social contract and inflicting misery on the bewildered, Murdoch-controlled masses.

Meanwhile, spiritually flawless metro-leftists, virtue signalling like holy beacons, attach consecrated safety pins to their robes, tag their entire beings with *#NeverTrump*, *#StrongerIn* and *#HopeNotHate*, and await beatification.

YOU CAN'T OWN PRONOUNS AND CULTURES, SO DON'T PRETEND THEY'RE YOURS

November 22nd 2016

Contrary to social justice radicals' attention seeking hollers of oppression, and their palpable longing for the impalpable patriarchy to crumble, in the Western developed world we're living with far reaching social mobility and open mindedness. And within this liberal environment, there are no stronger enclaves of freedom from persecution than university campuses —they're oases of fairness within an ocean of tolerance. All of which makes furious on-campus calls for compulsory *bias training* and the like seem ever more absurd. It's like going to the Vatican, protesting that it's not Catholic enough, and insisting the Pope enroll on the Alpha Course.

Within our generous societies there are, though, a few mean-spirited groups. They're attempting to disrupt the spirit of openness, and chief among them are the deeply regressive social justice warriors themselves. One way they display their misanthropy is through a sense of weird proprietorship, in which they claim ownership of things which either belong in the public realm or which demonstrably cannot be owned by anyone.

Something they're constantly trying to put restrictions on is language itself. At the moment they're going after pronouns, with regard to what they like to call gender neutral pronouns. One aim is to make everyone use the words *they/them/their* incorrectly—to refer to a single, known person. Even worse, they're also trying to enforce the use of clumsy, made-up words, such as *xe/xem/xyr*, along with other similarly unfamiliar variations, to which new sets can be infinitely added.

At the University of Toronto, Professor Jordan Peterson is taking a stand against this, and in doing so drawing a line in the sand on political correctness as a whole, by refusing to be forced into hindering his own clarity of expression with agenda-driven, PC authoritarianism. During a disagreement with protesters some time ago, one of them yelled at him childishly, "those are my pronouns!"

Well here's a little news—no, they're not. You have a name, which is chosen, and which you can change if you wish. That belongs to you, and you will of course insist on being called by it. You can correct anyone who gets it wrong. And you'd be justified in feeling aggrieved were anyone to deliberately misname you.

But pronouns are not an individual matter, they're linguistic tools that are beyond ownership. There's a reason why language has evolved pronouns connected to biological sex, and not connected to internally shifting, subjective perceptions. It's because biological sex is constant and identifiable, whereas latching pronouns onto internal feelings would render them confusingly baseless, liable to unexpected alteration, and detached from observable reality.

Essentially, they'd no longer be pronouns. State that you have a name and three personally specified pronouns, and you're effectively saying that you have four different names, to be chosen from depending on the sentence, while it's strictly forbidden to refer to you by actual pronouns. To insist on that would be several long, shaky bridges too far.

And then there is *cultural appropriation*, another example of grabby SJWs attempting to claim ownership where none exists.

Take hairstyles or ways of dressing. Wear a dashiki with your hair in cornrows, and if you're not of a designated acceptable ethnicity then you run the risk of being tiresomely harangued by a squad of whiny victimhood fetishists. What they steadfastly refuse to understand is that once a piece of knowledge or a way of doing things is out there, it belongs to no-one. You can copy someone's hair, copy their clothes, copy the way they speak, the way they walk, the books they read. You can copy anything you want, because when it comes to knowledge and customs—limitless, endlessly recyclable resources—the world is an all-inclusive free-for-all. And that naturally evolving and unpredictable exchange of ideas is a great thing, enabling creativity and innovation.

This is not to say that it's *always* a good thing to act that way—barge in and copy on-sight without a little prior consideration and you're liable to make a fool of yourself. But we don't need legislation outlawing social faux pas.

Which brings us back to Professor Peterson and gender neutral pronouns. Bill C-16, which would add gender identity and gender expression to the list of prohibited grounds of discrimination, has now passed in the Canadian House of Commons, but still needs to get through the Senate. This amendment could legally compel people to mangle their own speech with artificial new pronoun codes, or else risk contravening hate speech laws. Professor Peterson's battle against this deeply troubling piece of legislation is drawing huge support. Take a look at the clear and insightful videos on his YouTube channel to find out more about his principled defiance.

THE LEFT HAS SOLD ITS SOUL OVER BREXIT

November 23rd 2016

Let me begin by saying there's a minority on the left who have supported Brexit from the start: the Lexit contingent. This group have stuck to their guns on the issue of the EU. They've acted honestly and appear not to have been corrupted by the modern left's attachment to politically correct identity posturing.

But they're a minority. The new metropolitan left, on the other hand, is in thrall to identity politics, and has become publicly distorted by image obsessed, preaching celebrities. On the issue of leaving the European Union, it has confusedly painted itself into a thoroughly unenticing corner.

This is the left of Owen Jones and Will Self, Lily Allen and Bob Geldof, Eddie Izzard, Russell Brand and, well, pretty much any highly privileged actor, musician, comedian or academic you might care to mention.

For months now they've barraged us mercilessly with the idea that Brexit is a manifestation of bigoted, right wing populism —and the word populism is always employed as a euphemistic slur, insinuating a kind of neanderthal group-credulity.

In this world, Brexit is a cold-hearted exercise in rapacious capitalist exploitation, designed to enrich the few at the expense of—and this is the ultimate cruelty—those who voted for it.

But here is the real conceit. Despite having become utterly detached from, and disliked by, working class people, the modern left must still somehow maintain the pretense that it speaks for and works in the interests of these same people.

So how do they reconcile fighting for the working class interest with battling to overturn the working class vote? Well, they gripe solemnly that the poor, vulnerable unfortunates were ruthlessly manipulated by a powerfully dishonest Leave campaign. As a result, a lot of gullible saps went out and voted against their own interests, for something that they didn't really want. An astoundingly arrogant and insulting mantra of the Remain camp has been that Leave voters literally didn't know what they were voting for.

The modern left has repeatedly told working class voters, very slowly and deliberately, how stupid, easily controlled, and uninformed they were.

Not surprisingly, the voters have turned round and told the metro-leftists exactly where they can shove their presumptuous sanctimony, in no uncertain terms. The voters' rebuttal has been unequivocal—the vast majority knew exactly what they were signing up for by voting Leave (that Britain would exit the EU, even if a precise negotiating stance couldn't possibly be known in advance), that they possessed entirely valid, well-informed reasons for doing so, and that they have zero regrets about the result.

Despite nobody who voted Leave swallowing the left's unpalatable narrative, the left itself has become quite fond of it. After all, it allows them to continue pretending that they represent the working class, even if they must now do so directly *against the will of the working class.*

And now some concrete challenges to Brexit have come along. First, Gina Miller, a multi-millionaire investment manager, has undermined the UK's negotiating position and hindered the Brexit process by challenging the government in court. She contends that a Parliamentary vote is required before Article 50 can be activated, and the judges concurred.

Following that, we have news of the upcoming reappearance of Tony Blair, a man despised along the length of the political spectrum. Our obscenely rich former prime minister, who spends his days jetting around the world in the pay of sheikhs, oligarchs and dictators, is planning a new organisation to restate the case for the globalist ideology, which is intrinsically pro-EU.

At the same time, Sir Richard Branson, along with millionaire philanthropist Sir Clive Cowdery, who made his fortune as an insurance broker, will be partly funding a separate group, which is explicitly determined to stop Brexit from taking place.

Tony Blair is worth an estimated £60 million. Branson likes to pass the time on his private island in the Caribbean hosting movie stars and aristocrats. You can join them if you like, it's £40'000 a night, but don't expect to meet many humble socialists.

And these are the people with whom the left is now aligned.

More than that, in many ways, this now *is* the left.

Witness what happened when the Daily Mail attacked the judges in Gina Miller's Article 50 court case. Many left wingers threw an almighty tantrum, and demanded that the judiciary receive partisan coddling to selectively shield it from the non-genuflecting, pro-Brexit press. A puritanical whimper of campaigners calling themselves Stop Funding Hate rallied to cut off offending newspapers' advertising revenue, and snow-flake virtue signalers such as Gary Lineker, now adored by so-cial justice blowhards, joined the attack via social media.

This too, is the new left in action. It's a left that has abandoned liberalism, demands that dissenting points of view be cen-sored, and attempts to discredit elements of the media that challenge its agenda.

This left claims to be the voice of the oppressed, and yet it sides with the interests and representatives of the very wealthiest power brokers on the planet.

The members of this left wear the costume of radicals speak-ing truth to power, but attempt to silence criticism of judges.

So what the hell *is* the British left-wing now, on the issue of Brexit and beyond? By trying with all its might to keep Brit-ain in the EU, it's openly fighting *against* the working classes; ignoring their votes and over-ruling their voices. In this bat-tle against the people, the left is now allied and entwined with globalist billionaires, out-and-out free market capital-ists, and hyper-elitist technocrats.

It sneers at, contradicts, or ignores completely the hopes and opinions of the ordinary, working people it still—without shame or self-awareness—falsely claims to represent.

On the EU and Brexit, and more fundamentally, on democracy, the nation state and liberal values, the modern left has now lost itself completely.

MY LUCKY ESCAPE FROM THE CLUTCHES OF THE ALT-RIGHT

November 29th *2016*

"On one occasion I even, I am ashamed to admit…"

Even what..? Where might this suspenseful construction be leading?
…assaulted an Anglican vicar?

…ran over a guide dog and set fire to Oxfam?

Here's the full sentence:

> *"On one occasion I even, I am ashamed to admit, very diplomatically expressed negative sentiments on Islam to my wife."*

Oh. My. God. The horror.

Can you imagine expressing negative sentiments about a religion? I mean, the Catholics are fair game, obviously. And the

Church of England too, all fuzzy and liberal, yeah, fire away at them.

But Islam? The one with the Sharia Law, and the human rights offenses, and the radical offshoots that keep engaging in acts of unspeakable violence? Oh no, you keep your "diplomatically expressed negative sentiments" to yourself.

If you're wondering where that sentence was plucked from, it's part of an absurdist Guardian article titled,

"Alt-Right Online Poison Nearly Turned Me Into A Racist"

In many ways the article is a masterpiece. It encapsulates everything that is so wrong with the regressive left, head-in-the-sand, intolerant 'liberal' outlook. It appears to have been written for children, and it manages to passive aggressively slur a widely respected, best-selling author.

The anonymous writer opens with a glorious parade of not just his own impeccable virtue, but that of everyone he knows too:

> *"All my friends are very liberal or left leaning centrists. I have always voted Liberal Democrat or Green. I voted Remain in the referendum. The thought of racism in any form has always been abhorrent to me."*

How I aspire to be as ethically spotless as this. Not only does he explicitly declare that he's not racist, but he proves it too, by being neither a verminous Tory nor a despicable Leave voter, and by not knowing anyone who has different opinions. He's a model progressive, unblemished and pure.

But there lies something dangerous within him: curiosity.
The poor, flawed sod, why didn't he just stick with the people who all think in precisely the same way as him? They're obvi-

ously the good guys.

Alas though,

> "I was curious as to the motives of Leave voters. Surely they
> were not all racist, bigoted or hateful?"

What does he mean? Of course we're all racist, bigoted and
hateful—that's why we voted Leave! I mean, if we weren't we
would have voted Remain like him. The bloody idiot.

And so begins his descent, as after watching some videos on
YouTube, a Machiavellian, evil Leaver tells him to listen to
Sam Harris. Now, you may have thought that Sam Harris was
well-informed and considerate. A man concerned with facts,
who bends over backwards to avoid expressing anything resembling bigotry around controversial subjects. Because he
obviously isn't bigoted.

To the narrator though, Sam Harris is not simply a man, he's
a sinister, ideological gateway drug. After being "shocked" by
the entirely calm and rational Harris, the writer finds himself
sliding out of control along an oily, sinful snake:

> "YouTube's "suggested videos" can lead you down a rabbit
> hole. Moving on from Harris, I unlocked the Pandora's box
> of "It's not racist to criticise Islam!" content. Eventually I
> was introduced, by YouTube algorithms, to Milo Yiannop-
> oulos and various "anti-SJW" videos"

Yes, after being made aware of the entirely obvious fact that
"It's not racist to criticise Islam", he was led to a miscreant
even more treacherous than Harris, the fascinating character
known often just as Milo. And the writer's reaction to Milo's
videos?

"They were shocking at first"

This guy is easily shocked. First Sam Harris and now Milo. It's as if he spent his whole life locked in a cuddly university safe space drawing pictures of unicorns, and has only just been released into the community.

Just to be clear about what's shocking him, it's *other people opinions.* On YouTube. That he can turn off, or disregard, or laugh at, or do whatever he wants with.

Somehow though, despite the bewildering emotional cataclysm of listening to some ideas, he continues along the grisly path to damnation:

> *"the anti-SJW stuff also moved on to anti-feminism, men's rights activists – all that stuff. I followed a lot of these people on Twitter, but never shared any of it. I just passively consumed it, because, deep down, I knew I was ashamed of what I was doing."*

Oh god, the shame. The sacrilege of questioning third wave feminism. It's a wonder the guilt itself didn't destroy him, burning his guts and rotting his angelic, liberal heart until he simply fell down dead, face down at his desk with a frog meme flickering mockingly on the monitor before him.

It's at this point that he criticses Islam to his wife, and she gets a bit snooty, asking:

> *"Isn't that a bit... rightwing?"*

That's his ellipsis, by the way, indicating the pause during which his wife mentally scrolled through possible adjectives to describe her hubby's views: *fascist... literally Hitler... chaotic evil...* oh, I know–right wing!

He replies:

> *"Well, I'm more a left-leaning centrist. PC culture has gone too far, we should be able to discuss these things without shutting down the conversation by calling people racist, or bigots."*

A solid comeback, he gets it at last! Finally, the story has a happy ending. Oh, but wait, he then blows it completely by narrating retrospectively:

> *"The indoctrination was complete."*

That's the indoctrination of opening yourself to new ideas, allowing yourself to be challenged, realising that there are alternative ways to view the world, and that much of what you previously believed was inaccurate?

> *"This is exactly like a cult. What am I doing? I'm turning into an arsehole."*

Arsehole.

> *"I unsubscribed and unfollowed from everything, and told myself outright: "You're becoming a racist. What you're doing is turning you into a terrible, hateful person." Until that moment I hadn't even realised that "alt-right" was what I was becoming; I just thought I was a more open-minded person for tolerating these views."*

So, vote Leave, disagree with the social justice movement, question feminist theory, criticise Islam, even just listen to Sam Harris, and you'll turn into "a terrible, hateful person", you might be joining "a cult", and you're certainly well on your way to becoming a member of the alt-right.

While the penitent writer has bravely redeemed himself, if you should lean toward conservatism or stray from the liberal progressive agenda, then you are, as is always the case now, a bigot, a racist, and dangerously prone to extremism.

Just the usual slurs and insults then, but slightly repackaged. Unable to issue a straight 'you're racist', because it's been overused, we instead get a warped little pretend confession: *My lucky escape from the clutches of the alt-right.*

Here are the final couple of lines, just because they're so re-markably over the top and impossible to take seriously:

> *"I didn't think this could happen to me. But it did and it will haunt me for a long time to come."*

That's right, his flirtation with some ideas he doesn't agree with has left him in a state of profound existential discord. So be careful out there, heed the warnings and stay on-message… or it might happen to you too.

A HOAX OR A HOAXED HOAX ON THE GUARDIAN?

November 30th 2016

I greatly enjoyed myself yesterday putting the boot into Anonymous, from Brexit Britain, who'd pushed out a mind bending piece of writing at the Guardian claiming to have been sent into a right-wing, ideological death spiral by Sam Harris, Milo Yiannopoulos, and a YouTube algorithm.

But getting on Twitter today, it looks like I need to get my spider senses retuned, as one of the great troll-minds of our age, the eminently followable Twitter manipulator Godfrey Elfwick, has claimed responsibility for the Guardian piece.

But did he write it or not?

Here's the evidence he's provided so far:

[There was a Godfrey tweet here, but his Twitter account was long ago suspended by Twitter, for, if I remember correctly, calling Gary Lineker a cunt. So now I'm not totally sure what his evidence was, but it might have been a photo of the article text as an onscreen

Word document. Maybe.]

This in itself isn't really evidence. It could have been made at any time. There are a couple of things I notice about it too.

First, the headline is the same as the one on the published article. At a big organisation like the Guardian it would be usual for a sub-editor to write the headline.

Second, the text is *exactly* the same as in the published article, down to the punctuation style. Again, at a newspaper like the Guardian, a sub would usually make some changes, if only to make it fit the in-house style.

And then there's this:

[No idea. Another long gone tweet.]

This isn't strong evidence either, but it does make the following look a little suspect:

[Again, no tweet, but it contained a reference to having been inspired by some typically ridiculous, 2016-style Guardian articles by left-wing unintentional absurdist Abi Wilkinson.]

The two articles cited as inspiration were published *after* the parody was written (or started.)

I know, the 'inspired me' line could be just a joke, or maybe the inspiration was simply to turn some writing into a Guardian spoof. But either way, more evidence is needed to accept this as the brilliant hoax it might be. If it's real, then there must be some email correspondence with an editor at the Guardian. And if it's real, then why haven't the Guardian taken the piece down?

In a way, maybe a hoaxed hoax is better. It just underlines how far down the drain of nonsensical regressive leftism the Guardian has gone, when its articles seem more likely to be parody than real.

And Maajid Nawaz is right when he says this:

"∧ ppl asking for evidence, that's the beauty of it. "Anonymous" can't be proven& if the real snowflake comes forward, they're outed. Win/win"

Still, I'd like to know either way.

CONSERVATIVE POLITICS AVOIDS THE CELEBRITY SPELL

4th December 2016

When faced with a political dilemma my first reaction is always, what would Charlotte Church do? Sometimes she's busy planning a march or burning copies of the Sun though, and I can't discover her thoughts.

In those circumstances I get help by tuning in to the perspective of every other famous person on the planet. Superstars, has-beens, might-bes, can't-quites, it doesn't matter, because they all share a single, worn-out opinion. Whatever the circumstances, they favour the prescribed *liberal progressive* option.

The EU referendum wasn't a simple left/right binary, but unsurprisingly the likes of Benedict Cumberbatch and Keira Knightley lined up dutifully to back the totally anti-democratic fluffy liberal European Union, and the UK's zombified, eternal participation in it.

There were some famous names on the Leave side too, but

most of those in the contemporary spotlight backed Remain.

In the US election, Scarlet Johansson, Mark Ruffalo, and a roomful of other A-Listers made an unpleasantly twee video to support Hillary Clinton, while not-an-actual-gangster Robert De Niro threatened to punch Donald Trump, really hard, right in the mush.

It all worked a treat. Brexit was crushed and Hillary Clinton is poised to… no, not really. Of course it had no effect at all. Except, possibly, for the *exact opposite* to that which was intended.

Strangely, a troupe of studio-pampered millionaires offering unqualified support for the conveyor belt, establishment status quo doesn't quite ring true. It leads me to think that perhaps they're not made of twinkling stardust, and are just self-interested. The ingrained way of doing business has served them well enough up to now, so let's stick with it. For all our sakes. But mostly for their sakes.

Take a look at zany, Marxist lech Russell Brand. How does he think we react when he's frantically proselytizing? Utterly cocooned against hardship of any kind, Brand nonetheless bangs on about the perils of capitalism and the unfettered joy of command economies, and at some point announces that he's going to play right-on games with his child's emotional wellbeing by raising her gender neutral.

Although he pretends to be a revolutionary, he toes the line with ease. According to Brand we need to turn on, tune in and, erm, embrace metropolitan identity-leftism like every other Guardian reader in North London. Radical.

And this is where right-of-centre politics has the advantage. Thankfully, it's rare to find a celebrity who will raise themselves above the parapet in the service of anything not considered liberal progressive. We should be grateful for that, because in the world of politics celebrity endorsement is a bullet in the foot.

There have been a couple of notable exceptions this year though. First, Morrissey said that Brexit "was magnificent". This is not an endorsement of conservative politics by any means, but it does drive joyously against the grain of the vacuous liberal consensus.
Then, recently, Kate Bush praised Theresa May, and was spitefully harangued for it by narrow-minded zealots who can't bear differences of opinion.

These political statements didn't reek of the usual celebrity groupthink. They illustrate that on the rare occasions an artist moves away from the left-wing orthodoxy, their statements seem meaningful, for a number of reasons.

First, there can be no charges of hypocrisy or coercion. They're not instructing you to heed the message, stay in your lane, and stop being such a goddamn fascist (like the Hollywood set), and neither are they giving you a bullshit lecture about the illusory merits of a Marxist revolution, while raking in a vast personal fortune (like Brand).

In addition, a celebrity who voices conservative ideas will get savaged by so-called progressives. To anyone on the outside this looks like infantile vindictiveness. A clamour of trembling SJWs kicking someone on social media, or fretting over whether or not they're still allowed to like an artist's work, is not a good look. This pack mentality damages the image of its own cause.

Finally, knowing that they're going to be publicly flogged by the left, but expressing their views anyway, makes a speaker look principled. Their endorsement is obviously based on real beliefs because there's no personal gain to be had from publicising it. Their backing becomes worth having.

On a related note, just as the majority of celebrity endorsements are either without merit or of negative value, so celebrity threats to leave the country when an opposing candidate wins an election also amount to nothing more than throwaway attention seeking.

It's no shock that we're still waiting for an American exodus after Trump's victory. Wasn't Lena Dunham supposed to be leading the way?

REMAINERS PUSH FOR HARD BREXIT

8ᵗʰ December 2016

One of the false charges levelled at Leave voters is that Brexit is an act of self-harm. That whatever reasons a person might have for voting to escape from the European Union, the amount of damage caused will always outweigh the benefits.

But from where I stand, the only masochistic inclinations come from hardcore Remainers themselves, as they attempt to hinder or halt a clean, well executed departure.

As they snipe and circle in a constant, bad tempered performance, drawing attention to their own discontent like hormonal adolescents, it becomes clear that they'll try every trick at their disposal to oppose democracy.

An already impatient Leave camp is being made twitchy by the Remain contingent's obstructive posturing, but can the Europhiles do any real damage?

The most vocal Remainers are so entrenched and irrational that they've actually shifted general opinion toward the very thing they've spent the past few months ardently demonising: a hard Brexit.

There are Leave supporters who've consistently argued that the *only* real Brexit *is* hard Brexit, and Remain have unwittingly reinforced this view. In fact, the idea of simply repealing the 1972 European Communities Act and walking nonchalantly away as if we've never heard of Article 50 now has a certain nihilistic, up-yours attraction. It's the kind of thing Sid Vicious would do if he was in charge. Not so much a hard Brexit as a brick to the face Brexit.

That might give credibility to the charges of self harm though, and it's unlikely our politicians would have the poised recklessness to pull it off. Instead, given the space to play smart, our negotiators would do best to take that most composedly British of approaches, and play the long game.

And were we united behind Brexit, they could do that.

However, with Remain jabbering and poking in the background like irritating, spoiled children, the considered approach becomes less attractive. What Brexiteer would feel comfortable with such a cautious route now, in the knowledge that amoral Remainers would have more time to subvert the plan?

Suddenly we're a little less Roger Moore, and a bit more like John Cleese in *Clockwise*—quite prepared to steal a Porsche while dressed as a monk, as we race to trigger Article 50 before the entire glorious achievement can be stolen from us.

The upshot is that as time goes by and the Remain crowd stay as unreasonable as ever, the safest option, to ensure that we really do leave for good, is to get out quickly and completely, whatever it takes. And the nudge toward such thinking comes not from any external pressures, but from the internal threat of the Remain saboteurs themselves—those who least want to take that course.

There's no reason Britain can't make a success of any style of Brexit, but it's certainly not ideal that our hand is being forced by undemocratic elitists, and those elements of the media who turn into intellectually stunted dullards when attempting to get a handle on EU antipathy. ("Duh, shall we go with the racist angle again?")

Something these anti-democrats can never get their heads around is patriotism. The idea that a citizenry could be willing to risk a short-term financial hit in order to secure priceless, permanent sovereignty is apparently unfathomable.

They also have difficulty reconciling national integrity with being an outward looking, internationally-minded country, but of course there is no conflict between these things. Right now it's the EU that appears stagnant and insular, while an independent, agile Britain looks fresh and ready to do business.

Perhaps it's this intractable refusal to consider the value of nation states—in their most inclusive and forward thinking colours—that holds the Remainers back.

But that's their problem. They've had almost half a year, and deserve no sympathy if they can still neither adjust to change, nor make the effort to understand an alternative point of view. All we must now ensure is that their regressive tendencies are not allowed to affect our democratic choice.

GILES FRASER'S LOW EXPECTATIONS

12th December 2016

A recent Giles Fraser article in the Guardian, *Assimilation Threatens the Existence of Other Cultures*, asserts that wherever you might choose to live, you should feel no obligation to assimilate into the wider culture. He states:

> "I admire the resilience of a community that seeks to maintain its distinctiveness and recognises, quite rightly, that assimilation into the broader culture would mean the gradual dilution, and the eventual extinction, of its own way of life."

He's talking about a Jewish community in London, but unless we do away with equality and universal standards, we must assume that the same edicts apply to all.

That means no more derogatory comments about British expat communities on the Costa del Sol who don't bother learning Spanish. Fraser is clear on this, describing, back in the Yiddish speaking community:

> "a lad of 20 who has lived in the borough of Hackney all his life. He was born here and grew up here. And he's a bright boy – yet he speaks only a few very rudimentary words of English."

Fraser's feelings on this?

"I admire it."

So those stereotypes about the British abroad, shouting at waiters in simplified English, are to be admired. Thanks to Fraser, this can be embraced as a celebration of diversity.

I'm being disingenuous though. Everyone knows that double standards are a core part of the regressive left curriculum, albeit re-branded as 'cultural relativism'. In this model, there are no right and wrong, morals are inconstant, and the ground slips away from beneath your feet if you think too hard.

It's what allows third wave feminists to defend the burka, or has radical LGBT activists turning a blind eye to Islamic intolerance of homosexuality.

In that earlier quote Fraser said:

> "[a community's] assimilation into the broader
> culture would mean the gradual dilution, and the
> eventual extinction, of its own way of life"

The expectations here are set desperately low. How stupid does Fraser think minority groups are, that they're not capable of engaging with two cultures at the same time? You adapt to the wider culture, and you stay connected with your local one. Bingo, you've succeeded. I assume that Fraser would have no difficulty doing this himself if necessary, so why imply that minorities should find it a problem?

Regarding immigration, if a new arrival's relationship with their home culture does change over time, what's wrong with that anyway? We don't carry our cultures around the world with us, freeze dried, to set up and preserve like museum pieces wherever we hang our hats. People shift and develop with time and circumstance. It's called being adaptable, and it's a positive characteristic. Fraser apparently wants to put a stop to all that though, preserving minority communities in amber, and walling them off from functional inclusion in wider society.

When you live in a new country, the expectation that you should have fitted in is actually a huge compliment. It says 'you're one of us now'. It's a kind of acceptance. By contrast, being told that you needn't even bother trying is utterly disheartening. It's a sign that either your hosts are xenophobic, and will never fully accept an outsider, or that you personally seem unable to learn.

Mawkishly informing minorities that you don't expect them to assimilate is a pat on the head. You've judged them to be incapable, so you'll treat them like a family pet instead of an equal, to be coddled and cared for, and then left to their own unknowable devices.

This culture of low expectations, in which minorities are exempt from normal criticism, reeks of genuine prejudice. It's the kind of slant that goes unacknowledged because it hides behind sympathy, smiles, and the illusion of good intent. The kind which says nobody should ever break from type, or expect to be judged solely on the content of their character.

Immigrants who've thrived in the UK do so by fitting in to what's already here. And when that happens, the establishment is perfectly capable of bending a little too.

But by suddenly lowering the bar of our expectations, we devalue the hard work and decency of previous generations of successful migrants, who recognised the mutual necessity of integration.

Here's what Fraser says about Muslims:

> "They are serial offenders in their resistance to the hegemony of integration. They won't allow the Borg-like values of secular liberalism to corrode their distinctiveness. They seek to maintain their religious convictions and way of life. They refuse all that nonsense about religion being a private matter. They stand strong against the elimination of diversity."

Did you catch those parts about secular liberalism, and religion as a private matter? He's arguing that one group of people, whom he apparently views as a homogenous block, should be uniquely excused from fundamental ('borg-like') social tenets. Again he has low expectations, but now they become more explicitly dangerous, as he casually rejects the crucial accord that all must be treated equally, and that if no-one is to be discriminated against, then no-one must be favoured either.

Fraser's ideas help nobody. Minorities are instructed to resist integration and live in segregated ghettos. Everybody is forced to live in an increasingly fractured society, against their will. And our fundamental values are subverted and undermined by some incoherent moral contortions.

The only beneficiary is the delicate conscience of over-sensitive progressives, as they load up on virtue and balm their misplaced liberal guilt.

NO STUDENT VOTING—FOR THEIR OWN SAFETY

15th December 2016

In September 2015, student union officials at the University of East Anglia prohibited the handing out of sombreros at a fresher's fair, on the grounds that the headwear comprised "discriminatory or stereotypical imagery".

In April of this year, a survey found that two thirds of British students support the 'no-platforming' of speakers. This means denying controversial people the right to participate in on-campus debates. We've seen the exclusion of dangerous hate preachers such as... Germaine Greer and Maryam Namazie, a human rights campaigner.

Following US trends, growing numbers of British universities are now issuing 'trigger warnings' to let students know if upcoming course material will make them fall over in gasping convulsions. This has included archaeology students at University College London being forewarned darkly of "historical events that may be disturbing, even traumatising". Yes, *traumatising.*

And at City University London, Plymouth University, and Queen Mary University in London, student unions have banned the sale of a terrifying clutch of evil publications. You may have heard of these sinister journals, they're called the Sun, the Daily Mail, and the Daily Express. Going into a shop selling right wing newspapers is simply too much to handle for many of today's students.

Look across the Atlantic at what happened when Donald Trump took first the piss, and then the White House. There was complete meltdown. Distraught students were excused from class, while feebly named *cry-ins* were organised. Tutors cancelled exams and emergency support services were provided. On campuses across the United States, the sky came crashing in. It appeared that many students had been scarred for life, unable to forget the black day when—brace yourself— a candidate they didn't like won an election.

Clearly, such wrenching pain mustn't be allowed to inflict its trauma on Britain's youth. I care deeply about the emotional well-being of our idealistic young sunbeams, as they delicately strive for intersectional justice, while crushing all forms of dissent along the way.

So I have a proposal to guard their fragile, progressive intellects, in line with their fondness for politically pure safe spaces.

In order to protect them from the potentially lethal shock of not only encountering different opinions, but maybe even losing an election to them, I propose that while the legal voting age of 18 is appropriate for the general population, university students should have their voting rights suspended until after they graduate.

Sorry, suspended is a strong word. They should have their voting rights placed, like a fluffy, gender neutral kitten, into the temporary care of a state assigned thought-comrade.

Please understand that this is entirely for the benefit of the students themselves. Remember that safety is paramount, and that words are violence.

Put yourself in a snowflake's crystal slippers for a moment. Can you imagine the deadly potential of encountering a conservative opinion? Of going up against a libertarian in debate? Of voting for someone, that person not winning, and then having to just *accept* the result, even though you know your choice was better? It's all so upsetting, it simply doesn't bear thinking about.

I fully understand that what matters most are feelings. Not the feelings of straight, white men, obviously. The most important feelings belong to people who are definitely right, such as Marxist NUS officials. It's wonderful that their leftist ideas go unchallenged in the academic environment, and it would be a horrendous, shattering tragedy were students who cherish such ideologies to have their thoughts tainted by *the real world*.

After all, there are right-wing thinkers out there. As university students can't even look at a copy of the Sun without their eyeballs bursting into flames, it would be unfair and incredibly dangerous to make them participate in elections, overflowing as they are with terrifying, never before encountered opinions.

Emerging from the incubated political bubble of university life after graduation could in itself be troubling, and a period of decompression may be necessary. I suggest that graduates at first be given just a tenth of a vote, increasing by a further tenth year on year, until after a decade of exposure to reality, when they're comfortably acclimatised and deprogrammed, they'll be able to enjoy complete democratic participation.

I look forward to my proposal receiving the full backing of student unions and LGBTQQIP2SAA solidarity groups across the land, and thank them in advance for their support. #Hope-NotHate. #HugsNotVotes.

YOU WOULD SAY THAT, YOU'RE A WHITE MAN

20th December 2016

I wrote recently about holy segregationist Giles Fraser's low expectations of minority communities. But look closely at identity politics and you'll find this kind of fatalism is deeply ingrained everywhere. I noticed it the other night when I went out for a drink and narrowly avoided, as Mrs Merton used to say, *a heated debate*.

In Shinjuku's eastern district—a do-as-you-like, all-night corner of Tokyo—I found myself in a tiny, crowded basement bar sipping lager from a can and listening to *Depeche Mode*. Assimilation indeed.

An American couple included me in their conversation, and soon began lamenting the election of Donald Trump. They became quite fraught as they went along, and after a while seemed bothered that my responses weren't chiming with their feelings.

"What do *you* think about Trump?" One of them eventually asked, a touch of accusation in her tone.

"I guess to me he's kind of a..."

Personal Jesus came on in the background.

"…I don't think he's going to be quite the disaster you're making out." I said, and then her reply put an end to any hope of a reasonable exchange:

"You would say that, because you're a white man."

And there it was, the same blunt delusion as has manifested so stubbornly around both social and traditional media: an improper knockout combination of battering ram prejudice and those recurring low expectations. I considered telling her that I'm gender fluid and she'd committed a hate crime, but resigned myself to a sarcastic "right, okay", and ordered another can instead.

There's nothing new in this kind of prejudice, other than who's directing it, and who's on the receiving end. The in-your-face bigotry of dismissing someone's opinions on the basis of race or gender is as invalid and meaningless now as ever.

And the low expectations implicit in this recently common dismissal? They're embedded in a rock bottom judgment on the critical thinking of all-who-disagree. The message is that vast swathes of people, incapable of objectivity, are barricaded into their own ideologies without even realising it. Our ideas determined entirely by our physiology, we look in the mirror each morning, grunt, and set off out the house down a predetermined behavioural path to—do what exactly?—further our own racial interests? Exclude and oppress? Commit general acts of self-serving cruelty?

This prison-cell view is horribly reductive, diminishing everybody by dictating that nobody is capable of thinking creatively. Nobody can choose their own intellectual route. And the scope of our reasoning is determined largely by our skin tone. Fall into this intellectual trap and you've subscribed to a grim worldview, in which we're nothing more than shuffling dimwits, enslaved to primitive groupthink.

It also contains a low expectation of humanity's underlying moral codes. The suggestion is that we can't act on anything other than our own basic wants, and only make decisions—such as who to vote for—based on what will be of the most immediate, selfish benefit. It's a way of branding everyone in the out-group as brazenly self-interested, with no concern for the wider community.

In the world of identity politics this becomes the norm, and we're reduced to nothing more than component parts of competing biological interests. Condemned to spend our lives sniping and swiping at each other in a zero-sum game, the best we can hope for is to gain an inch for the team we've been bundled in with. It's a hopelessly savage outlook.

A glaring problem with this philosophy is that it requires the existence of unspoken but globally understood group motivations, driving all members of each race and gender, wherever in the world they might be. We're supposed to believe, for example, that all white people, regardless of economic, social, and intellectual circumstances, share the same politics and want the same things.

The absurdity of this is apparent in the fact that the people writing me off for being a white man were both *white*, and that one of them was even, shamelessly, *a man*. How then had they broken their genetic programming? Were they further evolved than me? Maybe they'd come from the future.

If someone tells you that you hold your opinions because of your race or gender, then you can be sure that they haven't even tried to understand your side of the argument. And if they have no understanding of their opponent's position, they can never have more than a partial understanding of their own.

At the bar we were in, there are hundreds of CDs shelved up to the ceiling behind the counter. You can ask for songs, and the bartender will take down your CD and place it in a stacked up queue of requests.

I remembered **an article I'd read** about some distress caused, after the US election, when a grocery store in Brooklyn played a famous Neil Young-rebuking Southern rock classic, and I called out to the bartender,

"Sweet Home Alabama, thanks."

THE FARAGE OVERREACTION

21ˢᵗ December 2016

I don't know what to call them anymore. Progressives? Obviously not. Liberals? I sense no liberalism in their approach to dissent. Regressive left? Control left?

However you refer to them, the response of some parts of the left wing to yesterday's horrific events in Berlin and Ankara was remarkable.

Try Labour MP Jess Phillips' Twitter timeline. You'll find that quite some effort has gone into attacking not Islamism, but instead Nigel Farage, due to his spat with Brendan Cox, the husband of murdered MP Jo Cox. There are tweets like this:

"I've just seen Farage's comments to Brendan Cox.Don't know why I'm upset Farage is a lying racist in cheap suit of knock off authenticity"

There are running battles with Farage supporters, and something about not being "a monster". That's what she calls the former Ukip leader, while implying that he has never felt sadness or loss, or at least not on the same level as hers.

On the subject of the atrocity in Germany? Well, there's this:

"Awful news from Berlin. My thought with all in the amazing city"

And not much else. Anything on the actual substance of what lies behind the horrific attack? On how we reconcile mass migration with the reality that extremists are in among the innocents? No, of course not. After all, she's just an MP, why would she comment on things like that?

As so often with those commenting from left-of-centre, she asserts a monopoly on compassion, while offering nothing on how to address the problem which is causing the suffering.

Owen Jones--who else?--bashed out a quick piece for--who else?--the Guardian. The main thrust of his article was that if there's one thing we must take from the atrocities in Berlin and Ankara, it's to absolutely not become right wing. Not at all. Not even a little bit.

He explicitly intertwines right wing politics and Islamism:

> "Islamist terror fanatics and the west's ascendant populist right are now working in tandem. They are feeding off each other. They are interdependent. Their fortunes rise with each other."

Nigel Farage had earlier allocated blame for the Berlin attacks to Angela Merkel's immigration policy, so Jones then asks, about Farage,

> "What kind of contemptible individual mixes horror with vindication?"

But look back at that first quote. Could we not instead ask, what kind of contemptible individual mixes an understandable shift to the political right with acts of terrorism perpetrated by religious fanatics?

And if there is a link between mass immigration and security issues, is it not a politician's job to address it, no matter whether or not it makes Guardian columnists feel uncomfortable?

Jones states,

> "From Donald Trump to France's Marine Le Pen to the Netherlands' Geert Wilders, the populist right will now be carefully plotting how they will extract political dividends from the horror."

It seems we needn't worry about the terrorism then. After all, we've seen that before. A far greater nightmare, haunting all Europe no less, is the very frightening prospect of people offering political approaches which differ from those of Owen Jones.

If Jones and his followers don't like what right wing politicians have to say on the subject of Islamism, then here's an idea: *offer an alternative.* Because right now, what exactly is the left saying? Hope for the best? As you were? Put a German flag on your Facebook profile?

Apparently, when your political compass leans too far to the right, a klaxon sounds and "the terrorists are winning". If right wing politics—let's not use the now derogatory 'populism'—is ascendant, then we're told it's all because of terrorists, and is unrelated to the left bringing absolutely nothing of substance to the table, or being unable to shift an inch from their unpopular, open borders immigration policies.

In this alternative reality, ISIS' main agenda has nothing to do with caliphates, Sharia rule, and all that Koran-based guff, what they actually want is a majority Tory government in the United Kingdom.

Let's return to Farage. What exactly did he say that caused so many commentators to spit out their dummies?

First, as mentioned, he assigned blame for the attacks on Angela Merkel's open door immigration policy:

"Terrible news from Berlin but no surprise. Events like these will be the Merkel legacy."

To which Brendan Cox, the husband of murdered MP Jo Cox, replied:

"blaming politicians for the actions of extremists? That's a slippery slope Nigel"

Then, defending his comments on LBC, Farage said, among other remarks on matters such as the Schengen Area, that Hope Not Hate, and organisation Brendan Cox is linked to, are "extremists" who "pursue violent and very undemocratic means." Hope Not Hate then threatened to sue.

Farage has previously accused the organisation of disrupting his rallies, and they were recently shown to have exaggerated figures on online hate speech in order to further their own causes. They have also received criticism for their targeting of reformist Muslims.

But this steers away from the point: that even if Farage's comments were wrong, how is it that among some people they generated more rage and vitriol than acts of murder and terrorism? It's as if bashing Farage has become a worthier cause than confronting Islamism. This is justified by implying that 'populism'--which has become a vague, coded slur for anything that opposes the liberal agenda--is an existential threat on a par with acts of terror.

Could it be that on the left, some things just don't matter in the same way that they do to everyone else? Islamism and ISIS don't matter. Immigration and integration don't matter. The opinions of ordinary people don't matter.

Apparently, all that matters to the left, is the left itself.

Whenever an Islamist atrocity occurs, so-called liberal progressives ignore the facts, ignore the causes, and neglect to talk about security or prevention. Instead they do the only thing they know how--they line up to beat us relentlessly with the same hollow, self-serving orders: don't listen to anyone else. Don't question the narrative. And at all costs: keep to the left.

SLIPPERALS: OWEN JONES AND MARK STEEL

23rd December 2016

Brexiteers have copped a lot of abuse over the past few months for allegedly being swayed by emotion and ignorant of the facts. I no longer care about this palpably incorrect nonsense. The Brexiteers I know are sometimes almost obsessively well informed about the EU, in many cases far more so than the bovine whingers who plumped for Remain because the establishment told them to. (I know, I know, there are plenty of intelligent, democracy respecting Remainers too.)

So when it comes to the topics of radical Islam, and immigration, I have to note the glaring self-contradictions being belched out by slippery liberals.

When it suits their agenda, their instructions will suddenly be inverted. As in, stop looking at the facts and figures you heartless fascist, we must be tolerant, open our hearts, and *#HopeNotHate.*

As in, when it comes to immigration, we must make decisions based on compassion. Yes, some of the child refugees coming in to the UK earlier this year weren't really children, but only someone with antifreeze for blood would care about that. Have you no heart, no *emotions*?

When it comes to self-contradiction and double standards, the so-called progressives are shameless. The truth is that they don't really care whether you vote with your head or your heart, as long as you vote with them, and they'll cynically reverse their opinions, without conscience (or perhaps without self-awareness) as and when it suits them.

Which brings us to the ways that some commentators are overlooking Islamist terror in favour of taking swipes at the right wing. I wrote about Owen Jones' response to the Berlin and Ankara attacks previously, but in his new article he's gone even further.

He writes about the terror attacks for just one paragraph, and spends much of the rest of the piece lashing out at political commentators he happens not to like. James Delingpole, Raheem Kassam and Arron Banks are, with the aid of some cherry picked tweets, designated histrionically to be:

> "a political cesspit. They are almost farcically unpleasant comic book villains"

Got that? When Delingpole tweets (in the context of Cox's attack on Farage) "When are we allowed to say that Brendan Cox is a total arse?" it's double plus ungood. But when Jones writes

"These individuals are a political cesspit", it's acceptable. I know, I don't get it either.

We are then let in on some abuse that Jones has been given by online harassers. While this is vile and should be confronted, I'm absolutely certain that Jones isn't alone in receiving such unwanted attention, and it's most definitely not limited to liberal activists.

For the article's grand finale, these terrifying strands are woven together, and we are presented with the ghastly truth-- it's nothing less than the rise of shit-your-pants, apocalyptic, full-blown evil:

> "We face a great danger, and not even those who will suffer because of it have realised just how grave it is. Intolerance and hatred have been legitimised across the western world. Dissent is becoming treason. That is bad enough. But there are other violent extremists who are being both radicalised and legitimised across the west. If we don't take a stand now, new dark chapters are soon to arrive."

To which the only response can be... what? Does he genuinely not know what everyone else is concerned about right now, and why? Strangely, nobody thinks that famous Guardian columnists with Twitter followings over half a million are unable to speak their minds ("dissent is treason"!)

And the "violent extremists" and "dark chapters" which most people care about are those associated with radical Islamism. By the end of his column, Jones seems to have forgotten the awful tragedy which occurred in Germany, when twelve people lost their lives and many more were injured, in horrific circumstances, because of terrorism. It's simply incredible that Jones chooses to overlook this.

In the Independent, Mark Steel generates an effort of pure distraction, which has literally just one line alluding to the terror attacks in Germany. Seriously, one line. After that briefest of brief mentions, he launches vitriol at some of the same right-of-centre voices Jones has in his wobbly sights, primarily Farage, and makes a big issue about not hurting the feelings of recent widower Brendan Cox.

> "this week Brendan Cox suggested it was dangerous to blame politicians who helped immigrants for outrages such as the one in Berlin. A couple of years ago we'd have respected the opinion of a man whose immigrant-helping wife had recently been murdered. Not anymore."

What does it mean to respect his opinions? Am I allowed to say that I think Steel is misinterpreting his words, and that he appeared to imply that Farage bore responsibility for a murder? Here's his tweet:

"blaming politicians for the actions of extremists? That's a slippery slope Nigel"

Cox is involved in a divisive, crucial debate around issues of national security, in which all must be free to voice an opinion.

But again we have this weird shifting of priorities, where protecting selected people's feelings is considered more important than actually discussing the profoundly serious issues at hand.

As always, when it suits the left, emotions are of primary importance, but when it comes to, let's say, voting on EU membership, feelings are to be disregarded. Well, which is it? Why don't they make up their minds?

Steel also talks about campaign group Hope Not Hate, which Brendan Cox supports, being "completely opposed to fascism". Can we just get a handle on this? How many fascists do any readers here know? How many neo-Nazis? I'd hazard a guess at precisely ZERO. Because fascism just is not a pressing issue in the UK in 2016.

Islamist extremism, on the other hand, *is* fascistic, and is an issue, and is dangerous. If Hope Not Hate truly want to battle extremism, then why don't they get in touch with the Quilliam Foundation and take an interest in Islamic reform? How can they possibly justify going after Ukip rather than stopping Muslim hate preachers? It's incomprehensible, until you understand that they are driven primarily by far-leftism, rather than anti-fascism.

If, on the other hand, Mark Steel is implying that Nigel Farage, Ukip, or the party's supporters are fascists, then he is obscenely irresponsible.

I'm not a Ukip supporter, but I can see quite clearly that many of those who find themselves aligning with Ukip are perfectly decent people who feel that no other party currently represents their concerns. But we now have the sight of the left wing slinging mud at people who (in some cases) might once have voted for the Labour party. You know—the voters gormless Corbyn and his unpleasant cheerleaders are currently trying to woo back. By calling them fascists.

If Jones, Steele and their allies are serious about taking on Ukip, Marine Le Pen, Donald Trump, and others like them, then, well, *take them on.* That means you don't launch ad hominem attacks on them or their supporters. You don't slur them with insinuations of fascism. You don't search for victimhood because they tweet more cavalierly than you.

Here, let's make it easy, this is Farage's original tweet, the one that kicked everything off:

"Terrible news from Berlin but no surprise. Events like these will be the Merkel legacy."

Farage is saying, obviously, that unchecked immigration has increased the likelihood of terror attacks. It's not an uncommon opinion.

So, Mark Steele, Owen Jones, and those who admire them, why don't you address that? Do you agree wholeheartedly? If so, what should be done? Or do you disagree? Why is that? What are your suggestions with regard to preventing Islamist terror attacks? What, broadly, is the left's position on these issues? Are you willing to shift with popular opinion, or would you prefer popular opinion to shift with you? Do you accept that your open borders worldview is out of touch with the current mood, and that you might, just conceivably, have called this one wrong?

We know you hate Nigel Farage, but that's irrelevant. Just for once on this issue, try talking about policies, not personalities, and let's not get distracted by emotion. There is much more at stake now.

BREXITEERS ARE NEANDERTHALS

I thought things were going well. We were in the EU and Britain was being drained of its troublesome sovereignty as I, through my subscription to *Everyday Feminism*, was being radically unchained from my toxic masculinity.

Brussels knows best. Who needs to know the names of the suits in charge anyway? They're European, nice shoes, brandy on tap. They're just better at managing things than us. We're all Europeans now, of course, but they're a bit *more* European.

Then it happened. Those... *people,* up north. In Grimhampton or wherever. They all ruined it with their feckless Leave votes. I mean, I feel sorry for them, because they don't have proper books, and the Guardian probably isn't sold up there. Why the hell didn't we send them some copies of the Guardian? We could've made an audio version, or made the words a bit simpler. The Guardian informed us quite clearly to vote Remain. And the BBC too. They get the BBC, don't they?

The thing is, they didn't know what they were voting for. They thought the EU was going to ban darts, and they're all racist anyway. They don't understand that having national borders is racist, because... let's see, what did the Guardian say..? Yes, that's right, it's racist to have borders because borders are racist.

Perhaps we could have written that on the backs of scratchcards, so they'd have got the message.

If we could just get them to understand our liberal thinking. It's simple: progressiveness is all about keeping things exactly as they are. But when we tell them leaving the EU will *change* things they seem pleased. I just don't get it, is it because they're low information? Or post-truth? Or—did anyone mention?–*actually racist.*

I'm ashamed to get my passport out now. I must show that I'm not a bigot. I changed my Facebook profile picture to an EU flag, and even did my Remainer friend's online survey that was shared around our Remainer group, to see which way we'd vote if there was another referendum. I clicked Remain and do you know what? Remain won! This could be an effective format for a second referendum.

A further tragedy is that 2016 has taken so many of our most revolutionary artists. I feel certain that if Ronnie Corbett were alive now he'd be marching to overthrow democracy and enforce the result that I personally favour.

Some say it's better to accept a fair outcome and move on, rather than fatally undermine democracy forever, but they're just bigots. I know, historically, it's dictators and tyrants who've shown contempt for democracy, but there's a big difference: they were *bad guys*, whereas I'm almost religiously convinced of my own moral and political infallibility, so, what could go wrong?

The most important thing for next year is that we absolutely do not change our political strategy. We need to let people know that they're wrong and stupid. We must spell out to them what their true motives were in voting incorrectly, and reinforce that they're wretched, provincial neanderthals. That way they'll soon come over to our way of thinking.

They seem to take in messages written on the sides of buses, so I thought something like, "Hey, racists, do as you're told" might work.
Also, it's vital that they only read approved news. A hopeful and positive goal we can all work together on is crushing dissent by banning off-message newspapers.

I'm starting a new campaign group called *Good Not Bad*. I want to keep the message simple. We aim to change people's thinking and make them embrace love, hope, and inclusivity. We'll do this through mob harassment and public shamings.

If all else fails, then there's a last resort. We'll put bad voters in camps and make them watch groupthink-compliant satirical panel shows, until their opinions are safely neutered and they can be released back into their boggy, un-European natural habitat.

PART TWO

2017:
INTRODUCTION

This is the year when I was most utterly consumed by online politics, and didn't stop writing about it, while getting into endless Twitter spats and occasionally having a tweet go viral. Follower count growing the whole time, but in the external world—the only one that matters—abandoning the norms of how to lead a balanced life.

Staring at my phone, thinking about inconsequential online drama, frustrated at how wrong so many people were. But rarely considering that I might be mistaken, or acting weird, or that everyone might have become mistaken and weird, or that it very often just didn't matter either way.

And not noticing that I had completely forgotten even the notion of presence. Not online presence. What I had forgotten was how to be present in my surroundings, with the people around me.

It's really not good to fall asleep looking at Twitter, and then follow an urge, as soon as you wake up, to check Twitter.

And it never occurred to me that the solution was simply not to do what I was doing. Which seems incredible, looking back. How did I not get that?

In the news it was, of course, Brexit. And also terror attacks, Islam, free speech, transgender arguments, identity politics... all the things it would be better *not* to think about, day after day, week after week, but on which I was—absurdly, claustrophobically—constantly focused.

What strikes me now is the repetition, and my own willingness to bury myself in recurring themes, talking endlessly about the left-wing and its faults, for no significant reward, material or otherwise.

And another thing I'm aware of, in retrospect, is how even as I imagined I was some kind of free thinker, able to see all angles having defected from the left, I was nothing of the sort. Not even close. I had simply exchanged one cast iron ideology for another. Contempt for the outgroup hadn't been exorcised, it had been reconfigured as contempt for a different outgroup.

And what an over-opinionated and rigid bubble I was constructing. One that, just like all the others, believed itself to be essentially different from all the others.

I was addicted, and addiction strips away perspective, but curiously, I can't define what, exactly, I had become reliant on.

THE DANGEROUS COWARDICE OF CENSORSHIP

1ˢᵗ January 2017

When you shut down free speech, thereby removing the right and the capability to dissent openly, then the methods of expression left available for those who have been silenced become out-of-sight, resentful, and, taken to the extreme, violent. The recent trend toward de-platforming and censorship is reckless and ill-informed.

Conservative journalist Milo Yiannopolous, who delights in provoking thin-skinned authoritarians, has just earned himself a $250'000 book deal with the publishers Simon & Schuster, and predictably, elements of the illiberal left are coughing and spluttering with indignation.

The Chicago Review of books tweeted this:

"In response to this disgusting validation of hate, we will not cover a single @simonschuster book in 2017."

Seemingly forgetting that their Twitter bio says, "The Chicago Review of Books is dedicated to diverse voices in literature."

And there's Hollywood star Judd Apatow, who's fully hitched to the anti-free speech bandwagon, and sends out tweets like this *[in response to a call to get Simon & Schuster to "back down"]*:

"I am in! In these times we can not let hatemongers get rich off of their cruelty. Shame on @simonschuster !"

Or comedian Sarah Silverman, who tweeted this *[referring to Yiannopolous]*:

"The guy has freedom of speech but to fund him & give him a platform tells me a LOT about @simonschuster YUCK AND BOO AND GROSS"

Apatow also wrote of Milo:

"He has the right to speak, we have the right to protest".

Some variation of this argument is commonly heard from those attacking free speech, but it doesn't in any way justify removing a speaker's platform.

Yes, of course we all have the right to protest, but that's not actually what Apatow wants—he's moving to have Milo's right to be published removed. If he were in a public debate with Milo, and after having said his own piece he then removed Milo's microphone, claiming that he were exercising his right to protest, that wouldn't be considered a valid strategy. And we are all in a constant public debate—we benefit greatly from a democratic, unrestricted exchange of ideas, both good and bad.

Apatow needs to understand that you protest against opinions by letting them be heard, and then countering them with your own opinions. This is the only effective, trusted, civil method.

Cutting off your opponent's opinions at the tap can't be considered a protest, because if you do that then there is nothing to protest against.

Apatow might claim that his stance is based on what Milo has said previously. In that case he should clearly and precisely challenge what has been said previously. But he can't protest against what Milo hasn't said yet, because it *doesn't exist yet.* Silencing people because of what you think they might say sounds more than a little bit tyrannical.

I would love for the Apatows and Silvermans to stop for a minute, and extrapolate where we would end up if their approach toward restricting opposing views were to become the norm. It's staggeringly short-sighted. Once censorship is in place, it's in place for everyone, including those who called for it in the first place.

They might say this is fine, because their views are the 'right' ones. But how about if someone who disagrees with them about a few things comes to power, and some alternative views become popular? Congratulations A-Listers, you're now vulnerable to being shut down using your very own erroneous justifications. An irony in the Milo case is that someone they're opposed to, Donald Trump, *is* about to take office, and a common fear is that he's hostile to a free press. So what on earth is Apatow doing by harassing publishers, getting the ball rolling for the incoming president?

The crying over Milo's deal echoes the anti-democratic stance of hardcore EU Remainers in the UK, or Never Trumpers in the US. There's a palpable sense that they'd rather subvert the values of democracy than concede a loss, showing no sense of perspective, and no realisation that any damage done by their actions would inevitably come back and bite them too.

Ultimately, shutting people down is a form of cowardice. If Milo's detractors can't combat his ideas with their own ideas, then we have to ask, what have Milo's ideas got that theirs haven't?

After all, if they're so utterly confident that he's wrong, so very certain to the point where they feel he *shouldn't even be published*, then what do they have to fear? Why not let his ideas be exposed, and then show the world how faulty they are?

If their reasoning is sound, then it shouldn't be difficult for them. After all, Apatow is totally convinced that his ideas are better, he has a public platform significantly larger than Milo's, he's more famous, richer, and he has more influence.

So I wonder, just what is it that he's scared of?

HATE CRIME: NO HATE REQUIRED

14th January 2017

On Thursday, Joshua Silver, a professor at Oxford University, was comprehensively taken apart by Andrew Neil and Michael Howard on the BBC's Daily Politics.

As a recap, scruffy Europhile Silver had freaked out and reported home secretary Amber Rudd to the police, for a speech and briefing at the Conservative party conference last October, in which it was suggested that companies list their foreign-born employees, ensuring that vacancies can be filled by British workers. It's an idea which came to nothing.

The absurdity doesn't end with Silver contacting the police though, as it turns out that his time-wasting appeals weren't dismissed. Although the police didn't investigate the deluded academic's complaint, they actually recorded Rudd's speech as a hate incident.

Due to the nonsensical nature of the affair, Professor Silver was unable to defend his antics, and was instead made to look like a shambling chancer during his BBC appearance. However, I feel that we should also extend some gratitude to the slovenly campus lurker, as his willingness to make an arse of himself on national television dragged some important issues into the light.

First, it debunked one of the elitist fallacies that has been thrown around since the Brexit vote last June: that the higher a voter's education level was, the more likely they were to have voted Remain, and so therefore Remain must have been the more intelligent choice. While it's true that a majority of university graduates backed Remain, Professor Silver, who is a physicist, is living, just-breathing proof that having the skills necessary to thrive in a university setting certainly does not equate with having good judgment, common sense, or the ability to understand simple political back-and-forth.

The professor's behaviour also serves as a reminder of just how politically sealed off university campuses can be. There's a substantial left wing bias throughout the education industry, reinforced to the point of distortion by the looping echo of the university bubble. Considering stories of **universities instructing staff to vote Remain, and offering counselling services** to feeble-minded academics traumatised by the referendum result, it's fair to say that universities are unlikely to have engaged in a balanced exploration of the issues around EU membership. In this kind of environment, a sizeable majority in favour of Remain is indicative of the pressure to conform, and of a lack of viewpoint diversity.

Further to this, look at Professor Silver's words (after admitting that he didn't even watch the speech) when he says: "I've read the speech carefully and I've looked at all the feedback." He also refers to how Amber Rudd's speech was "interpreted".

I'm going to go out on a limb and suggest that he didn't travel far to gather that "feedback" on how the speech was "interpreted". When the only opinions you hear come from your fellow Oxford doctrinaires and the Guardian comments section, you're not going to develop a particularly rounded view of the world.

So on matters of policy which affect a nation, I'm inclined to think that whatever the majority view in universities might be, it's likely to be based on wrong decisions. If safe spaces, no-platforming and newspaper bans continue to proliferate on campus, this will only become more true. University should be where students learn to value objective truth, but at the moment academia appears biased to the point of dysfunction, ideologically warped, and horribly infantilised.

The second point highlighted by Silver's petulant appeal to the police, is that the reported rise in hate incidents following the Brexit vote can now be firmly dismissed as unreliable. The so-called spike in hate crime has been a rhetorical cudgel used against Brexiteers, but no more. If Amber Rudd's speech is a 'hate incident',

then we can consider the term 'hate incident', along with 'hate crime', to have been rendered meaningless.

It's evident that there's a critical flaw in the police's handling and recording of these 'hate incident' complaints.

Police reporting rules state that all such complaints, whether from the victim or someone else, must be recorded "irrespective of whether or not there is any evidence to identify the hate crime incident". And so Silver's complaint has been logged, in the words of West Midlands police, as a "non-crime hate incident".

Or to put it another way, even if it isn't a hate incident, it will be recorded as a hate incident. Welcome to your head-spinning, words-have-no-meaning, post-modern dystopia.

This kind of creepy fixation on unfalsifiable alleged biases was once limited to mentally unstable social justice warriors, but it seems that their corruptive lunacy has now leaked out into wider society.

Here's hoping that Amber Rudd's own inclusion in the meaningless hate incidents statistics might give her cause to look into how such incidents are defined, or if such a category is even necessary at all.

SCHOOLS SHOULD EDUCATE, NOT INDOCTRINATE

17th January 2017

If you were uncertain about whether your kids were being imparted with a balanced, impartial view of the world by their school teachers, then you can stop doubting and be sure: they definitely are not.

Over at the TES (formerly the *Times Educational Supplement*) a little while ago, Oliver Beach (pictured below), a former economics teacher and part of the BBC's *Tough Young Teachers* series, laid out his educational call to arms. Casting aside old-fashioned notions of neutrality and open-minded inquiry, he makes clear that it is the mission of schools to indoctrinate your children into the faux-liberal, broken leftism that is currently being put firmly back in its box around the Western world.

Early on, he lets us know that he is scared.

"The past year has been frightening."

I thought maybe he was going to tell an anecdote about being mugged at knife point or wrestling with alligators, but no, it turns out that this trembling millennial is all of a fluster because, you guessed it... *Brexit.* And..? Yep, the incoming new POTUS.

Despite the fear, and with a heavy heart, he courageously breaks the news that we have been deceived:

"An unquestionable sum would go to the NHS each week," remarked Boris Johnson and Nigel Farage, or a "tumultuous wall will be built by Mexico" boomed Trump. To the naive voter, these promises were catalytic to ballot-box decision-making. Decisions based on lies."

Yes, while Beach and the other intellectual giants of our school system could perceive beyond the smoke and mirrors, us naive dimwits who plumped for Leave are now kicking ourselves at having been duped by evil pied piper Nigel Farage and his malevolent cronies.

Never mind that a lot of Leave voters had made up their minds about European integration long before the referendum campaign had even started, some as early as 1972. Never mind that a good number of Leave voters thoroughly disliked the Leave campaigns. Never mind that in polls to ascertain why people voted Leave, nobody ever says, "duh, the red bus." Never mind that Remainers appear to be the ones who didn't do their research, and instead spent their time shitting bricks at the government approved Project Fear, which was carelessly disseminated by a partisan media.

And as for Trump, really? You still don't know why people voted for him? You missed the discussions on the utter failure of bankrupt, widely despised identity politics? You didn't pick up on many voters' justifiable contempt for the know-it-all illiberal-liberals sanctimoniously dominating the cultural discourse? You didn't notice what an unequivocally awful candidate the Democrats fielded?

No, you're just going to put it all down to the wall. Sure, let's go with that. After all, if it's all about the wall, then saintly Hillary backers needn't introspect, or change course, or take a solitary moment to consider their own faults.

Beach's oblivious lack of self knowledge hints that Trump has 2020 in the bag already. However, I can agree with him on the next part:

"The importance of young people being empowered and encouraged to challenge and question cannot be understated."

Very true, but what he doesn't grasp is that in 2016, that's exactly what voters did. The aloof suits in the EU are the overreaching, unpopular authority being challenged and questioned. In fact, in a minor way, Oliver Beach and others like him are the authority being challenged and rejected, and not before time.

And in the US? A non-politician just took on an entrenched Washington insider who belongs to the party that's been in power for the last eight years. And he won. So what do we think, who is challenging and asking questions in that equation? Here's a hint: it's not the dodgy career politician whose sole plan was to insult a large section of the electorate, stick with the program, and change nothing.

That's the beauty of being "empowered and encouraged to challenge and question", it means you can challenge anyone. Including—and this is the fun part—the up-themselves, holier-than-though new left.

Beach tells us, referring to the "Right" (all those not agreeing with his point of view):

"The success of the Right in gaining the highest political power with a narrative of pro-guns, anti-gays, limiting women's reproductive rights and building physical national borders will give new momentum to those with similar views here and across Western democracies. "If he can do it, why can't we?," they'll cheer as they grab their pitchforks."

Got that? We're dangerously close to staggering out of our ditches, grabbing our pitchforks, and engaging in some crude mob savagery. You may have thought that all that occurred last year was enacted fairly through the very same robust democratic institutions that have previously delivered victories for the left. But no, 2016 was actually just rambunctious, farm tool wielding yokels barging around and messing things up. Oh, and if you voted differently to Oliver Beach, you're quite likely to be a trigger happy homophobe, so sort yourselves out, peasants.

We're then informed:

"In recent years, it need hardly be said, we've seen vast strides of progress in achieving social and civic liberties for under-represented groups."

He neglects to mention that any such advances are currently being undermined by a strain of ferocious, illiberal identity politics which has turned pathological. Far-left radicals are corrupting their own movement by lashing out at all who disagree with their garbage post-modern theories. The very notion of social justice is being subverted from within, while potentially sympathetic allies are pushed away.

In a hypocritical closing flourish totally lacking in any modicum of self-awareness, Beach tells us:

"We must reject echo chambers, post-truth proselytes or sycophants. We don't need more Donald Trumps, Nigel Farages or Marine Le Pens; we need Martin Luther Kings, Harvey Milks and Rosa Parks. And we need them now."

Well, it's up to each individual to make their own decisions on Trump, Farage, Le Pen, or any other politician. But when I think of progressive giants such as Martin Luther King, Harvey Milk, or Rosa Parks, I can't imagine how such profoundly inspiring figures could possibly emerge from the modern, groupthink left, with its stifling intolerance and lack of common decency.

If the 'liberal' bubble isn't the very essence of "echo chambers, post-truth proselytes or sycophants" then nothing is.

Through its double standards, lack of respect for individual freedoms, and shameful attacks on those who have differing opinions, the left is regressing. Increasingly cult-like, lashing out under scrutiny, and incapable of self-reflection, this wayward group cannot seriously call itself liberal, or lay claim to any kind of moral high ground.

Beach says this:

"Educators must be curating minds that question their realities, not just accept them."

And he's right. Enable young people to think freely, without indoctrination, and we can make certain that future generations won't be gulled and manipulated by shamelessly irresponsible classroom ideologues like Oliver Beach.

LAUGHING AT VOTERS, WITH JONES AND CLEGG

18th January 2017

Have you seen the new method that liberal progressives have come up with to get all us wayward peasants back on board the love train?

It's inspired. They get together in front of a camera, openly laugh in our faces about what feckless, naive cretins we are, and then widely distribute the recording.

The idea, I presume, is that if it's drilled into us constantly that we are hopelessly stupid and unable to make logically coherent decisions for ourselves, then we'll be happy to hand consent over to the enlightened, better-than-us leftists, and not meddle oafishly in their global masterplans anymore. They can get on with sainthood and erasing human misery, and we can get back to our pints of mild.

Have a look at earnest saviour of the oppressed Owen Jones' interview with radical totalitarian Nick Clegg in this new video. *[Included in the article was a link to a discussion on Owen*

Jones' YouTube channel, titled "Owen Jones meets Nick Clegg, 'I warned David Cameron over failing Brexit strategy'".] Take in the five minutes on Brexit from the forty second mark.

We get an anecdote about a simple-minded Yorkshireman (file under *didn't happen*), Jones and Clegg laugh smugly at how stupid Leave voters are, and then Clegg, with the apparent agreement of Jones, comprehensively fails to understand the reasons Leave won, and blathers on about geography. And yes, inevitably, the much-abused NHS funding line is dragged out yet again. How many times do Remainers need to be told? Leave didn't win because of the NHS funding claim. The Remain side bullshitted too.

And Clegg's case *for* the EU? Safety. That's it. The coddling security blanket that only Mother Brussels can gift.

Are you convinced? Are you going to join Momentum, now that you've been dismissed as a laughable dupe? Or how about Clegg's Liberal Democrats? They've still got an insipid cluster of MPs and the cool thing about them is, when they don't like how people vote, they try and void the result.

Here's what's really irritating though. Owen Jones and his ilk carp on incessantly about the terrifying danger of the 'far-right' (meaning anyone who disagrees), as if Guardian journalists are being rounded up and imprisoned on a daily basis. I wrote previously about his shameless opportunism in using last year's Berlin terror attacks to demonize the right wing, while he showed no interest in the terrorism itself, or in the very real oppression that is a part of radical Islam.

It's clear that Jones and the rest of the illiberal new left are fixed on a weird political course, but that they fail to understand how any general shift to the right has been partly caused by the repellent irrationality of their own position.

There's a clear pattern though.

The new left has unpopular policies, such as being pro-EU, supporting open borders, deflecting attention from radical Islam, talking down their own country, hindering enterprise, putting useless oddball Jeremy Corbyn in charge of the Labour party, and being generally miserable killjoys who insist on total ideological conformity.

Voters understandably look for alternatives, which means either the Conservatives or Ukip. By choosing those alternatives they by definition move further to the right.

The new left, seeing this shift, change nothing about themselves, and instead start yelling about an incoming far-right/ populist Armageddon. They spitefully berate anyone who has left their horrible, faux-liberal cult as a racist/bigot/Islamophobe/etc/yawn, or tell us that we are stupid and inferior, and must come back and follow their orders.

Not surprisingly, this results in more people abandoning the hysterical leftists, and jumping on over to have a look at the alternatives.

Which in turn causes the left to get even more worked up about the impending apocalypse, and call some more people stupid racists. This process is repeated until the left runs out of people to alienate.

And what will happen then, when they've insulted everyone? They appear incapable of self-analysis, and are so deeply invested in their warped ideology that they're unable to recognise their own profound faults. Perhaps, in order to avoid acknowledging the flaws in their worldview, the process will end in Waco-style self-annihilation.

For now though, the only thing to do is sit back, pour a drink, and marvel as they block-headedly engineer their own route to total left-of-centre oblivion.

WHY PROGRESSIVES GET VIOLENT

24th January 2017

Before the US election, some on the political left predicted that Donald Trump supporters would be violent if they lost. This can now be seen as an act of psychological projection, as the opposite has actually happened.

Immediately after the results came in there were violent demonstrations, including property damage and burned flags. Later, a young Trump supporter in Chicago was kidnapped, tortured and racially abused for being white.

Trump's inauguration was accompanied by rioting on the streets, a burned out car, and further property damage.

All the while, Trump supporters have been abused online, and celebrities expressing anything other than hostility toward the new president have been **spitefully insulted**. Performers who were considering playing at Trump's inauguration were intimidated into changing their minds. It was reported that opera star Andrea Bocelli received death threats.

At last weekend's Women's March, a demonstration of anti-

Trump sentiment, **Angela Davis was a speaker**. If you're not sure about her, she has a history of supporting political violence, and aligning with brutal Communist regimes.

And then there's Linda Sarsour, one of the event's organisers, who has tweeted repeatedly **in favour of Sharia law**, and expressed disapproval of state anti-Sharia bills. Take a look at how women are treated in countries where sharia law is in place, and ask yourself how that fits in with gender equality.

Absurdly extreme slurs are tossed carelessly at anyone not on board with the progressive agenda, while at the same time the left excuses real violence, from the petty to the tyrannical, when it suits their own ends.

Look at the reaction from some left wing establishment politicians to the death of psychotic dictator Fidel Castro last year. Jeremy Corbyn called him a "champion of social justice". Canadian Prime Minister Justin Trudeau expressed "deep sorrow" for a "larger than life leader who served his people". And celebrities who like to chip in on politics had their say too. Russell Brand tweeted the Castro quote, "La historia me absolvera".

How did this happen? When did human rights become a pick-and-choose concern, relevant only when politically expedient? What became of respecting different opinions, and why are personal attacks and violence being excused and validated so casually by progressives?

As I see it, there are several factors underlying the left's comfort with hostile confrontation and physical violence.

First, there's the way the academic liberal left seals itself off and prohibits dissent. University safe spaces illustrate this. In the safe space there can, by definition, be no opposing views.

Through no-platforming speakers who don't cleave to the progressive consensus, entire campuses become safe spaces. But 'safe' is an inappropriate term. In a sealed chamber, theories and ideas feed back on themselves, becoming inbred and extreme. There are no checks or balances. There's no open marketplace of thought in which only the best propositions can thrive. An environment like that is liable to spawn ignorance and extremism, and allow fallacy to go unchallenged.

From there we get the demonization of political opponents. If liberals don't meet any conservatives on campus, at work, or in their circle of friends, then it's easy for them to fall into the trap of thoughtlessly placing all right-of-centre thinkers into a distant outgroup, never to be engaged with. Tribalism takes over, and opposing arguments get automatically rejected without ever being heard out or considered. Fair criticism of Black Lives Matter is shouted down as racism. Critical discussion of the Women's March is sexist. Taking exception to advocates of sharia law is Islamophobia.

It's a simplistic caricature world, of activists and allies on one side, and of the dreaded *straight white man* on the other.

Alongside this, a far-fetched narrative has been sold, through which we live in an oppressively structured tyranny. Intersectional feminists such as Laurie Penny **refer to it constantly**. Their sketchy ideas leak out from unhinged gender studies departments into the wider discourse, and suddenly there's a magical explanation for everything that's wrong with the world: *the patriarchy*.

The very fabric of our society becomes the enemy, and we find ourselves living in a fantasy world. Guardian columnists and their acolytes are cast as virtuous insurgents, while those who refuse to nod along with their dubious concepts are condemned to play imperial goons, marching to the tune of a global cabal of villainous capitalists.

In this world, personal responsibility is diminished and victimhood reigns. Things not going well for you? Blame the patriarchy. Life's unfair? Tilt your head up to the next rung above you on the ladder of privilege. You're being oppressed.

Identity politics becomes key. You're allocated a block, and receive oppression/privilege points accordingly. Nothing is your own responsibility, because everything is structurally decided.

In such a reality, why would there be anything wrong with violently trashing the system? If the patriarchy is to blame and you're trapped in an unjust cultural prison, property damage becomes an act of emancipation. And sometimes you can attack people too, as long as they've been labelled—through skin colour, gender, religion, sexual preference or political persuasion—as oppressors.

We get deindividualized and played off against each other, but crucially, those in the progressive group are always the victims, no matter what they do. Crushed by circumstance and unburdened by personal responsibility, they're never to blame for anything.

LEARNING FROM LIBERALS

27th January 2017

In the interests of balance, I chose this week to open my mind to the liberal progressive cause, and learn about social justice.

Ready to be tutored by my liberal superiors, I've watched the bewildering, right-on bedlam being played out, seemingly unscripted and without any discernible purpose, by the zany, arsonist left. There was much to grapple with and it was terribly frightening, but I've been schooled well and am now ready to join the progressive struggle.

First there was the Women's March. Here I learned that gender equality is old hat. Feminism now is entangled with Islam, relaxed about Sharia law, and might even defend Saudi Arabia from time to time.

This confused me. In some Sharia enforcing countries punishment lashings are handed out by judges. Women can be sentenced to death for adultery. Homosexuality may be a capital offence.

It made no sense to me that these horrors could be defended, and by women's rights campaigners of all people. I puzzled over how putting on a hijab for a day could represent equality, when in some places such garments are a tool by which a real patriarchy exerts control over women.

Thankfully, some old tweets from Women's March organizer Linda Sarsour put me right. Amazingly, what Sharia law is really all about is interest free personal loans.

"You'll know when you're living under Sharia Law if suddenly all your loans & credit cards become interest free. Sound nice, doesn't it?"

And as it happens, I just haven't understood Sharia well enough. Apparently, if I dig a little deeper then the sexism, homophobia, imprisonment, whippings, and executions will all make sense.

"If only my fellow liberals understood what Sharia Law actually is. Smh. #ScaliaLaw"

In Berlin, a group of march participants even had a public 'Allahu Akhbar' chant. A surprise at first, but leftists know best. In fact, the ideal way to show dedication to the progressive cause right now would be to throw away your inhibitions, replace them with some controlling, theologically sanctioned ones, and enthusiastically convert to Islam.

Liberalism has allied with the illiberal. If we follow Linda Sarsour's example, we should fight the patriarchy by being apologists for the most authoritarian patriarchies in the world. Anything to deal with manspreading, right?

"10 weeks of PAID maternity leave in Saudi Arabia. Yes PAID. And ur worrying about women driving. Puts us to shame."

Moving on, I discovered that although we're engaged in a daily struggle to rid the world of injustice, it's absolutely fine to punch people in the face. And I'm not just talking about the well documented attack on deeply unpleasant white nationalist Richard Spencer.

At a Women's March in Edmonton, Canada, a male feminist appeared to punch a female reporter, before disappearing into a protective crowd of astonishingly sanguine third wavers. It takes a special kind of dedication to the feminist cause to actually punch women who don't like post-modern gender theory, and this guy wasn't going to shirk his progressive responsibilities.

He's been charged now, but I'm sure that when the cops realize he's just phenomenally selfless and liberal, he'll be free to go and assault some more gender traitors.

And finally, there was social justice fop Ewan McGregor, who you may know for his excellent and inspiring Davidoff adverts. He was due to give an interview on ITV's Good Morning Britain, but after arriving at the studio cancelled the whole thing in a fit of chivalrous pique because he didn't like interviewer Piers Morgan's way of thinking. Morgan had committed the sacrilegious transgression of making fun of the Women's March the previous day.

McGregor has taught us all a constructive life lesson: do not listen to wrong opinions. You'll know opinions are wrong when they're different to your own, which, if you're a good progressive, will always be right.

Should you be at all hesitant about the correctness of your own views, then you can use Meryl Streep or Mark Ruffalo as an ethical spirit level. Check their latest pronouncements, recalibrate your mind to be in alignment with their beautiful wisdom, and you'll soon be back on track.

What a relief to know that by following McGregor's example I'll never have to waste my brain on bigoted wrongthink ever again, and that my pristine ideological bubble won't get polluted by ungood hate speech.

Stick to this method, and you might even get a celebratory tweet from Brussels-loving scruff-buster Captain Jean-Luc Picard, a man whose unfeeling treatment at the hands of the Borg may have rendered him unusually vulnerable to groupthink.

Having taken in this carbon-friendly wealth of moral brilliance, I now feel very optimistic about the future. It's clear that for Europe to avoid the tyranny of right wing populism, and for the Democrats— peace be upon them—to regain the White House, all we need do is embrace Sharia, punch people, and never, under any circumstances, speak to Piers Morgan.

ANTI-TRUMP FURY AND PROGRESSIVE PREJUDICE

30th January 2017

At the weekend Donald Trump authorised a 90 day temporary ban on people entering the United States from Iraq, Iran, Libya, Somalia, Sudan, and Yemen, and an indefinite ban on Syrian entry. This is similar to when Barack Obama imposed a 6 month entry ban on Iraqis in 2011, except that Obama received no vilification. The purpose of the current ban is to ensure security while the new administration reviews the vetting process for incoming refugees. Many observers argue that this isn't reasonable justification. Others say the opposite. As it happens, America just held a free and fair election to determine who makes the decision.

As always among the anti-Trump wing the reaction has been a lot of shouting, no clarity, and a misrepresentation of the facts. It's exhausting to witness, and a problem is that with Trump being so unpredictable there might actually, beneath the social justice rhetoric, be something worth objecting to. But when there's so much deafening yelling going on, it becomes difficult to tune out the static and identify the important points.

A troubling part of the events which unfolded were reports that people who've already been vetted strictly enough to have green cards were among those detained at airports. This is unjust, unnecessary, and unlikely to win over skeptics who dislike Trump but are willing to give him a chance.

However, the official line is that the ban doesn't apply to green card holders, and there's provision in the Executive Order for cases to be dealt with on an individual basis as required. This is something that needs scrutinizing, along with the treatment of travellers with dual nationalities. In these regards, the White House has created an unacceptable amount of confusion.

Had those who oppose Trump calmly pointed out such problems, they'd receive greater support along more of the political spectrum. But instead, they went into full hysterical revolutionary mode, striking their most heroically indignant poses while feeding on and stoking emotion.

Misleadingly, protesters called the Executive Order a 'Muslim ban', which it evidently isn't. How can it be, when over forty other Muslim-majority countries aren't facing restrictions? And that includes countries which have larger Muslim populations than the ones in the order, such as India and Egypt.

Note also that the seven countries affected are those which were designated as being of special concern, without any media commotion, when liberal favourite Barack Obama's administration was in charge. In fact, the Executive Order doesn't even name the countries, it simply refers back to the legislation made during Obama's time in office.

But none of that stops the kneejerk hyperbole erupting all over social and mainstream media. Tellingly, some of the people broadcasting their opposition to the order have expressed what looks like Islamophobia, while indicating, as is becoming the norm on the left, a propensity for violence.

Here's Kumail Nanjiani on Twitter. He's got a blue tick and 937'000 followers, so he must know what he's talking abou... oh wait... he's an actor. And a comedian, in the modern sense.

"How to make terrorists:
1. Ban everybody from a certain group from entering the country.
2. Wait."

He's saying that if 'certain group' is restricted from travelling to the US, then they will become terrorists. In Nanjiani's opinion, 'certain group' is on the edge of committing brutal acts of indiscriminate violence. As well as placing Nanjiani in alliance with actual Islamophobes, this tweet also unwittingly makes a case *for* the travel ban. After all, if he were correct, and a significant number of the people being banned were on the brink of embracing Islamist terror, then you probably wouldn't want to let them in the country.

Or how about Sunday Times writer India Knight? She got the ball rolling with a light-hearted, homicide-themed tweet. Subsequently deleted, it read "The assasination is taking such a long time."

Having garnered attention but turned off anyone who isn't so much into political murder, she then came out with this stunning piece of anti-Islamic stereotyping:

"...he's making 100 more homegrown terrorists every time he opens his idiot mouth."

"He" refers to Trump, and according to outraged, trigger-happy Knight, Muslims are so thin skinned and eager to blow things up that they can be radicalized in their hundreds just by listening to the American president speak. In her world, followers of Islam might be liable to kill people whose politics they disagree with. And bizarrely, just like Nanjiani, she is implying this as part of her argument *against* Trump's order.

Liberal progressives who like to throw around accusations of bigotry and racism are sometimes in possession of their own disguised prejudices. They mask them behind platitudes, while exchanging virtue signals with their co-saints. But as the above tweets show, you don't have to look hard to see their true nature. It's revealed not in expressions of hatred, but in conspicuous compassion, through patronising vast groups of people, by blurring individuals into demographic blocks, and through the simpering low expectations inherent in the fallacy of cultural relativism.

A concern now is that the mixture of virtue signalling, exaggeration, and ramped up outrage we've seen over the past couple of days sets the tone for the rest of Trump's time in office, and distracts from the real details. Perhaps more than any previous president, he must be held scrupulously to account. But there's only so much right-on fury that normal people can stomach, and placard wielding, angry marches are limited in both usefulness and wider appeal.

If the anti-Trump rage never subsides, and is accompanied by a constant undercurrent of physical menace, then it will quickly become little more than white noise, and would-be allies will start to melt away. Those who really want to make sure that Trump is kept under close scrutiny need to stick to the facts, cut out the radical posturing, and try to keep their emotions in check.

TRUTH OR NAZIS? HOW TO AVOID REALITY

31ˢᵗ January 2017

It's not often that one tweet totally encapsulates the political atmosphere, but comedian Andrew Lawrence managed it when he wrote this:

"Sad that Liberals are so bored with easy middle-class life that they've had to invent a neo-Nazi doomsday scenario to entertain themselves."

Lawrence is that rarest of professional comedians--one who appears at ease with annoying the liberal ingroup, and who doesn't conform to the self-censoring, left-wing drone mentality which has a stranglehold on arts in the UK.

To an observer it often looks like if you want to get ahead as a comedian in Britain, the main requirements are that (unlike Lawrence) you make piss weak, inoffensive comments in support of progressivism, act extremely smug, and maintain a hatred of poor people/Brexit/ideological transgression... you know, all those fascist things.

After the election of Donald Trump, I thought there might be a popular watershed. Suddenly people on both sides of the political spectrum were discussing identity politics and what a pile of shit it is, and it genuinely seemed that cultural sanity might be restored. Even left-liberal Hillary supporters were confronting the problem, as shown in the nail-hitting Jonathan Pie video that went viral back in November. (I have no idea how much of what fictional reporter Pie says reflects what creator Tom Walker really thinks, by the way.)

Regrettably, Pie's awakening wasn't universal, which brings us back to Lawrence's tweet. What's become clear is that many progressives are living in a fantasy world.

And maybe that's understandable. They have a tough decision. On the one hand they could choose to deal with reality. This means accepting that their identity politics is out-of-control. That while it once served a purpose, it's now counter-productive. It divides and discriminates, creates tension and misunderstanding, and ultimately leads to segregation and intergroup hostility. It does all the things that it was supposed to be fighting against.

Then they need to repeat this process of harsh critical analysis for intersectional feminism and political correctness. And face up to the thought control and lack of ideological balance on university campuses. Then factor in how disconnected and arrogant the liberal left has become. And perhaps admit there's no reverse-Candyman scenario in which radical Islamic terror magically disappears if you simply don't say the words 'radical Islamic terror'.

This kind of cleansing and renewal would be difficult if you'd spent your whole life surrounded by people who constantly echo every single one of your beliefs. If your worldview has been reinforced by every teacher and professor you've ever met, and by all the Salon, Vox, and Guardian writers whose columns you unquestioningly ingested. When 'safety' is valued over debate, and even to voice a dissenting opinion is condemned as a 'micro-aggression'--on a spectrum of hate with racism and homophobia--you may not want to voice disagreement.

In that situation, it wouldn't be easy to tear down all your beliefs and start again. So what's the alternative? How else do you rationalize the cultural and political changes taking place around you?

Well, you're already immersed in a fiction anyway, so why not make up a few more stories?

And that's what we're seeing played out. On the progressive left, Trump isn't simply a bad candidate, or a weird chauvinist. They're too fired up for these prosaic analyses. In the left's self-preserving construction, Trump is a Mussolini figure . On social media it's the 1930s again. Over at the Guardian, a black tide of fascism is rising and we're heading for apocalypse. Trump voters themselves, all 63 million of them, are actual neo-Nazis, and social justice fantasists are brave revolutionaries engaged in noble rebellion. They heroically battle tyranny, and then they tell people about it.

Take this option, and though the world outside transforms into a dangerous place, progressives' own sense of internal security is restored. With their ideological safe spaces intact, it's reality that disintegrates instead.

Have a look at this utterly freakish video from the Screen Actors Guild Awards last Sunday *[can be found on YouTube, "Stranger Things Cast: Acceptance Speech, 23rd Annual SAG Awards, TNT"]*. It's an acceptance speech by David Harbour, one of the stars of Stranger Things. As he becomes increasingly melodramatic and unhinged, he bears every resemblance to a deranged cult leader. He's cognitively dissonant. He says he will "cultivate a more empathetic and understanding society by revealing intimate truths", and then yells wildly that he and his fellow believers will "punch some people in the face when they seek to destroy the meek and the disenfranchised and the marginalized".

As he bellows, the transfixed congregation--pampered, immensely rich, cocooned from normal life--becomes excited. Their stares are locked on him, and when the words "punch some people in the face" salvo violently around the room, they rise to their feet and howl ecstatically.

BERKELEY RIOTS RESULTS ARE IN: MILO WINS

5th February 2017

The riots that took place at UC Berkeley last week were disturbing to watch. A thuggish combination of students, left-wing activists, and those calling themselves Antifa put on a chest-thumping display of violence and intimidation. With their faces covered and dressed in black, they acted out their faux-revolutionary wet dreams, playing the big man in a totally safe environment where they faced no opposition. With pack-mentality cowardice they started fires, smashed up businesses, and savagely beat those they disagree with--in this case, visiting speaker Milo Yiannopolous' intended audience. Video footage shows them surrounding Milo fans and beating them with flagpoles, or spraying them in the face with Mace.

The brutality was unprovoked and potentially fatal. One piece of footage showed a baying mob pummeling a face down, unconscious man.

Adding to the revulsion caused by these images is the knowledge that their underlying motives were profoundly illiberal: they are opposed to free speech, and will use extreme violence to prevent non-left wing speakers from being heard. In this case, their target was the aforementioned writer and cultural commentator Milo Yiannopolous. They call him a fascist, or a white supremacist, but such slurs are absurd when he openly condemns such things. Remember that the extremists who were rioting on Wednesday night call everybody they disagree with a fascist, a Nazi, or a white supremacist, and then declare that anybody labelled as such deserves to be physically attacked.

Amid the flames, Milo's Berkeley speech had to be shut down, and the myopic, puffed-up rioters claimed victory. But now that the dust has settled, it's clear that the unarguable beneficiary of all this is Milo Yiannopolous himself, along with his politics, his ideas, and his influence.

He has, as always when anybody tries to silence him, gained an enormous amount of publicity, this time perhaps more than ever before. Advance sales of his as-yet unreleased book soared by 17'675%, and he was invited onto Fox News' Tucker Carlson show where he gave a strong, lucid performance.

Speaking on camera, Milo came across as likable, intelligent, and entirely persuasive. Because while there's no doubt that he's sometimes been deliberately offensive, the principles he stands for are sound and resonant.

Here's what he appears to believe in: Freedom of speech. Reigning in identity politics and out-of-control political correctness. Gender equality over intersectional feminism. Not allowing the left wing to strangle academia, the media, or public discourse. Upholding the American constitution. The free marketplace of ideas.

Contrast this with the violent thugs who shut down his speech. What do they stand for? The collective over the individual. Civil disruption. Restrictions on speech, expression and thought. Ideological conformity. Intimidation and political violence, from property damage to serious physical assault. Marxism.

Throw a light on these two opposing sides, and there's really no contest. Add to the equation that Milo is audacious and funny, while his opponents are grim faced, angry zealots, and the contest is over.

You have to wonder what the Antifa numbskulls were thinking. When a video shows a normal looking, lone young woman surrounded by masked hyenas in black beating her with flag poles, what do they think the reaction is going to be? Are millions of Americans going to leap from their couches and pledge to join the mob in assaulting innocent people in the streets, in order to silence dissent and install a Communist dictatorship? I'm no marketing executive, but I can't imagine queues forming round the block for that one.

Milo gets criticism from all sides. Leftist ideologues spasm at the mere mention of his name. Conservatives think he gives them a bad reputation. Airy, hyper-rational types don't really like anyone. But the reality is that free speech has been under severe assault, on campus, in the media, and in wider society. You might not like Milo's tactics. You might think that at times he's been cruel, and crossed the line of decency. But he has certainly never endorsed violence. And at the risk of stating the obvious, in the trench warfare of the culture wars his methods are working. And that's a good thing.

The Berkeley riots showed more people than ever the dark, authoritarian brutality of which the modern, activist left is capable. They showed us that our principle mechanism for thriving as a civil society--free speech--is under threat. And when Milo was given the platform to express himself on Fox News, a substantial audience saw that although he has been savaged and demonized by the progressive media, in reality he is standing up for essential values.

Is Milo careful to always strike a balance and play nicely? Obviously not. But unlike his opponents, he uses words, not violence.

POLITICAL TRENCH WARFARE

8ᵗʰ February 2017

Which are you, a neo-Nazi or a Stalinist? Would you prefer alt-right white nationalism or soc-jus Marxist absolutism? Do you want that with chips or rice?

As the political landscape fractures and shifts, and the not-really-progressive left continues to handle actual change very badly indeed, an extreme polarization has taken hold. Issues are being divided into a competitive binary, around which you must plant a flag and dig in.

It's curious that this atmosphere of polar opposition comes at a time when political correctness tries to close certain avenues of discussion, and the education industry's left-liberal bias becomes ever more pronounced.

Children are taught that there are no winners or losers (or genders), but that everyone lost in the EU referendum. Quotas promote equality of outcome over equality of opportunity, as part of a controlling, top-down style of social micro-management. And university safe space culture retards students' natural abilities to face opposition and embrace debate.

This malignant, mollycoddling culture of low expectations dilutes competitive competence, and extinguishes the combustive sparks which come from clashing ideas together.

Such artificially engineered conflict avoidance might be expected to create an arena of blithe agreement, but instead it's brought into play the precise opposite: political and cultural debate is turning into extreme trench warfare. We have the emergence of blind partisanship on steroids, manifested through over-simplified binaries, and a widespread inability to make concessions, or even listen to those on the other side of the debate.

While a culture of 'safety' existing side by side with irreconcilable, heartfelt disagreements might at first appear contradictory, it actually makes sense. A risk-free environment, in which the sanctity of each individual's feelings (no matter how delicate) is valued over facts and logic, leads to a critical handicapping of efficient, objective thought. When abilities to reason and compete become severely diminished, then the path of least resistance is to retreat into base tribalism. And tribalism leads quickly away from any possibility of normal conversation.

Left-wing identity politics is defined by division, and has penetrated every sphere of debate, disrupting formerly powerful unifying forces such as class solidarity.

The alt-right too is little more than an inverted version of social justice clan building, taking the groups ostracized by the SJWs and meme-shaping them into a competing category of their own.

What we're left with is a total breakdown in functional public debate, and when compromise through civil means goes out the window, then we're really in trouble.

An indicator of the seriousness of this deterioration is the lurch toward violence the American left has taken since Donald Trump's election victory. As unsettling as the violence itself is the liberal media's reaction to it. Commentators have played down or even, astonishingly, approved of the use of violence. There have been infantile public discussions about 'punching Nazis'.

This is what polarization leads to. Since Trump's inauguration, the name calling from the left toward anyone they don't like has escalated from bigot to racist to Nazi. And the definition of who it might be acceptable to physically assault keeps on widening.

In the UK, the announcement on Monday by the Speaker of the House of Commons John Bercow that he won't invite Trump to speak in Westminster Hall fits seamlessly in with these facile trends. It's a grandstanding display, fully in line with the tiresome excesses of histrionic Student Unions when they no-platform visiting speakers or ban sombreros. Bercow's exasperating performance serves no purpose to the country, and makes it look like even Parliament has now given in to irrational, feelings-first virtue signaling.

It's time for a conscious effort on all sides to stop polarizing current affairs, and to restore some nuance to public debate. In the long term, it's critical for schools and universities to address their lack of political diversity. Too much progressive bias in education, with an emphasis on a very warped form of social justice activism, leads to ignorance of alternative viewpoints, and to the dehumanization of anyone who holds a dissenting point of view.

Address these imbalances, tone down the hyperbole, and we might in time be able to end the siege mentality.

JIM JEFFERIES, PIERS MORGAN, AND EVERYTHING WRONG WITH THE LEFT

11ᵗʰ February 2017

For an indication of how astonishingly badly the left is doing right now, consider this terrifying fact: they're making Piers Morgan look good.

In this clip from Bill Maher's Real Time *["Piers Morgan & Jim Jefferies: The Lesser of Two Evils, Real Time with Bill Maher (HBO)" on YouTube]*, Morgan is verbally barracked by Australian comedian Jim Jefferies. Morgan's crimes? First, like 63 million Americans last November, he doesn't agree that Hillary Clinton would make a better president than Donald Trump. And second, he correctly stated that Trump's Executive Order on immigration can't accurately be called a 'Muslim ban'.

In other words, Morgan had the temerity to disagree about politics, and to point out a fact.

In the face of this counter-progressive heresy, Jefferies lost his rag and, with the exception of setting a building on fire, ticked every box on the disturbed angry-left checklist, all in under a minute.

First, he interrupts Morgan's point on the travel ban by telling him to "fuck off." Then, rather than explain why Morgan is wrong--which he can't do because Morgan is right—he comes out with this cringeworthy hyperbole:

"Hitler didn't kill the Jews on the first day, he worked up to it."

Really Jim? You're going to draw comparisons between a three month travel ban and the Holocaust? The actual Holocaust? Do you not see any problems with this? Or are you deliberately chanelling Rick from The Young Ones for a bet?

There follows an exchange in which Morgan points out the hysterical nonsense that Jefferies is spouting, to which the sensitive Australian pokes at Morgan with a personal jibe: "you won the apprentice and you have a famous friend", before raising a *truly devastating* middle finger and leaning back in his chair.

And that's it, that's the extent of his soggy, meaningless 'argument' against Morgan, against the immigration order, against Trump, and against millions of voters across America.

As I said, almost everything that is wrong with the left is on display here.

There's aggression. Spite. A lack of emotional control. A total lack of courtesy. Ad hominem attacks. The inability to listen to or respect differences of opinion. Playing to the ingroup. Conviction of moral superiority. Factual inaccuracy. Denial of the truth. Incoherence. Failure to address the issues. Childishness.

And to top it all off perfectly there's a ludicrous reference to-- who else—*Hitler!*

It's worth noting that Jefferies got big cheers from the crowd for his performance, and it's worth noting also that this indicates a further problem on the left. No doubt some Never Trumps will hear that cheering as vindication that they're in the right, and have the popular support to prove it. But Jefferies is soaking up adoration from a rigidly partisan crowd, who will happily cheer on anyone that echoes and reinforces their own beliefs. They're all deep in the bubble, somehow *still* convinced of their own infallibility.

Meanwhile, outside the clique, ordinary people who value fact based, adult discussion are utterly repelled. Just as they were by the Berkeley riots, and the viciousness directed toward Trump's young son on social media, and the violence around the new president's inauguration, and the mindless hollering to 'punch Nazis', and all the other yelling and crying and threats and intellectual dishonesty, and on and on and on.

We're less than a month into Trump's presidency and the

left is already beyond meltdown. They've turned gaseous and manifest as a noxious belch of self-righteous, demented fury.

And amid the obnoxious tantrums, one thing becomes clear: if the left doesn't get a grip, then Trump is a nailed-on cert for a second term in office.

NORMALIZING THE EXTREME BY REDEFINING WORDS

15th February 2017

Stumble accidentally into a social justice dominated forum and you'll find yourself dizzied by various barked phrases which don't mean anything. That is, you'll recognise the words, but their meanings will be hollowed out and corrupted.

This is because the activist left has a habit of twisting words to serve its own purpose. There's a basic disrespect for language, and an unwillingness to be precise. Buzzwords abound, and if you don't know what they mean, then your ignorance may itself be taken down and used in evidence against you.

This mangling obfuscation comes perhaps from the left's fatal entanglement with post-modern thinking, in which nothing means anything and we may as well all just give up, deny the existence of gender, and spend our days berating strangers for not being gay.

Manipulating language leads us into a very Orwellian realm. Controlling what people say is a means of controlling their thoughts and behaviour. And redefining words can lead to dangerous places, in which subversive actions become normalized.

Anyone employing these practices—redefining language, obscuring the topics, eschewing clarity—should be regarded with deep suspicion. Here are some words and phrases whose meanings change when they're employed by misanthropic leftists.

Violence

You can't have missed that the left has been enthusiastically embracing violence recently. It's a characteristic of left wingers that although they denigrate the military, oppose the Second Amendment in the US, and advocate 'safe spaces', they also harbour an elemental yearning to put dissidents against a wall and shoot them. We're seeing a bit of this formerly repressed blood-lust at the moment, for example in this month's Berkeley riots, and one way that the mob attempts to justify its latte-fuelled aggression is by sneakily redefining the word 'violence'.

They've decided that words are violence. And not embracing gender neutral pronouns might be violence. We hear about 'structural violence', whereby just existing in the world can render one a victim of assault and battery.

And as a counter to that, it becomes acceptable for activists to use real violence. But this—burning things, smashing windows, beating people—is no longer *bad* violence. It's self-defense. Or a legitimate expression of dissent. Or an act of noble resistance.

So the activists—just through existing in society, or knowing that somebody, somewhere is listening to some contraband words—are reconfigured as victims rather than aggressors, even as they crack skulls with metal rods.

Unsafe

This means that you're uncomfortable with something someone has said, or with an opinion you don't like, or perhaps even with someone's mere presence.

Of course, if someone explicitly threatens you, or blocks your path and cracks their knuckles, it would be fair to say that you feel unsafe. But this kind of palpable danger isn't required in social justice world.

The words which make you feel unsafe can be nothing more than a difference of political opinion. You can feel unsafe about someone's presence even if they're far away and you haven't seen them. In US universities conservative speakers have been prevented from even setting foot on campus.

Using this logic, all that's required to enforce your agenda by having dissent removed is that you claim a nebulous, subjective lack of emotional security. Opinions are presented as existential dangers, and again, words and ideas are conflated with physical threat.

Check Your Privilege

This means shut up, your opinions are not welcome. It means that you don't get to have a say on the matter in hand, because you look/think/act wrong. That is, you belong somewhere on the nefarious side of the cis-hetero-white supremacist-gender conforming-Satanist-patriarchal-neo-Nazi oppresion spectrum. If you're told to check your privilege then you should consider yourself persona non grata and stand silently in the corner facing the wall. The social justice caste system has declared you unclean and inherently guilty, and you're permanently expelled from the debate.

Be aware though, that you're not being discriminated against, because discrimination has also had its meaning changed. It now means what conservatives do all the time just by existing in the world, while it's literally impossible for progressives to be guilty of discrimination. Because they're the good guys.

Hate Speech

This can be anything. Seriously, it means absolutely anything you want it to, as long as your complaint comes in pursuit of the left wing progressive agenda.

Hate speech regulation is a crude bludgeon used to silence naughty people who have their own ideas. It puts anyone who isn't an intellectually jellified PC drone permanently on edge about saying what's on their mind. It prohibits looking at the evidence before your eyes and articulating it in words. If you have the urge to express yourself in this way, you should report yourself to the authorities immediately.

Hate speech doctrines also function as a de facto blasphemy

law, but only with regard to one religion. Can you guess which one? I'll give you a hint: you can say what you like about Justin Welby, and the Zoroastrians are fair game, but if you were to, for example, drunkenly make fun of five-times-a-day prayer rituals *[a reference to Louis Smith]*, you'd be in an awful lot of trouble.

It's not so bad being accused of maliciously spewing raw, primordial hatred though, as you'll find yourself in respectable company. Just last year the police added our very own Home Secretary Amber Rudd to the list of people-who-say-bad-things. She's actually in charge of the police, so if they can get her, they can get anyone.

5 THINGS ANTI-TRUMP PROTESTERS ARE GETTING WRONG

16th February 2016

Donald Trump's election has sent progressives into a tailspin, and there have been numerous protests against the new president. But not everyone shares the sense of imminent catastrophe. Marches and demonstrations are viewed with cynicism by many, and if those opposed to Trump want to engage with people outside their activist groups, they need to address some critical problems in their movement.

Violence

I never expected to hear people sincerely asking if it's 'ok to punch a Nazi', but as this is happening now, then here's the answer: it's ok if you're fighting in World War II.

But nobody's fighting in World War II. And the people we've been advised to punch are not Nazis.

Look at Milo Yiannopolous' intended audience at UC Berkeley, where protests turned into riots. There's nothing to suggest that the people assaulted there have any connection with fascism, and the same goes for Milo himself. Some of them stated they were present

to show solidarity with the principle of free speech—a principle antithetical to fascism, which actual Nazis would trample under their boots.

But the supporters of free speech were beaten unconscious. By *anti*-fascists, who then sent out a tweet boasting that they 'control the streets'. Controlling the streets being, of course, entirely normal and not at all *oppressive and authoritarian*, right?

There is simply no grey area around the violence issue. If you believe in little details like human rights, democracy, and living in a civil society, then it's not acceptable to use violence for political ends. And yes, that includes toward actual racists like Richard Spencer.

In fact, it especially includes the worst cases. It's easy to defend free speech when nobody is saying anything that bothers you, but to keep your cool when baited by truly extreme views shows conviction to your principles.

And as Maajid Nawaz said recently, "violence coupled with a sense of moral righteousness is precisely how terrorists emerge."

Liberal progressivism has been the dominant political ideology for as long as some voters can remember, and the trend toward globalism has seemed unstoppable.

But it just stopped.

Whether this is a positive or a negative shift depends on your point of view. But here's the thing, the move toward globalism was a democratic one, and the move away from it is also a democratic one. Underpinning it all is democracy. It would be nonsensical to revolt against the core mechanism that allows us to live peacefully, just because it throws up results you don't like sometimes. After losing a vote, you pick yourself up, accept that a democratic majority has disagreed with you, and work out where you went wrong.

Alternatively, in the event that a majority has chosen to go against you, you could sweepingly write off the opinions of everyone on the opposing side, and conclude that there's a problem with the system. But that would be myopic. After all, the system worked just fine when your guy was winning, didn't it?

So maybe the flaws lie elsewhere. And logic dictates that it's the losing side which will, by definition, be in need of an overhaul.

Hyperbole

This relates back to the first point about punching Nazis. Trump is not Hitler. The revolution will not be televised and neither will the alt-right propelled global apocalypse, because neither is happening any time soon.

People get sick of hearing exaggeration. They tune out. So keep at it with calling people fascists and Nazis, and the only change will be that the words become meaningless. Nobody will care and we'll be left with some very important language that doesn't work anymore, because it's been recklessly misused.

So be precise. Be honest. State the facts as they are and people will keep listening. Contrary to the insults, Trump supporters are open to debate and perfectly willing to listen to opposing points of view.

In fact, some Trump voters don't particularly like Trump either, but have perfectly coherent arguments as to why he got their support anyway. Talking to people who have differing political views can only be a good thing, so rather than demonizing people, try engaging with them.

Double Standards

Trump isn't judged by the same standards that Barack Obama was. Among progressives, the bar has been set preposterously low for Obama, who often receives only the gentlest of scrutiny for his time in office. For Trump, on the other hand, there is no bar, as everything he does is deemed inherently barbaric. Obviously, there's a point in the middle of these two extremes at which we should place a neutral marker.

An example of this bias is when Trump's first military raid in Yemen was widely reported as having killed up to thirty civilians and a Navy SEAL. This is grueling news which we should all know about. But looking at some reactions to it, you'd have thought that US military action in Yemen had started on the day that Trump took office.

Obama was ordering drone strikes in Yemen for years, with predictably devastating consequences. Unsurprisingly, I don't remember this generating an uproar among progressives. And that's because of double standards.

Moral Outrage

You don't like a sexist remark Trump made ten years ago in private? That's understandable, but the reality is that a lot of people will never give it much thought.

You think Trump gives odd, rambling speeches, and is liable to be crass and unprofessional? Ok, I agree. But his weirdness and general demeanor aren't cause for mass protest.

These aspects of Trump's strange persona aren't worth discussing if the purpose is to gain wider support . Neither is it reasonable to simply protest 'against Trump'.

People care about specific issues, such as the Executive Order on immigration, so be clear about defined grievances, and explain what the alternative might be. Emotion is subjective and mutable, so avoid it and stick to concrete policies. Skip the moral outrage—a lot of people don't share it—and then we might have a meaningful exchange on our hands.

And keep in mind that constructive discussions involve opposing points of view. If you're only talking to people who nod their heads and agree, then you're doing group therapy, not politics.

THE INCREASING IRRELEVANCE OF CELEBRITY POLITICS

22ⁿᵈ February 2017

It's easy to become frustrated by right-on celebrities like JK Rowling and Gary Lineker. The kind of reverend preachers who dissolve moronically into the regressive left cultural soup like soggy croutons in a rancid onion broth.

Aloof, blinkered, and dismissive of ordinary people's opinions, they seem willing to put lives and liberties in danger for no other reason than to preserve their own warped ideology.

But take a breather and you remember that they're not deliberately nefarious. They believe earnestly that they're doing the correct, moral thing. And that is at once chilling, and simultaneously a paradoxical reminder of all that needs protecting in Western democracies.

It's chilling because it illustrates their unknowing indoctrination into the rigid cultural orthodoxy of the modern left.

And it's a reminder of what's at stake. It's the freedom for ideas to swell and ebb, move in out of fashion, assume prominence and then be overwhelmed by something new, that has allowed such an insidious philosophy to assume primacy. The post-modern, self-contradictory mindset of the left is a harmful one, but its presence is part of living in a free exchange of ideas. Not all of the ideas will be good.

The unconstrained marketplace allows that bad ideas should, given time, be beaten and cast aside, and we're seeing the long belated arrival of that process now. We see it in the rejection of the worst purveyors of identity politics—the Labour Party, and the Democrats in the US—and we see it in Brexit too, which is a restorative breaking away from the relentless homogeneity of the EU project. There's a libertarian crackle in the air, and that's the very antithesis of the smothering PC blanket of the regressive left.

Politically correct modern progressivism carries a disguised threat. It falsely presents itself as an ideology of niceness.

Inoffensiveness. Morality, modernity and manners. When Gary Lineker supports ending the free press through Section 40, he's killing freedom in the name of politeness and decency. In the pursuit of *goodness*. If you asked Lineker about the tabloids, he might opine that closing down the Daily Mail would be a great way to stop intolerance. Staring into the abyss, his make-believe battle to combat extremism turns him into a mini-extremist.

The refusal by many on the left to discuss the Islamic part of Islamist terror, or any problems relating to Islam at all, is due in part to as prosaic a motivation as blithe courtesy. To simply wanting to do the right thing. Nobody wants to be called a bigot. Nobody wants to *be* a bigot. And it's very easy to buy into the idea that if we treat everyone nicely, then everyone will treat us nicely too. Celebrities are still doubling down on this misapprehension, but outside their rarefied bubble the long overdue shift in attitudes and behaviour is occurring. There is less fear of saying the wrong thing now, and less willingness to acquiesce to the progressive orthodoxy.

It feels like the ice is breaking, and that no topics are off limits now. It turns out there's only so long you can get away with admonishing people for discussing the realities in front of them. The thaw hasn't reached the celebrity sphere yet, and it might not ever, because they don't appear to occupy the same world as the rest of us. That's fine though. The more isolated they become and the less they understand the grounded discussion taking place among ordinary people, then the more freakish and hypocritical they will appear. And as their detachment grows, their influence will evaporate.

MARINE LE PEN: THEATRE WITH A MESSAGE

22nd February 2017

You can't fail to have noticed a fair number of opinion pieces in the liberal media questioning why the left is in trouble, and how it is that right wing, populist movements are in the ascendant. Still lumbering creakily along in the wrong direction after the cultural upheavals of 2016, some cranky progressives remain blankly unable to recognise the staggeringly obvious.

But French presidential candidate Marine Le Pen has just done a helpful favour to baffled liberals, by demonstrating exactly what they're missing. If you want a short, effective illustration of why politicians such as Le Pen are gathering momentum, all you have to do is watch Tuesday's video of the Front National president arriving to meet Lebanon's Sunni leader, Grand Mufti Abdel Latif Derian.

Le Pen was informed she'd have to put on a headscarf to speak with him, in line with his Islamic customs. She refused, politely and in good humour, and left briskly. She may well have known in advance what would happen and had her response planned, in which case it was a piece of theatre. But it was theatre with a message.

Contrast this with Sweden's self declared 'feminist government', who've also tried their hand at performance politics. They made a big deal of their gender after Donald Trump was inaugurated, posting a morally immaculate photo of their undeniable femaleness, in apparently deliberate contrast to images of Trump flanked by men while signing Executive Orders in the Oval Office. However, the Swedes were then roundly mocked when they visited Iran, and rather undermined their gender warrior credentials by lining up wrapped in head scarves, a perfect picture of signalling over substance, and hypocritical obeisance.

Or compare with the Women's Marches last month, when demonstrators donned hijabs as a sign of resistance. That is, they wore tools of patriarchal control to protest against the notion of patriarchal control. And they did so in free countries where they aren't patriarchally controlled.

Or take a look at the teachings of intersectional feminism. Or is it third wave, or fourth wave feminism? Whatever it calls itself, with its reliance on post-modern trickery, victimhood fetishization, and the reduction of society to segregated special interest groups, it crumbles under scrutiny, and speaks to very few outside its own cultish circles.

Marine Le Pen, as far as I'm aware, doesn't call herself a feminist. But, whether pre-planned or not, by publicly refusing to wear the scarf she appeared to make a bigger statement on gender equality than intersectional feminist writers such as Laurie Penny have ever done in their entire careers.

Le Pen played out a kind of feminism which people who aren't interested in feminism instinctively understand. It isn't anti-intellectual, it's just common sense. We needn't even call it feminism, since it just means gender equality. And the vast majority of people fully support that, without having to go anywhere near a university gender studies department.

Of course, the other thing Le Pen did when she refused the headscarf was to unambiguously reject Islamic rules. For years, Western politicians have kowtowed and capitulated to Islamic sensitivities. Up to a certain point, this can be seen as normal political expediency, and serves a purpose.

Up to a certain point.

But the growing opinion in Western democracies is that we're now well past that point, and that it's time for a reassertion of secular values. Forcing women to wear a headscarf in order to join a conversation is fundamentally incompatible with egalitarian principles. Le Pen made a show of upholding those principles, well aware that centrist politicians have become incapable of doing so.

And that's quite incredible, that it falls to the leader of a previously toxic, far right wing party to speak up for liberal values, because the nominal liberals are too scared of their own politically correct decrees to stand up and be counted.

Progressive parties and social justice marchers apparently

don't grasp the strength of feeling among voters who are tired of having legitimate concerns evaded. Should the French elections tip in Le Pen's favour, then adherents to the liberal consensus might finally start to understand some hard facts. Primarily, that her victory would be a shock of their own making.

ZERO PITY FOR
THE BBC

1st March 2017

The BBC, along with CNN, Buzzfeed, and various other media outlets, has every right to be upset at being excluded from the White House's off camera press briefing last week. But there's something important the corporation should consider. A significant number of licence fee payers either don't care, or are positively enjoying the fact, that the broadcaster was left out in the cold.

Aren't we supposed to love Auntie? Shouldn't it give us a reassuring glow as it broadcasts in good faith from around the world? Not any more, it seems.

When a lot of observers think the BBC has got what's coming to it, that should give it cause to sit up and think. After all, we're talking about people who fund the BBC through their taxes, celebrating their own broadcaster being denied access to the American government.

And viewers feel that way because, contrary to its own proclamations, the BBC is far from impartial. In the increasingly intense culture wars, it can sometimes appear to be a media wing of the progressive left. And as the progressive left has lost the plot lately, that doesn't bode well for its state funded mouthpiece.

A turning point, at which many already dissatisfied viewers felt they could take no more, was the EU referendum, when the result was greeted by our state broadcaster as if it were a national catastrophe. It was the largest mandate in British history, and a victory for democracy and self-governance. The country mobilised to decide its own fate, and as 17.4 million citizens celebrated, the Beeb went into mourning. Remain lost, which meant almost everyone at the BBC had lost. With little respect for the viewers, the corporation didn't bother trying to hide its maudlin wetness.

And then there's the BBC's position on Donald Trump. How can this even need spelling out, Auntie? You don't take sides in US elections. When you greet the announcement of a new American president as if you're on the losing team, you renounce all credibility.

The BBC has positioned itself as pushing back against Trump's reported authoritarianism, but it does so only in the hope of carefully replacing it, like an anaesthetist applying the gas, with its own softly woozy, Islington-inflected dogma.

The broadcaster has enormous power, but it becomes diluted if it isn't used selectively. And right now it's been reduced to homeopathic proportions. Nobody's listening anymore, because since Brexit the BBC has been eroding its own influence through the law of diminishing returns. As a result it must bear the brunt of what it has self-destructively invoked: indifference. Who would want to stick up for the BBC now, when it embodies everything that so many people are voting to get rid of?

The Beeb is shot through with political correctness and identity politics. It runs on quotas, and is creepily obsessed with race and gender.

But we all know that bigotry is vile, and we don't need the state broadcaster to drive the obvious home. It's also perfectly clear, in a recruitment context, how to beat racism and sexism: don't hire people based on their *race* or *sex.*

In modern Britain, affirmative action is bigotry by stealth. The statement it makes is that whoever is hiring has such low expectations of women and minority groups that they don't believe such applicants will be able to get a job on merit. The left likes to throw around accusations, so let's follow suit: through employing affirmative action the BBC is racist and sexist. Its bigotry extends, through a combination of pat-on-the-head box ticking and point blank exclusion, toward *everyone*—men, women, any of the other 31 bathroom-commandeering genders, and all the races on Earth.

If the BBC must insist on being committed to targets and social control though, then here's a scheme I could get behind: promote diversity of thought. Hire creative people who aren't left wing. Get some conservatives on board. Go wild and recruit a libertarian capitalist. Just do anything, BBC, to melt the suffocating, liberal progressive crust which currently entombs your coagulated form, before you become any more tiresome and unrepresentative.

Sort out your biases and people outside your diminishing liberal circle might start to like you again. They might even get on side next time you want to stick it to the American president.

THE OBSESSIVE RACISM OF THE NEW LEFT

10th March 2017

The new left is racist. The middle class, holier-than-though, Europhile left. You know the ones. The millennial, mud-slinging narcissists, fixated on skin colour and marching for Islamism. Look at their progressive media and you'll find endlessly carping think pieces on their perpetual hang up: race. They have a creepy obsession and ambiguous motives.

In a recent assault on basic reasoning from the BBC News site, it's proposed that arranging chopsticks incorrectly is a micro-aggression. Micro-aggressions are a newly made-up thing that don't exist. But just having the term in circulation allows left-ist control freaks to hypocritically call anyone and everyone a bigot for microscopic violations of the incomprehensible, ever-changing PC code. After all, imagine the damage done by not putting your chopsticks in the right place before you take a photo. The horror.

The new left works outward from the miserable premise that

all white people are racist. An obvious flaw in this statement is that it's racist. But its proponents use sophistry and codswallop to get around the contradiction, falling back on the lie that we live in a white supremacy in order to excuse their prejudice. This is misdirection, and has nothing to do with the dictionary definition of racism. But they're vandals, and would happily do away with dictionaries altogether if it aided their crooked ends. They claim that racism can only be perpetrated by people who have an inbuilt societal advantage. A societal advantage that now exists solely in the obsolete imagination of the left anyway.

So we're foisted with a fictional definition based on a fictional view of society, but they'll pretend it's all valid. And the progressive media, overrun with sympathetic zealots, gives credence to the lie.

Go tell an unemployed person on any predominantly white council estate that they benefit from structural advantages and were born racist. Tell them they're inherently privileged, and should feel guilty for their ancestral sin. See how far that line of argument works in the real world. Oh, and let's say a big well done to Barack Obama—it's quite an achievement for a black man to serve two terms as the democratically elected head of state in a white supremacy.

For a look at some real racism, you need to focus on the people who can't stop talking about the subject. Cast your attention leftward. The racism of the left is practised in full view, with the support of the popular media and mainstream academia, and without censure or challenge.

As an illustration, watch journalist and Islamic reform activist Asra Nomani's recent appearance on Bill Maher's show in the US. Nomani voted for Donald Trump, and has spoken of the vicious abuse she's endured for doing so. Maher's partisan, left-liberal audience will bay and jeer at anyone who doesn't condemn Trump, but Nomani is too smart to be caught out.

Before explaining the logically consistent reasons for her vote, she states gently that she's a Muslim and an immigrant, and this instantly buys her some respect. The audience's minds are wrenched open a millimetre or two, and they listen. In other words, in this confrontation with identity politics, she has no choice other than to employ identity politics. To the audience, her opinion becomes more valid because she belongs to groups they classify as oppressed. It doesn't matter how comfortable her individual circumstances might be, because the categorisation process is absolute. Remember that to a racist, individuals don't matter—they only care about groups.

The new left judges how much time, attention and respect they will grace on a speaker based on the speaker's race, gender, and religion. And they make no apology for it. In fact, they actively disseminate the ideologies which foment such bigotry, through academia, activism, and the liberal progressive media. Racism is inherent to how they operate, and they'll use toxic, charlatan theories to legitimise it.

Incredibly, they do all this in the name of tolerance, fairness, and social justice. This is real life doublethink in action, and it's disturbing to watch.

MR O JONES'S DIARY: EDGE OF REASON

15th March 2017

It's been a busy few months campaigning against democracy, and having achieved nothing I think I've earned a break. Actually I'm confused. I just don't understand the abuse I get online. I dedicate my life to telling people they voted wrong and we shouldn't do what they've chosen, and I get grief for it. Is it bad to remind Brexiters that their hatred and bigotry have enabled a wave of hatred and bigotry? Don't Tories want to know how evil and degenerate they are? And as for Trump, I clearly told Americans to vote for Hillary. Weren't they listening?

And now my own lot have turned on me too. It's so unexpected. All those weird extremists loved me when I backed Corbyn. But now I've had enough of him, they've gone all weird and extreme. Why are they being like that?

And even the normal lefties are having a go, just because it turns out Jezza isn't very good at being Leader of the Opposition after all. They're so ungrateful. If I hadn't campaigned to get him in the job, we'd never have known he wasn't up to it. Nobody could've predicted he wasn't suitable. I mean, thousands of people I blocked on Twitter might've mentioned it, and all the journalists in England, and everyone who didn't pay 20p to join the Labour Party, but come on, they're all just vile, right wing trolls.

Anyway, I have to do some research. I'm on the BBC later and I must find something to get indignant and worked up about. Some of the people they get on to disagree with me have that, 'we're calm and brought some objective facts' approach to discussion, but that's bobbins. I'll just get all agitated and act morally superior. A bit of smirking, huff and puff a bit, and I can always just storm off if they don't think I'm right about everything.

What they don't get is that they're on the wrong side of history, so their facts don't matter. I used to be sure the voters understood this, but in hate-filled Brexit Britain, rife with spiteful people being mean to me, I'm not so sure. All I hear these days is people talking about disgusting, fascist ideas like sovereignty, independence, and global trade.

But then, not everyone has my insight. I want to save the world, but how can I when the evil, right wing media is controlling everyone? We really need to get a grip on that. We should put Breitbart writers in, maybe, not prison, but... camps..? Could we do that, if we were in charge? I'll ask Seamus. I'm sure he'll say yes.

Still, for now I'll stick with my usual debating formula: virtue, flounce, and a bit more virtue. If nothing else I must show that I'm a good person. Signal it, if you like. If I make it clear that we're talking about morals, not politics, then anyone who disagrees will look like a thoroughly villainous type, and I'll win. Then it's a surge in the polls for Labour and a taxi home, what could go wrong?

Actually, I should use public transport. Look humble and all that. But I'm in London now, not Brexit country. And thank god for that, they're a bunch of racists up there. I mean, hard working, Northern racists, whose honest determination I admire very much, despite their rampant xenophobia. Sometimes I wish I could be a proper Northern coal miner, with dirty hands and everything, but the reality is that my true vocation has chosen me. I am not a miner, but I will chip at the hard face of injustice with my nice, liberal pick.

That's why I connect with the working class, I'm the same as them! Except for their vile bigotry and disgusting small mindedness, obviously. Why the fuck won't they vote Labour? If we could just ban all right wing press and get the Brexit dimwits to read only our opinions, they'd have to vote for us. Maybe we could threaten them..? Will check with Seamus.

Back to my research though, and I've found some reports that are genuinely shocking. They're all about Islamic extremism. They recount the sickening atrocities being committed around the world. The concert goers and cartoonists mowed down by gunmen in Paris. The trucks ploughed through crowds of innocents in Nice and Berlin. The victims in ISIS-held territories being raped and slaughtered. The suicide bombers, the burning cars, and the axe wielding murderers. I look at the carnage and the bloodshed, at the inhumanity, the barbarism, and the clearly encroaching danger, and the message is clear: I must write an article attacking Nigel Farage.

STEALTH BLASPHEMY UK

23rd March 2017

As was discussed a few days ago, the BBC Asian Network went a little off kilter last week. In case you missed it, they sent out a cheerful message in which presenter Shazia Awan, who just arrived from the middle ages, vacuously requested listeners to call in with their views on the appropriate punishment for blasphemy. The corporation had to cope with a backlash, and in the end Britain's glorious state broadcaster apologised. Our selfless moral guides at the Beeb are no doubt now fretting over whether their lack of conviction with regard to persecuting sinners might have serious consequences in the next life.

It's telling that the BBC could have put out such a question in the first place. How is it that there are staff on their books who wouldn't have seen a problem with legitimizing blasphemy laws? Don't forget that the question wasn't should there be punishments, but *how* should we punish people.

Which is not to say that asking if we *should* have punishments would be ok either. Such a debate would be deeply regressive and a waste of everyone's time and money. So it should come as no surprise, if you keep up with the BBC's state-funded pandering to theocratic, modern leftism, that on the Asian Network's website they're still asking precisely that question.

And let's be clear that when we have to talk about blasphemy, it's not the Church of England which is driving the illiberal, unpleasant conversation. Of course, it's all about Islam. The Asian Network's programme was made with reference to Pakistan, where blasphemy is punishable by death. But the very fact that they framed the issue as they did—not as a critical report, but as a topic that's up for debate—highlights the creeping imposition, in secular Western democracies, of blasphemy policing by stealth.

Think back to last year when a video became public of Olympic athlete Louis Smith drunkenly pretending to engage in Muslim prayer as a joke. Smith was forced to offer the following apology:

> *"I am deeply sorry for the recent video you may have seen. I am not defending myself, what I did was wrong. I want to say sorry for the deep offense I have caused and to my family who have also been affected by my thoughtless actions. I recognise the severity of my mistake and hope it can be used as an example of how important it is to respect others at all times. I have learned a valuable life lesson and I wholeheartedly apologise."*

He also grovelled on ITV's Loose Women, was dragged round some mosques, and still received death threats anyway. The threats weren't, as far as I know, from the BBC Asian Network, but there might have been some Guardian journalists toying with the idea.

Which brings us to the current incarnation of *useful idiots*—arrogant, left wing barmcakes who are attempting to normalize brutal religious extremism and who fit right in at, for example, the BBC.

These self-righteous cultural relativists are pompously dragging us into an oddly right-on religious dark age. Convinced of their own virtue, they'd blithely dispose of our basic human rights and throw us all under the bus in the name of diversity, inclusion or some other such cynical misnomer.

People like London Mayor Sadiq Khan, who has stated that terror attacks are "part and parcel of living in a big city", a statement no self-respecting Londoner should put up with.

Or like those who blindly follow dodgy fake feminist Linda Sarsour, a woman who's hijacked American feminism as a vehicle for her own Sharia-apologetic agenda.

Or supporters of motion M-103 in Canada, which is sold as tackling Islamophobia, but which critics say affords Islam with a uniquely protected status. If the motion passes then fair criticism might be reclassified as hate speech, and free expression will be curtailed.

Such developments are alarming, as is the fact that they're underscored by fear. There's the physical fear that opposition might bring violent reprisal from Islamists, but there's also a tangible social fear, of being slurred, castigated and abused by the left, which currently believes itself to be battling some kind of apocalyptic fascist uprising. They're caught up in this delusion because they lost a couple of votes, along with their grip on reality. They'll call you racist, or deplorable, or actually a Nazi, if you step out of line. And much like the Islamists themselves, they won't tolerate any criticism of Islam.

And so the perverse Left/Islamist coalition supports restrictions on free expression. If in the UK blasphemy is outlawed again, it won't be done explicitly. Rather than calling it blasphemy, it will be called hate speech. But though 'crimes' against (one particular) religion might be rebranded to fit in with the aesthetics of the Millennial activist left, the end result will be the same. Our rights eroded, and a safeguard against religious tyranny removed.

The progressive mob went after Louis Smith, and now they nod along with discussions about punishing those who speak incorrectly. They can do all this without hesitation or reflection, because they've categorised Muslims as a class of oppressed people to be protected under the banner of social justice.

Ironically, considering progressives' self-proclaimed opposition to bigotry, they draw no distinction between moderate Muslims and radical extremists. The nominal liberals are doing the very thing they warn others against—putting all Muslims into one homogeneous block, and as a result tarring the moderates and coddling the extremists.

Blasphemy laws were finally disposed of in the UK in 2008. But now we appear to have the threat of unofficial, de facto blasphemy policing taking their place, bolstered by expanding, repressive hate crime definitions. The BBC is enabling this process, while left-wing activists stifle dissent with unfounded cries of Islamophobia.

The danger contained in illiberal theocratic encroachment isn't something to be kicked down the line or covered over for fear of causing offense, because the longer it's avoided, the more difficult it becomes to address. And we can be quite sure of one thing: if we don't confront it then it will, in the end, confront us.

THE DUMB DEFAULT

27th March 2017

In response to last week's terror attack in London, we saw a swift, strong, and efficiently targeted official response. It's reassuring to know that our media and government are working in finely tuned coordination to protect us. The process has gone like clockwork, so let's take a moment to reflect on how it works.

First, criticism of Islam is cracked down on. This is necessary because, as always in cases of Islamist violence, it's unconnected to Islam. Obviously, when someone makes the step from being a normal Muslim to being a Muslim who interprets their faith literally and kills people, they cease to be a Muslim. This means that Islamic violence is, by definition, non-Islamic. It's a logical impossibility: Islamic violence doesn't exist because Islam isn't violent. In fact, the more violence that is committed in the name of Islam, the less violent Islam becomes.

Second, There will be strong statements from the authorities reassuring communities that they are safe and protected. Muslim communities, specifically. Everyone else, on the other hand, can refer back to Sadiq Khan's words a few months ago on the subject of terror attacks:

> "Part and parcel of living in a great, global city is

you've got to be prepared for these things."

Extreme carnage? Get used to it, you're in a great, global city #VisitLondon.

Third, attack the right wing. This means anybody who says either of the dreaded I-words: Isl*m or Imm*gr*tion. Such degenerates must be relentlessly bludgeoned with rhetoric and insults. We must not be fearful of terrorism, but we should be very, very afraid of Tommy Robinson, who often does frightening things like opening his mouth and sometimes even uses facts and figures which are true. Finger pointing and fear mongering are perfectly acceptable when directed toward the right, so don't worry about breaching any hate crime regulations. They don't apply to the left, because the left made them up.

Fourth, there will be a mass mobilisation of the people in response to these cowardly acts of violence. Virtuous, tolerant progressives who are willing to stand up and be counted will gather courageously. In numbers, with passion and solidarity in their hearts they will:

- Light candles.

- Project the flag on to the Brandenburg Gate.

- Hashtag tweets with #PrayForLondon.

- And, most important of all, yell ISLAMOPHOBE at anyone who breaks from the official narrative and starts slagging off *the religion of peace*.

Fifth, to emphasise that the attack is—has it been mentioned? —nothing to do with Islam, the media will focus on any other characteristic of the attacker besides his religion.

He is a British terrorist. A homegrown terrorist. A British-born, homegrown terrorist. A left-handed terrorist. A misunderstood terrorist who was called names and picked on when he was growing up. The Guardian will give away a free poster of the terrorist, and have a go at you for being murderphobic.

Overall, the central, driving theme which we must all internalise and obey is this: Not Islam. It's just nothing to with Islam. So don't read, speak, or think about Islam.

Repeat: IT'S NOT ISLAM. OK?

And with that self-evident and entirely common sense point made clear, please empty your mind of negative thoughts and return to your life of mindless tax slavery in the multi-cultural, rainbow utopia.

Have some sushi.

Let us do the thinking for you. You're not enlightened enough to understand the program anyway. That's why we've cooked up this dumb default for you in our social cement factory.

And above all, don't rock the boat. It's not you that's been blown up, beheaded, tortured, shot, stabbed or run over, so why are you even concerned? You're not one of those Islamophobes are you?

GOODBYE TO THE EU, BUT NOT TO EUROPE

30th March 2017

After several months of waiting, Article 50 has been triggered. Britain is leaving the EU and the reaction has been exactly as you'd expect. Celebration among those who voted to leave, acceptance from Remain backers who are now comfortable with the result, and a strange mixture of negative emotions among intransigent Hard Remainers, who've expressed anger, despair, and a significant amount of bitterness.

A deeper sentiment expressed by some in the pro-EU camp is a feeling of loss because they feel not simply British, but more like citizens of Europe. This really indicates how profoundly the EU succeeded in influencing self-perception, to the point where people feel aligned with a nation that doesn't exist.

That isn't normal. Feeling like a citizen of your own country is essential for society to function well. Without citizenship and shared community, we're not a nation. That doesn't mean being jingoistic, holding street parties for the queen, or wrapping yourself in the Union Jack, although you can do those things if you want. It also doesn't mean stopping other people from entering. It simply means respecting a sense of community and shared values, and expecting newcomers to do the same.

It means, if you live in the UK, being liberal in the classical sense of the word. That means respecting the results of elections and referendums, whether they go for or against you. It means accepting other points of view, valuing diversity of opinion, and not projecting the worst of motives onto those with whom you disagree. It means recognising that progressivism falls apart without a sporting respect for the conservative counterbalance. And it means valuing the freedom of the press, and understanding that the Daily Mail has as much right to be provocative, rabble rousing, and right wing as the Guardian does to be sanctimonious, breathless, and Blairite.

These liberal values are an area where the EU falls conspicuously short. It's demonstrably less democratic than its member countries. It introduces an extra layer of governance, which is more distant and less accessible. It re-runs referendums, until it gets the result it wants. And it's obstinately unwilling to offer concessions, as we saw when David Cameron was unable to secure the reform deal he wanted a few months before the referendum. This latter flaw was surely fresh in many voters' minds when Britain went to the polls.

Considering these things, we have a problem if you've been made to feel less a citizen of your own unique, respected, and heritage-laden country, and more a member of, well, what exactly? We can't accurately define the EU. It's not a nation. It's both supra-national and inter-governmental. It might have federal ambitions. It's certainly far from a simple trade bloc. But whatever it was, is, or wants to be, it's subsuming sovereignty, and incrementally replacing real nations with itself.

If you love all the countries and colours of Europe, then the EU is anathema. The EU, for all its pompous statements of peace and goodwill, has little respect for the cultures and people of Europe. In fact, it's worse than that: the EU has come to believe that it *is* Europe, and that is an act of unacceptable conceit. The EU has sought to water down and undermine everything that defines a nation. It operates a deliberate process of homogenization, rounding the granite edges of regional identity until there is nothing left but the featureless corporate platitudes of the EU enterprise.

Those who take pleasure from cultural differences, and can celebrate diversity with a proper grasp of what such a principle entails, showed two fingers to the self-serving philistines of Brussels last June, and let out a cheer with the triggering of Article 50. And let's hope that spirit spreads across our familial, shared continent, causing our neighbours to remember that Europe is not the EU, and that the EU must not be allowed to pretend otherwise.

For an example of how this mixing up of terms has taken hold, look at the various 'Marches for Europe' that have taken place since the referendum. They weren't Marches for Europe at all. They were Marches for the EU. Marches for the Commission. Marches for Jean Claude Juncker and his meticulous technocrats.

After Theresa May's Article 50 triggering letter had been delivered, Donald Tusk spoke to the media, and his final words were ordinary and yet touchingly sentimental.

"What can I add to this? We already miss you."

It was unexpectedly moving. But don't worry Mr Tusk, we're not going anywhere. We're just over there on the other side of that thin stretch of water, where we've always been.

Because, sincere and regretful as Tusk might have been, the fact remains that the EU and Europe are two different things. Europe is beautiful, resilient, diverse, and will, of course, long outlive the EU project. In the United Kingdom, we're all just as European now as we were on the eve of the referendum last year, whether we like to think so or not.

Brexit isn't about turning our backs on the rest of the continent, it's about restoring the best possible relations with our closest friends and neighbours, and none of us, in any nation, should need a rubber stamp from Brussels to do that.

At the same time, as citizens of this distinctive, disruptive island off the rainy north west coast of our shared continent, we can celebrate that we're finally, rightly, taking a more optimistic, globally connected path.

The future might not be smooth, but it's wide open now, so Happy Brexit.

PROGRESSIVES' BARMY UNIVERSE

6th April 2017

The more you listen to modern liberal progressives, the more you can feel like you're losing your mind. Let yourself get sucked into their barmy universe and the only way to survive is by letting go of reason and logic. So, it's worth asking if progressivism nowadays is a form of mental disorder, and if, perhaps, we should give consideration to having the whole lot of them sectioned.

For Liberal progressivism involves believing in all manner of directly contradictory things at the same time:

1. Islam is a religion of peace, but we mustn't do anything that might provoke Islamists into killing us. According to the left, anything other than the blind acceptance of any and all Islamic practices is likely to cause mass radicalisation and some amount of carnage. But, simultaneously, there is no reason to fear Islam, and the slightest criticism of its doctrines means you're a horrible racist. This amounts to a weird proposition. Say the wrong thing and you might provoke violence, but complain about the threat of violence and you're a bigot (who's provoking violence). In other words, if you want to discuss Islam in less than glowing terms, keep your opinions to yourself.

2. On a related note, while progressives are deeply concerned about the rights of women and LGBT people, they're not that bothered about the rights of women and LGBT people under Islam. Put it down to cultural relativism: anything non-leftists in the West do is inherently oppressive, imperialistic, and mean. But if anything bad happens in the name of Islam, then we mustn't judge others by our own Western imperialistic standards. Because that would make us, as usual, villainous bigots. So, for example, we mustn't concern ourselves too much with gays being executed under Sharia law, but questioning the wisdom of gender neutral bathrooms is a crime against humanity.

3. Racism, sexism and homophobia are bad. Nothing to argue with there. But at the same time, if someone you disagree with is white, male and straight, you may use those characteristics to invalidate anything and everything he says. Simply spluttering the words "straight, white man" can clinch any argument, on the grounds that the leftist's interlocutor is inherently and utterly wrong about literally everything. In fact, he's worse than wrong, the very fact that he's voicing a dissenting opinion is, in the terminology of the left, problematic.

4. Mass immigration should be accompanied by no expectation of integration. So throw open the borders and let everyone in, but insist that to advocate integration is somehow intolerant. Any notion that shared values are a good thing for everyone, both those coming in and those already here, should be dismissed as nationalistic and narrow minded. Ghettoization and a fragmented, tetchy

society? Yeah, why not! Diversity is our strength, and it's not like it matters if the country loses all sense of cohesion and disintegrates into conflicting group interests.

5. There are an infinite number of genders, and you can choose a different one every day if you like. While we used to have the word 'sex', of which there were two, we've now added 'gender', of which there are as many as you can imagine. You can invent a new one if you like. And they are all real, distinct, and carry an inherent threat: that if you look confused and suggest that this all sounds made up and unscientific, then you're probably guilty of a hate crime. HSBC just introduced ten new gender neutral titles for customers to choose from (including the useful Pr for 'person' and Mre for—seriously—'mystery'), but this is woefully inadequate and only serves to prove the bank's tone deaf ignorance. After all, if you compare with the law in New York City, then HSBC is 21 genders short, and that's extremely transphobic.

6. The working classes are all uninformed, racist scumbags who never actually know what they're voting for. Oh, but the progressive left is on their side, and hopes to get their votes.

This is a big problem for the left right now. Progressives are incapable of masking their visceral contempt for ordinary workers, anyone who didn't go to university, and people who don't live in London. Metropolitan liberals seem astonished that they should have to share a country with low-life Brexit backers, and like nothing more than to sneer and cackle among themselves about how stupid and unsophisticated the proles are.

But with Islington Europhiles and Oxbridge philosophers

making up a regrettably small percentage of the electorate, the Labour Party is going nowhere without the support of a few actual labourers. Who've been thrown under the bus and laughed at. Oh dear.

So, as the progressive left lurches further away from tangible political power, its madness intensifies. They double down and lash out. They stamp their feet and rail against the media, against free speech, and even against democracy itself, never pausing to recognise the flaws in their own broken ideology.

And with every furious temper tantrum and frazzled denial of reality, they appear a little worthier of an entry in the DSM.

STOCKHOLM: SAME OLD SCRIPT

13th April 2017

Don't bother turning off the lights on the Eiffel Tower, or turning on the lights on the Brandenburg Gate, or lighting a candle and photographing it poignantly.

After the Islamist atrocity in Stockholm last week, does anybody still care about these overly familiar, increasingly mechanical routines? It looks like theatre now. Like a jaded actor sadly going through the motions. Projecting his lines, pitch perfect and with not a vowel out of place, but signifying absolutely nothing of consequence. Or nothing other than that we can all shuffle on, herd-like, to the next phase in the worn out, melancholy sequence of response. Which is to do nothing, as if this were all the most natural thing in the world, like paying the bills or forgetting to put the rubbish out.

Go to work. Change the subject. Wait to see who gets killed next.

And even if some of those tweeted platitudes and Facebook pleas for something-or-other are actually sincere, then so what? What's their purpose? Anesthetization? Therapy? Just read, retweet, and forget about the dismembered bodies, and the lives ripped apart.

Or maybe that other tribe of peculiar airheads will make an appearance. The ones who dribble on predictably about how all religions are the same, or that 'the Right' is coming to get us, or who perversely, perniciously wrench reality out of shape so that actually it's us, the people being attacked, who are to blame for the fact that we're being attacked. Because of imperialism, or privilege, or not caring enough about savage, shoddy superstitions of a variety we outgrew centuries ago. Or whatever the current charge might be.

I say us, but it's obviously not me or anyone reading this that got torn in half by several tons of metal in Stockholm. And it's not any of the cold-hearted con artists, or the misguided naifs, or anybody else that chooses to distract from the truth of the matter, ramp up the danger, and stand in the way of putting together a responsible course of action. The only role such people serve is to complicate a difficult situation further, leading to an increased possibility of yet more bilious carnage.

People like the Irish Times' correspondent in Sweden, who wrote an article which, rather than focusing on the actual horrors taking place there, chose instead to ignore the bodies, and warn us of a hypothetical future in which the far-right makes political gains. As if it were the far-right that had driven a truck into innocent shoppers, or left a grotesque trail of misery along Westminster Bridge, or gunned down concert goers and cartoonists in Paris, or blown themselves up in an Egyptian church, or hacked, knifed, raped, maimed and murdered their way into the global consciousness. And as if using tragedy to push an agenda—while dismissing genuine shock and fear—isn't exactly the kind of repugnant behaviour that will drive rational, intelligent people as far away from the calculating, self-interested Left as they can possibly get.

Think back to last month's Westminster attack. It might seem long ago, because the atrocities are coming thick and fast now. After that one, George Eaton, of the New Statesman, tweeted this:

"A snapshot of London's magnificent diversity in those injured: French, Romanian, Korean, German, Polish, Irish, Chinese, US, Italian, Greek."

And what a staggeringly inhuman take on events that is. What kind of desperate, ghoulish mind would take the still congealing blood in a stack of mutilated corpses, and use it to grease the spin on their own creaking, fractured ideology?

On the Sunday after the Stockholm attack, thousands gathered in the city to, in the words of Sweden's official Twitter account, "show that peace and love will win over violence and hate".

Which sounds just wonderful, but frankly, I didn't care about peace and love before I heard about a truck being driven at speed into pedestrians, and I don't care about peace and love now either. In fact, what on earth have peace and love got to do with maintaining national security and ensuring that Islamists don't murder people?

Imagine instead if the crowds were gathering in city squares for something meaningful, such as to demand an unapologetically robust response to Islamic extremism. Or to show that we can be fair and decent, but remain unflinching against the mindless vitriol of the politically correct mob, and give not one inch to illiberal doctrines. Imagine how much better we might be able to deal with the problem of Islamism if we could finally call time on the restrictive political constraints imposed by the progressive left.

Or shall we just stick to that worn out, overly familiar script?

Go to work. Change the subject. Wait to see who gets killed next.

VEILING THE ISSUE

28th April 2017

There was something troubling about sections of the media's sneering reaction to Ukip's statement on the subject of face veils on Monday. The party wants to prohibit the custom of completely covering one's face in public, as practised by some Muslims. As it's the widely maligned Ukip who proposed it, the idea was met with a significant amount of derision.

"Does this ban apply to all face coverings, like beekeepers?" queried Christopher Hope, of the Telegraph.

It's a funny line, to be fair. How about welders? And the local fencing club, do you want to lock them up too?

Of course, Ukip will always be more vulnerable to journalistic prodding than other parties, and if we can't snigger at politicians then we're doomed. But if the mainstream media were to stop and look around for a moment, they'd find that there is a quietly smouldering issue at the heart of all this, and it's not cooling down.

This topic cuts to the bone of the overtaxed 'liberal elite' trope, which might be a cliché, but is as true now as it was last

June when Brexit descended, filing its nails and grinning conspicuously, from the midsummer heavens. The metropolitan bubble never actually burst, and within it, concerns about Islam are dismissed, entirely wrongly, as a form of bigotry or narrow mindedness.

On the outside though, among the majority of the population, the wearing of face veils can be spoken about openly, and it's a custom that's certainly not welcomed with open arms.

Is that bigotry?

Well, ask yourself this. If you were walking down the street and the black-clad person approaching you was wearing their black hood up, with their black scarf pulled up tight so you could see nothing but their eyes, would it be bigoted to feel uncomfortable?

Is it bigoted to acknowledge that physically disguising oneself, so you cannot be visibly distinguished from others in your similarly attired group, is disconcerting for others?

Is it bigoted to state that we need greater integration between communities so that we can live together cohesively, and that if one group of people conceal their identities every time they go out in public, it's disruptive to that process of integration?

Is it bigoted to note that burkas are worn only by adherents to a radically devout form of Islam, which in no way treats women as equals, and which is fundamentally incompatible with liberal ideals?

The media can go ahead and take the piss out of Ukip to their heart's delight. Snarking and sniping is the British way of dealing with things and I wouldn't want to change that for a moment. But they should also be aware that it doesn't matter how much they ignore this issue, or laugh at it, or temporarily misdirect people's attention, it will still be there, and it's growing.

Wait a few years and it won't just be Ukip discussing this, it will be all the major parties, and the beekeeping gag might not get rolled out. If it seems unlikely that the issue will gain wider traction, just look at how Euroscepticism used to be treated: as a fringe concern, toxic to the electorate. How misguided that false consensus looks now that we're actually leaving the EU, for good, because it turns out that actually, most people are Eurosceptics.

Discussing face veils also raises vital issues around free speech and Islam. The establishment consensus is that there will be no burka ban, but at the same time there's a risk that we'll become constricted by hate speech regulations, which could prevent us from discussing Islam in a robust and open manner. Just recently Sadiq Khan implicitly warned us to wash our online mouths out with soap and holy water, or else prepare for a knock on the door *[a reference to Khan launching an 'Online Hate Crime Hub']*. But logically, you can't make the liberal case for the freedom to wear the veil (or the freedom to be forcibly veiled) while simultaneously endorsing hate speech rules, which are fundamentally illiberal.

A core part of the argument not to have a burka ban is that the state has no right to tell anybody what they can and can't wear. This ignores the issue of coercion, but can nonetheless be framed as an authentically liberal argument. And authentic liberals know that the liberties they espouse extend to everyone, even those with whom they disagree. It's very easy to defend liberalism when you're only dealing with people on your side. It's when you have to extend those liberal rights to your opponents that the true test comes. Put simply, if banning face veils is illiberal, then so is monitoring and restricting people's speech.

If we aren't to deal with the regressive elements of Islam through bans and state enforcement, then part of the alternative is to use reason and argument. And also jokes, ridicule, disrespect, trolling, baiting, and heckling. The same as we've done with every other overbearing religion, dysfunctional political system, and thin-skinned authoritarian.

But our ability to do any of this is hindered if we must be constantly wary of crossing arbitrary lines on what is and isn't acceptable speech. We end up with what amounts to blasphemy policing, and are quickly left with no further method of critical engagement. Give a free pass to Islam in this way, by cracking down on those who peacefully confront it while also dismissing the idea of legislative intervention, and you're on the path back to a theocratic dark age.

QUILLIAM FLAWED

4th May 2017

You may be aware that this week, relations between Tommy Robinson and Maajid Nawaz's *Quilliam Foundation* broke down completely. For those not up to date on what happened, here's a summary.

First, there's Tommy Robinson, former leader of the English Defence League, and outspoken campaigner against Islamic extremism. Robinson is a deeply controversial figure about whom you can find two competing descriptions:

One is that he's nothing more than a loudmouthed, racist thug. According to this view, he hates all Muslims (and probably other minorities too) and lacks intelligence, but through his posturing attracts the adoration of similarly minded trolls and extremists. He's a violent, hard-right street agitator with a criminal record, who seeks to whip up anti-Muslim prejudice.

And then there's the alternative, growing view. That while Robinson doesn't have a clean record, he's a man who now, in his thirties, is a legitimate political voice. This view holds that far from being racist, Robinson, through harsh personal experience, has identified deep seated problems in Muslim communities, which are threatening to wider society. Issues such as mosques disseminating extremist views, Islamist radicalisation in prisons (don't forget that he's been in prison), and the operation of rape gangs, such as were exposed, infamously, after the Rotherham cover up.

My advice is to look into Robinson's story for yourself, and listen to what he has to say in his own words. If you're not harbouring any weighty preconceptions, you'll find that the former description of him seems increasingly wide of the mark. Even if you still don't like him, two things will become clear: he's not a racist, and he's well-informed about Islam.

And we also have the Quilliam Foundation. This is an organisation set up by campaigner and former Islamist extremist Maajid Nawaz which works to fight extremism of all kinds. Its primary focus has been on Islam, and it aims to help facilitate an Islamic reformation, aligning the religion with the standards of twenty first century secular democracy. Recently though, it launched its new Circle initiative, which aims to combat extremism on all sides, and it's become more concerned with right wing, nationalistic movements. The foundation has employed a mix of characters in the past, some sound and some more dubious.

In contrast with Robinson's public reputation, Nawaz portrays himself as a thoroughly respectable figure. He has his own LBC talk show, appears as a political commentator on television, wrote a book with Sam Harris, and has become, in the UK, a go-to authority on Islamic reform.

Where Robinson and Nawaz's paths cross is when in 2013 Robinson publicly abandoned the EDL and began working with the Quilliam Foundation. This was seen as a victory for Quilliam, but Robinson eventually rejected the organisation, regarding them as unproductive. He has also raised questions about the motivations involved in the relationship, stating that he needed the financial support Quilliam could offer, while it benefited Quilliam to be seen as having de-radicalised him.

Cut to 2017, and Robinson's popularity is surging. His book, *Enemy of the State*, is an Amazon bestseller, and he's working for the libertarian conservative organisation *Rebel Media*. Crucially, his robust, untrained style, which cares absolutely nothing for political correctness, and explicitly rejects both the mainstream media and left wing ideology, connects with people in a way that a newspaper such as the *Guardian* could only dream of.

Things get interesting when, at the beginning of April, in the wake of the Westminster terror attack, he calls up his old pal Nawaz on the latter's live LBC phone-in. While Robinson makes points about a Home Office approved extremist imam, Nawaz is concerned that Robinson should articulate the difference between Islam and Islamism, and they talk across each other. I believe that Nawaz's distinction is significant. But at the same time, non-Muslims are under no obligation to expend energy thinking about such matters, and in most cases never will. Something anyone can grasp immediately though, is a problem such as the authorities being duped by an extremist preacher. Which is precisely what Robinson was talking about.

Nawaz doesn't disagree with Robinson at all, but he moves the conversation over to the fact that far-right groups are on the rise. Robinson in turn doesn't disagree with this. But if there's a rise in the far right, then it's precisely because critical points like the one Robinson was making aren't being properly addressed by the political centre.

Then, this week, Quilliam's senior researcher, Julia Ebner, wrote a defamtory article for the Guardian in which, without evidence, she calls Robinson a white supremacist. Here is the passage in question:

> "That the far right has moved from the fringe into the mainstream demonstrates the massive support that white supremacist movements have attracted from digital natives. Their online followership often exceeds that of mainstream political parties: with over 200,000 followers, Tommy Robinson's Twitter account has almost the same number of followers as Theresa May's."

When confronted on Twitter about this, Nawaz denied that the article says Robinson is a white supremacist. But it does, and if you don't think so, read it again. Or alternatively, read this, in which well known podcaster Stephen Knight has changed a few words from the paragraph for illustrative purposes:

[Knight wrote, "That Islamic extremism has moved from the fringe into the mainstream demonstrates the massive support that Islamist movements have attracted from digital natives. Their online followership often exceeds that of mainstream political parties: with over 130,000 followers, Maajid Nawaz's Twitter account has almost the same number of followers as Theresa May's."*]*

I wonder what Nawaz would make of that. And let's take a look also at the line which comes directly after the offending paragraph of the article:

> "Neo-Nazis outperform Isis in nearly every metric, a 2016 report by the Institute for Strategic Dialogue found."

It immediately references neo-Nazis, as if they're connected to Robinson. While not as explicit as in the first passage, the implication is clear, and the effect of further smearing Robinson is reinforced.

This looks like a cut and dried case. It really shouldn't matter whether you sympathise with or loathe Robinson, the article is an effort to discredit him. And not just through nods, winks and insinuation, but with an outright lie: that Robinson is a white supremacist.

Working for Rebel Media, Robinson has a new approach to dealing with such libels. In journalistic fashion, camera crew in tow, he doorsteps the writer. Just recently he did so at the newsroom of Wales Online.

And that's where it gets a bit messy. When he did the same at Quilliam, he was refused entry, but managed to sneak into their office. The confrontation became heated, Quilliam's staff appeared to take some of the media crew's equipment, and eventually the police arrived, escorting Robinson and his crew out of the building.

Soon afterwards, Nawaz tweeted out news of the confrontation in what can only be described as a sensationalist manner:

"BREAKING: Extremist Tommy Robinson raided @QuilliamOrg office & intimidated staff. Police escorted him off"

Bear in mind Robinson took action because he'd been defamed as a white supremacist, the kind of false accusation he has to deal with constantly. And he's then immediately labelled by Nawaz as an 'extremist', who 'raided' and 'intimidated'. It's hardly difficult to see the pattern in which Quilliam is depicting Robinson.

Watch the video and it doesn't look much like an *intimidating raid*, particularly considering there are members of Quilliam who know Robinson personally.

I write all this as someone who has admired Quilliam and

the work that Maajid Nawaz has done since his Hizb ut Tahrir days. It's not intended to bash them. But it's impossible to see Ebner's Guardian article as anything other than an attempt at defamation, and it's troubling to see Nawaz defending it.

I can't help thinking that the Ebner article – and the Quilliam Foundation's public statement over the affair – will turn out to be an own goal. The people who think Robinson is a racist will still think so. And the people who have done a little research and know he isn't will still know he isn't. But it's now apparent that Quilliam isn't averse to acting in an underhand manner. And if there's one tactic which the general public is absolutely sick of right now, it's the throwing around of baseless accusations of bigotry, racism and the like. After his run-ins with the Southern Poverty Law Center, Nawaz should know about this more than most.

PITY THE SHOWBIZ SOCIOPATHS

21ˢᵗ May 2017

First there was Brexit, and now the local elections have confirmed it: the British people are no mugs. To the know-it-all celebrities who have the biggest platforms and the loudest voices, the message has come through loud and clear: screw you.

The rich and fabulous love nothing more than to emote tragically on how Brexit is the end of the world, Tories are evil, and Socialism is wonderful. Selflessly, like Jesus, they provide constant public guidance on what steps us unwashed serfs should take to improve ourselves and vote correctly.

The problem with this is that celebrities are idiots. Even the once clever ones are now bottom of the class, because they're trapped in a showbiz alternative reality. Money is thrown at them and they're surrounded by sycophantic bumlickers. So even the tiny minority who did have some latent intelligence quickly lose it, as their brains become rotten and squelchy through being constantly told how wonderful they are, when in fact, they're not.

Viewed through the flat screen of social media, politically judgmental celebrities become two dimensional caricatures.

Every feeble brain twitch they have is amplified dramatically. Each lopsided ejaculation of politically correct slop gets notched up to 11, when the best place for it would be down the shitter. Every flaw in their thinking is exposed mercilessly, and the vacuous one-sidedness of their position slaps you in the face.

Bothering to understand only one side of the argument, celebrities are horribly partisan. And they're the very worst kind of partisans, not schemers who spin deliberately, but dunces who project their bias because they're simply ignorant of the facts, and have no wish to consider any opinion that challenges their worldview.

The worst case proselytizers dehumanize and fail to understand their opponents as a matter of habit because, being sociopathic big shots who always get their own way, they've forgotten that other people's ideas are just as valid as their own.

And so the caricatures solidify as the luvvies entrench, mutating into blustering, megaphone voiced bullies, understanding almost nothing of the world, but spitting out their pompous messages nonetheless, day after day, stopping not once to listen to alternative points of view.

Recently, some of them have set themselves up as courageously facing down a tide of authoritarianism, but in fact, it's the dissent clubbing celebs themselves who are the authoritarians. They despise democracy because it keeps throwing up results they don't like, and spoiled brats can't handle not getting their own way.

What kind of two bit tyrant would rail against democracy and then brand themselves as the good guy? Answer: a celebrity idiot. They thought they were the misfit rebels, but the truth is the precise opposite: they are the establishment conformists. They are the fat cats, sneering at the workers. They are the conceited, inbred aristocrats, sniffy and disdainful of the rabble gathering outside. They've become everything they might once have despised, before they were famous. They're maddened and neurotic, flabby and ensconced, and too precious, unhinged and uptight to ever realise what they've turned into.

Here's an example of a famous gobshite you might once have thought was reasonably smart, but who has over-reached, and revealed that she suffers from disrupted cortices. Ladies and gentlemen, Caitlin Moran:

> "As Labour collapses across the country, I can't think of anything I regret more than voting Jeremy Corbyn as leader. I'm so sorry, my kids."

Oh dear, didn't you realise he'd be useless? Didn't you notice all the political commentators explaining exactly what would happen? Because even the turgid drips at your beloved Guardian warned you about this dud candidate, and I've been hearing since Brexit that cool and rational left-liberal geniuses *always* take stock of expert opinion.

But what did Caitlin think about Corbyn's past record?

> "I'll vote for a leader who's more left-wing and less media-trained!" I thought – not bothering to find out what he was actually like."

Oh, I see. Even leaving aside specifics though (such as Corbyn supporting terrorists), it's striking that anyone could be that unaware of how electorally toxic the hard-left is. Until you remember that we're dealing with a celebrity. Only by lacking completely in self-awareness, and having an absurdly trumped up sense of self-importance, could anyone be so oblivious to the majority opinion in the real world.

How about a considerably more famous writer, JK Rowling? She must be on the ball, she wrote some books about a wizard. And she has an incredible platform: 10.3 million people who don't particularly like reading follow her on Twitter. So how did she reach out and engage with their vibrant diversity of opinions?

Well, she's spent several months spouting incessantly about what an almighty disaster Brexit is, and how we're all doomed, and Trump is going to harvest our organs, and the abyss is nice and warm so let's just throw ourselves into it now, and on and on, tweet after godforsaken, egomaniacal tweet. She was so distraught after the referendum that she clattered unfortunately into over-wrought sixth former mode, and used the F-word:

"I'll use my influence whatever way I want. This country needs to be freed of fascists on both right and left."

What she forgot, like Moran, is that most of us inhabit reality, and it's quite nice down here. The sky isn't falling in. We speak to people who have different opinions. We might—*gasp*—be rather fond of Brexit, or at the very least know someone who is, and not think they're a deplorable racist.

Rowling can no longer perceive day-to-day life beyond her elitist cocoon, inside which the only acceptable behaviour is to worship blindly at the altar of liberal progressivism. Crucially, she forgot that a lot of people are naturally optimistic about the future. And even if they're not, they have no problem honouring the democratic wishes of their compatriots, and can do so with magnanimity. And that whatever happens, they'd prefer to roll up their sleeves and make a go of things, rather than congealing into a sticky blob of po-faced, self-righteous morbidity.

Scratch the surface, glimpse the void underneath, and the same pathology applies to them all. To Gary Lineker, Lily Allen, and any comedian the BBC can countenance hiring. To Damon Albarn, Michael Sheen, and Emma Kennedy. To Patrick Stewart, Billy Bragg, and the rest of the spitting, spoiled, self-obsessed cry babies. Wherever they once came from, none of them has the faintest idea how ordinary people live now.

Rather than becoming annoyed, perhaps we should pity them instead. The sad truth is that even with their obscene bank balances, monumental arrogance, and grotesque egos, there's nothing they can do to reverse the damage done to their own minds: their critical faculties have been permanently turned to mush by life in the spotlight.

But please, celebrities, don't take this to heart. Don't ever change. Carry on with your snide, sniffy, ignorant, intolerant, head in the sand, high and mighty, laughable, la la land, bubble-wrapped bullshit.
Because as you can see from recent results, it's working perfectly.

LONG LIVE THE TRAITORS

21ˢᵗ May 2017

The right looks for converts, the left for traitors. So runs the famous saying and it's true, but feels incomplete. The modern left sniffs around obsessively for racists, homophobes, pronoun-skeptics, Islam-doubters, and any other kind of careless bigot you can imagine, with the possible exception of anti-Semites, to whom the hard left is more likely to give a free pass and an inclusive wink.

Losing sight of its founding principles, the left has largely given itself up to identity politics and grievance representation. It has defined itself by what it's opposed to—discrimination and inequality—so when it turns out that what it's opposed to is in increasingly short supply, the left has no choice but to invent it, which is how it winds up turning on its own one-time members.

The current generation of haughty leftists flounces round the political scene like a wheat intolerant Spanish Inquisition. They combust, mortally wounded, at the slightest digression from their peculiar brand of moral commandment, weaponising their own emotional delicacy to justify the abuse of anyone who breaches their anti-intellectual safe space. People who at one time supported the left, but who now hold proscribed opinions, are directly in their line of fire.

So contrary to Theresa May's matter-of-fact statement, Brexit does not mean Brexit. It means a Tory deception now, a way for the hard-right to refashion Britain as a predatory economic dystopia, in which children will be sent to the workhouse, hospitals demolished, and forests burned down for fun. Never mind that many Leave backers are people who'd usually vote Labour. And never mind that Brexit is not, and never was, a left/right issue. If you're in favour of leaving the EU, then the new left-wing purity police will put you on their watchlist.

But as hard Remainers continue their public breakdown over the imagined consequences of Brexit, they fail to recognise that they chose, by themselves, to relinquish their own influence over the process of leaving the EU. They did this when, rather than immediately accepting the result in an adult manner, and getting on with the task at hand, they chose instead to throw an almighty tantrum.

It's the new left that lost emotional control and tried, with pathological selfishness, to subvert democracy. They misrepresented Leavers and their reasons for voting out. They cast around for heretics to throw stones at, repelled former Labour voters, and in the end did nothing other than remove themselves, in a fit of ridiculous, misplaced indignation, from the real debate.

Still they don't see their own role in driving people away from the left, but why would any Leave voter go within a million miles of the Labour Party now? The Labour Party whose media cheerleaders have made it clear that they viscerally despise Leave voters, and would dismiss the referendum result if only they had the power to do so.

And how about another pressing national concern, immigration? The most common opinion is that it should be lowered. After all, what reason is there to think that the current rate is perfect, or that it's always too low, and must only ever go up? Surely there's nothing wrong with simply presenting for discussion the idea that immigration could be set lower.

But these normal opinions are abhorrent to the Islington Left, who've been conditioned to reject such thinking without consideration. Talk to them like this and you'll be regarded with suspicion. You will become, of course, a racist. A word which, when uttered by a millennial leftist, simply serves as an indicator that your opinion is beyond the limits of what they've been enabled to process.

And then there's the small matter of Islam. Perhaps this is the issue around which Labour have destroyed themselves the most comprehensively. There are so many problems that it's difficult to know where to begin. Maybe with Sharia Law's incompatibility with secular values. Or with attitudes to homosexuality, and apostasy. Or with women's rights, and the burka. Or with enabling cohesive integration. Or with violent extremism, and how to defend against the bloody wave of terror attacks breaking across Europe.

This is a defining issue of our time, by which Europe is being reshaped. So what do those on the left, who are always so assured of their own intellectual and moral capacity, have to say? What is their expert input to this profoundly significant debate?

Well, as it happens, their contribution is to cancel the debate. They not only refuse to engage with the issue, but they actively, aggressively work to prevent anyone else from talking about it either. Even in the immediate wake of an Islamist terror attack, they will move quickly to discredit anyone who criticises Islam, defaming them with Islamophobic motives. Or alternatively they'll wrench the discussion over to some weird, out-of-place discourse on the workings of the 'far-right'.

And as with 'racist', 'far-right' now has a new meaning. It's anyone who doesn't go unquestioningly along with the progressive agenda, no matter how irrational and out-of-touch that agenda becomes. Far right means dissenter. Far right means traitor.

So on three of the big issues of the moment, Brexit, mass immigration, and Islam, the left have removed themselves entirely from the conversation. In fact, worse than that, they've huddled on the sidelines, from where they pelt everyone else with insults, bang pots and pans, and moronically attempt to derail the normal conventions of civil discourse. The left doesn't present its case anymore, it simply tries to stop anyone else from presenting theirs.

The Labour Party now is a weird amalgamation of two of the most voter repellent groups in politics. On one side is the hard-left faction, which has at various times shown support for Hamas and Hezbollah, the IRA, and North Korea. It's Jeremy Corbyn, John McDonnell, and Andrew Murray. These are real-life political extremists, who have nothing good to say about the West. They're the kind of people who address Stalinists under a hammer and sickle, or who were members of the Communist Party of Britain just *five months ago*.

And on the other is the creepy, Guardian-fed, millennial faction. Thin-skinned Marie Antoinettes who can do little more than berate and belittle anyone who happens to hold a differing opinion, while ignoring entirely the atrocious beliefs of those in charge of their party.

Both groups have worked ceaselessly to root out noncon-formity. They've alienated and abused people who spent a lifetime supporting Labour, while leaving moderates who feel naturally at home on the centre left in a state of perplexed despair.

So it's truer now than it's ever been. The right looks for con-verts, while the left hunts traitors. And the left has done a sterling job of it. These days, the traitors outnumber the true believers.

A LINE IN THE SAND

25th May 2017

Here's the sand, now draw a line. Where do you want to put it?

After 9/11, or the Madrid train bombings? Or should we focus domestically, on 7/7?

We were shaken profoundly by the murder of Lee Rigby, but still no line.

Over the channel but close to home there was Charlie Hebdo, the Bataclan, Nice, Berlin, and Stockholm, but the sand remained undisturbed.

Westminster sickened us, and candles were burned, but we carried on as normal, as the liberal consensus always decrees.

And then Manchester. The deliberate targeting of children and teenagers, at a pop concert, with a nailbomb. Burning nails driven through children's shattered bodies.

Can we draw the line now?

Can we draw the line when not doing so means neglecting to defend our own children? Or are we so weak, in a state of such abject submission, that we can't protect the most innocent, vulnerable people in our families?

In our community.

Because the most vulnerable people are the ones being buried, or in pieces. After years of horror and abuse, are we going to guard against the enemy, or shall we guard instead against *'islamophobia'*. Shall we look after our own families, or shall we look after the feelings of the politically correct Guardian strata?

If we're going to make a stand, then first we must redefine the parameters of debate. The conversation around Islam has been shaped entirely by the left, and the borders they've drawn are so narrow as to make effective discourse impossible. So let's reject their pointless regulations. They can no longer be permitted to police the debate.

There were voices from the left in the aftermath of the Manchester attack who were more outraged by things being said on Twitter than by the massacre of children in a British city centre. These people are deeply confused, so let's clear things up for them: getting angry because a brainwashed psychopath has committed mass murder is normal. Talking about the ideology that drove him is normal. Searching for solutions is normal. To have been galvanised, frustrated, and furious all at the same time was normal.

The people driving this public conversation are not the bad guys. *The terrorists are the bad guys.*

Have you got that, do-gooders? Don't attack people for condemning atrocity, and searching for ways to stop it recurring. Don't sneer, high and mighty, because people demand *real* justice, rather than your contradiction-ridden, power grasping *social* justice.

If we can speak freely, then all options are on the table, and it's perfectly acceptable to explore outlying ideas. Ideas that may not be enacted, but which it's valuable to articulate because that's how discussion works. You go too far in one direction, get pulled back, improve your thinking, try again.

If it's fine for head-in-the-sand Marxists to suggest open borders, the dissolution of the nation state, and cheerful side-by-side co-existence with a murderous Caliphate, then it's equally fine for others to suggest, for example, a total ban on immigration from majority Muslim countries.

It's OK because we understand free speech, and these ideas are simply part of the reasoning process. They're too extreme to be enacted, but that doesn't mean it isn't beneficial to consider exactly why they wouldn't work. That process of back-and-forth leads to a sharper, more refined understanding of what *would* work, and for what reasons.

Hurt feelings, linguistic transgression, micro-aggressions, and all the other incoherent, intangible nonsense that the social justice left obsesses creepily over should be rejected. It's a waste of time, doesn't stand up to scrutiny, and hinders progress.

So what changes can we make in our approach to Islamic extremism?

Ideologically, we must abandon all ideas of cultural relativism. We follow the rule of law, and Britain is a secular country. No group of people, no matter their ethnicity or number, receives special favour on cultural, theological, or any other grounds.

More concretely, the problems of known extremists, and of British born jihadis returning from armed conflict in the Middle East must be addressed. Colonel Richard Kemp, a former member of Cobra—the government's emergency response committee—wrote about this from a position of expertise yesterday:

"All non-British citizens involved in extremism must be deported – that includes those preaching, financing, supporting or preparing for terrorism. Dual citizens must be stripped of British citizenship and deported.

Those who leave the UK to murder, rape and torture with the Islamic State or other jihadist groups must not be allowed to return. They are the most dangerous – blooded in battle and trained in sophisticated acts of mass violence."

He continues:

"Internment must be seriously considered for British citizens who cannot be deported or prosecuted yet intelligence shows are involved in terrorism.

These are draconian measures and they may well infringe the human rights of terrorists. But better that than to leave them free to violently deprive innocent British men, women and children of their lives."

Are these appropriate measures? As Colonel Kemp states, they appear draconian. But they're on the table now, to be taken apart and assessed.

Another area of concern is the influence of Wahhabi/Salafi mosques, funded by Saudi and Qatari money, radicalising through extremism. In an article from 2015, Iain Dale argued convincingly that they should've been banned from receiving foreign funding. He includes a disturbing quote from Islamic studies expert Dr Denis MacEoin, in which he describes "a huge amount of "malignant literature" inside as many as a quarter of Britain's mosques", allegedly all Saudi linked:

"Among the more choice recommendations in leaflets, DVDs and journals were statements that homosexuals should be burnt, stoned or thrown from mountains or tall buildings (and then stoned where they fell just to be on the safe side). Those who changed their religion or committed adultery should experience a similar fate. Almost half of the literature was written in English, suggesting it is targeted at younger British Muslims who do not speak Arabic or Urdu. The material, which was openly available in many of the mosques, including the East London Mosque in Whitechapel, which has been visited by Prince Charles, also encourages British Muslims to segregate themselves from non-Muslims. There is, of course, nothing new in such reports. Investigative journalists have over the years uncovered all manner of material emanating from Muslim extremists in various parts of Britain. Earlier this year an undercover reporter for Channel 4 filmed preachers and obtained DVDs and books inside mosques which were filled with hate-filled invective against Christians and Jews. They condemned democracy and called for jihad. They presented women as intellectually congenitally deficient and in need of beating when they transgressed Islamic dress codes. They said that children over the age of 10 should be hit if they did not pray. Again the main mosque chosen for exposure was influenced and funded from Saudi Arabia."

That makes for chilling reading, and shows exactly what we're dealing with. There can be no place for any of it in a modern, open society, just as there's no place for violence.

Which leads to another message I'd like to offer the apologist left: don't ever tell us that Islamist terror is something we must learn to live with. Don't dismissively opine that it's normal.

The view from the left seems to be that it's a price worth paying, but a price worth paying for what? To maintain a failed, left-wing ideology that most people don't subscribe to? And what exactly do we get in return for bowing in reluctant consent, a pat on the head from the BBC? A cheap seat at the back of the unrocked (but leaking) multi-culti boat? I can pass on those, thanks.

Immediately after a terror attack, something strange happens if you start making forceful statements condemning Islamism. You might say it must be kicked out, punished, and defeated. Despite not being abnormal reactions to news of a mass killing, there are elements of the left who'll turn on you for saying such things.

To clarify that, you run the risk of being viciously criticised for expressing anger at child murderers. That's right: *for expressing anger at child murderers*.

But the terror situation is getting worse, the attacks more frequent, and the methods more barbaric and stomach churning. After a pop concert for teenagers, what might be the next target? Do you think it likely that someone in the UK is planning an attack on a primary school, right now? How far along in their preparations might they be? Is whoever made the nail bomb in Manchester gathering materials for his next hideous device now, and how many children could it kill and maim?

The left appear incapable of processing such thoughts, their memories seemingly clear of the most recent attack by the time the next one comes along. They're desperate to move on, perform the candlelight vigil, change the story. But let's not go along with that anymore. The myopia the left displays is, literally, fatal. And it's fatal to all of us.

We have to take a more pragmatic approach. Paradoxically, in order to preserve the tolerance that's at the core of our liberalism, we're going to have assume an intolerant attitude. Not too much, just enough to keep our precious, hard-won values intact. Intolerant enough to remain tolerant. Because the alternative is that we co-habit with homicidal authoritarianism, an option which would have unthinkably dire long term consequences, and which must be avoided at all costs.

Austria just banned the face veil in public, following France, Belgium, the Netherlands, and Bulgaria. Since 2009, Switzerland has restricted the construction of minarets on mosques. The latter seems a minor decision, but both are indicative of public feeling.

When policy institute Chatham House did a survey earlier this year across ten European countries, they found that on average 55% of respondents agreed with the statement, "all further migration from mainly Muslim countries should be stopped". And only 20%, on average, disagreed with the statement. In the UK, the figures were 47% and 23% respectively.

This isn't to say that enacting an immigration policy to reflect this data would be either desirable or viable, but rather to show that the idea of taking much more robust action—on immigration, citizenship, extremist mosques, burkas—is not a fringe opinion.

Open borders are particularly unpopular, and mass immigration has breached consensually acceptable limits. Excessive displays of religious faith make people uncomfortable, and clash with our non-negotiable secular standards. When the religion threatening our values is sexist, homophobic, and has links with violent extremism, why should anyone be happy with its more zealous adherents flaunting their devotion? Britain has evolved past theological deference, and if the liberal left expects us to go backwards in order to appease Islam — a foreign faith to which Britain has no affiliation— then they're simply deluded.

The will for change is out there. The vast majority of people understand the issues and what's at stake. Either mainstream politicians start acting on the realities of what we're facing, or their semblance of control will come apart at the seams.

PUT DOWN THE PITCHFORKS

2nd June 2017

Can everyone please stop trying to get everyone else sacked?

Here's what people used to do when they were annoyed with someone: ignore them. Fume quietly. Or maybe even go right ahead and tell the offender what you think.

But what you would never do is cry victim and appeal to a higher authority. Snitching to teacher was viewed as cowardly in the extreme, and to do so would mark you out as feeble and undignified.

And yet this, and worse, happens all the time now. The go-to punishment that the mortally offended immediately grasp for is that their tormentor be sacked, without caution or appeal. That's a draconian punishment for often doing nothing more than ignoring the boundaries of the ingroup *opinion corridor*.

Going for someone's job and livelihood is below the belt, and in normal circumstances would be considered out of the question. I might despise you and your opinions, but I don't wish to see you out of work (and I certainly don't want to *cause* you to be out of work).

So I can only conclude that we're not in normal circumstances anymore, as a fair wedge of people have no problem with such morally out-of-whack tactics. It's a familiar routine: whoever is the current pantomime villain voices an outlandish opinion, uses naughty words, or fails to kneel before a sacred cow, and the mob will be after them, rooting for their destruction in the hope that they'll be rendered forever unemployable.

In Britain, the most high profile recent casualty was Daily Mail columnist and former LBC shock jock Katie Hopkins. Except she isn't that shocking at all, unless you've spent your whole life only talking to people who agree with you.

Has she said unpleasant things before? Certainly. A column in the Sun comparing incoming migrants to cockroaches was a low point. I'm surprised that went to print (it was later taken down), and she was rightly condemned for it, with even a UN high commissioner weighing in.

But she also, entirely rightly, never apologised. Let me be clear, I don't mean she was right not to apologise because the column she'd written was in any way reasonable. It wasn't, it was contemptible. But it was right of her not to apologise because she *isn't sorry*, and you can't force people's thoughts to conform with your own, no matter how disagreeable theirs might be.

The now deleted rogue tweet that got her cast out of LBC last week suggested a 'final solution' to the problem of Islamic extremism. It doesn't need explaining that to couch one's views in the language of the Holocaust is provocatively nasty. But apparently it does need explaining that we are *allowed* to make provocatively nasty references, to *absolutely anything*, including, should you really want to, genocide.

And let's not forget, her tweet came in the profoundly emotional immediate aftermath of the Manchester bombing, in which an Islamic terrorist slaughtered 22 concert goers, including children. For so many people to have focused their anger on getting a media commentator fired over a tweet, rather than on the psychopath who murdered children at a pop concert, shows a worryingly skewed perspective. It indicates that when it comes to slicing out the Islamist cancer, we're not all on the same page.

You didn't have to wait long for the next burst of scattershot outrage. Earlier this week, sections of the Liverpudlian populace suffered fainting fits because of what one person thinks. Liverpool is usually a tough city, with no shortage of sardonic good humour. But there are times when it turns into Snowflake-on-Sea: highly strung and forever the victim.

So when Talksport presenter Mike Graham replied to a tweet about the Heysel Stadium disaster by calling Liverpool supporters who'd contributed to it 'murderers', it's not difficult to imagine what happened next. Inevitably, as always now, there were calls for him to be sacked.

Was his tweet inaccurate? Yes. If he'd written #InvoluntaryManslaughter he'd have had a cast iron defence, but perhaps that went over Twitter's character limit.

Those flipping out in anger hadn't lost their rag because he'd overstated the charges though. It was simply that he'd transgressed, and spoken in a way in which those complaining never would, indicating that he might hold opinions which they don't. A sackable offence? It's not any kind of offence.

Again, no apology was forthcoming, but Graham did delete the tweet, and he wrote this by way of explanation:

"My tweet from last night was sent to one individual who was engaged in a vile and abusive argument with me. I allowed my anger to cloud my judgement but it was only ever my intention to insult him, not all Liverpool fans....... Needless to say I have also removed the offending tweet."

And then, in a break from the familiar *right says something/left takes offence* norm, there was the Kathy Griffin furore in the US. In her now infamous photograph, the left wing comedian holds up Donald Trump's bloodied, decapitated head, creating an image deliberately evocative of ISIS jihadis flaunting their barbarism.

It's graphic, goes way beyond the conventions of mainstream political discourse, and is astonishingly badly judged. Reports that Trump's 11-year-old son Barron was disturbed by the image illustrate how gruesome it was, and that it should have been treated as adult material. Griffin was condemned across the board and quickly released a full apology, but was dropped from her hosting role at CNN anyway.

But let's not forget that she's a comedian, not a cross-cultural diplomat, and if we start dictating how comedians can and can't express themselves then we're going down a bleak, authoritarian road.

Part of her problem is that left leaning comedians (which means almost all of them) have critically restricted themselves in who they'll take aim at politically. I can't stand most anti-Trump humour because it's predictable and self-righteous, and conforms deadeningly to liberal conventions.

Griffin's reaction to public fatigue with the anti-Trump message was not to change the record, but to employ shock tactics and gore, revealing her lack of perspective. After months of increasingly drab Trump material, it's time for comics to expand their subject boundaries, not ratchet up the blunt intensity of their hatred. Ultimately, the incident might serve as a wake-up call that anti-Trump hysteria has gone off the rails.

But at the same time, if Griffin chooses to express herself through grotesquerie then that's entirely up to her. The liberty to be crass, to screw up, to articulate views beyond the pale and *not* offer an apology, is a vital part of what distinguishes a free society from a tyranny.

So I'll reserve my outrage for the real villains who, as it happens, take full advantage of our obsessive speech policing to further their own nightmarish agenda. They don't use strong language and abrasive references, they use bombs, trucks, and Kalashnikovs. And given the chance, they'd make sure you never said a word out of line again, on threat of losing more than just your job.

Now more than ever, no matter which side of the political spectrum we've each landed on, let's put down the pitchforks and value our shared freedoms, even when we don't value the sentiments they're being used to express.

LABOUR LOST, BUT THEIR EXTREMISTS ARE EMBOLDENED

13th June 2017

It's easy to distinguish the many decent Labour supporters out there—they're the ones who are alarmed by the rise of Jeremy Corbyn.

The ones who are as disturbed as anyone by the party leadership"s links to the IRA, Hamas, and Hezbollah. Who don't want a leader that always sides with Britain's opponents in times of conflict. A leader that voted against preventing ISIS fighters returning to Britain, and that has spent his entire political career entangled with a latent thread of vile anti-Semitism.

So what do moderate Labour supporters do, come polling day? Some abstained. Some were pragmatic, put tribalism aside, and selected an alternative. And some held their noses and voted for this profoundly tainted version of their party.

For centrist Labour supporters who'd like nothing more than to see the back of Corbyn, it could be argued that the worst possible result has now come in. That is, that Labour, by the standard of their reduced expectations, performed relatively well.

And that's bad news for the centre-left. It means that the extremists just cemented their position at the top of the Opposition. They won more seats than either Gordon Brown or Ed Miliband could manage, and increased their vote share by almost 10%, taking back supporters who'd migrated to Ukip as they did so. There was an air of triumphalism about the Labour leadership as they did their post election strutting.

But despite exceeding expectations, the reality is that we may well have hit peak Corbyn, in terms of the returns he can expect to get in elections. Turnout was high. He mobilized the youth vote very effectively. He remained unaffected by a constant stream of revelations about his ghoulish political past (not smears, all truths), and he promised the Socialist utopia, which a section of his audience—heavily conditioned by school and university into anti-Capitalist thinking—have bought into completely.

By contrast, Theresa May was uninspiring. Her campaign was self-defeating, and the Conservative manifesto couldn't have been more badly received. During electioneering, the overwhelming disruption caused by two horrific terror attacks made May's 'strong and stable' mantra appear platitudinous. In the end, Corbyn performed as well as he conceivably can, the Conservatives were awful, and despite all of this, Labour *still* ended up 56 seats short of the Tories, and 64 short of an overall majority.

Corbynism lost the election, but you wouldn't know that from the celebrations that followed the count. Labour and their supporters paraded around in a state of delirium as if they'd won a landslide. There is a certain cultishness about their behaviour, in which all negative information is dismissed as false propaganda (the work of external enemies), and any good news is fed back and amplified, until their feverish hysteria blows up out of all proportion.

In their minds, Labour's leaders have been vindicated—all those years on the margins and it turns out they were right all along. They're as wrong as ever, of course, but confirmation bias will reinforce their self belief. The hard left doesn't loosen its grip once it's got a hold on power, and their takeover has just been further consolidated. It's their party now.

Corbyn has spent his entire career on the fringes, rebelling against his own party's leadership. At times it's unclear whether he's a politician or an activist. He speaks and carries himself like a student protester, and has spent the last several decades defined mainly by what he is against, rather than what he would deliver given the opportunity.
And that description of Corbyn also describes what Labour has become under his leadership: a bloated protest movement, ensconced in Parliament, with enough support for those who've taken control to resist challenges to their authority, but not enough to secure an election win.

This is not a healthy state of affairs. And what's further troubling is the debasing effect on political debate which Corbyn's ascent has had. His supporters have been coerced into a horribly binary way of thinking, whereby anyone who objects to Socialist policy, or who identifies as a conservative, is considered to be below contempt. There's no gradation, and no room for negotiation. You're simply with us, or you're evil.

There has been a resurgence in anti-Semitism, aggression, and insults. You don't have to look hard on social media to find examples of increasingly misanthropic left wingers piling in to spit bile at anyone who disagrees with their ideas. This mindset has been legitimized by Corbyn and his allies, who spoke of a 'kinder, gentler politics', but have enabled anything but. What we actually see is a viciously intolerant pack mentality taking hold. The attitude on the Cobynite left goes something like this:

"We believe in empathy and compassion. And if you don't agree with us you're hateful scum."

And it's mainstream too. On the day prior to the vote, the award winning Sunday Times columnist Caitlin Moran sent out a tweet in which she declared that anyone who disagrees with her political choices is 'a cunt'. Now, I've no objection to swearing. Some people are indeed cunts. But the thing is, they have to have done something particularly bad to deserve being called that. On the hard left though, that's not the case. Over there, you're considered the lowest of the low for nothing other than voting Conservative. I don't believe that Moran is, at heart, of the hard-left, but her party now is, and its extreme perniciousness is seeping out and changing the political tone.

On polling day, some Labour supporters posted videos online of themselves burning stacks of right wing newspapers. That should ring alarm bells. It started with author John Niven (who was taken to task after the election by JK Rowling for his abusiveness toward Theresa May) and the trend caught on, with Corbyn supporters boasting of having cleared their local newsagents of the Sun and the Daily Mail. Just think about that. Burning newspapers because you disagree with the content. Burning newspapers because you want to ensure that other people are only able to read content which you personally have pre-approved. It's a downright totalitarian mindset. Or in other words, it's a hard-left mindset, and it's being normalized.

Food writer Ruby Tandoh boasted of binning newspapers in

bulk. But in addition to purging wrongthink media, she took to Twitter to abuse and harangue other famous chefs. She called Jamie Oliver a 'prick', and implored Nigella Lawson to voice support for Labour, asking her 'please speak up?' After the event that might sound funny, but it wasn't banter. She was deadly serious and her tone was spiteful as she went about publicly demanding ideological conformity. She used shame and insults as a stick to beat her victims, because shame and insults were all she had, but imagine if a group of people with her mindset obtained state power. What might they do with it?

For all these reasons, it's difficult to see how any centrist Labour supporter can take real joy from Labour's gains in the election. Had Labour crashed and burned, the Corbyn diversion would be finally over, and might act as a lesson to all who got swept up in it. Corbyn and his thuggish mob would be consigned back to the political fringes, and the Labour Party could get back to the business of engaging in respectable politics.

But as it stands, the extremists are now more firmly installed than ever, and it's difficult to see how Labour—a party which used to represent noble principles—can be wrenched back to lucidity any time soon.

The Corbyn movement was a cult before the election, and it's still a cult now. But they've become puffed up and emboldened, and are dangerously convinced of their own moral infallibility. They won't win any elections, but they've successfully hijacked the Labour Party, toxified mainstream debate, and popularised a crudely judgmental, aggressively partisan way of thinking.

DEMONISING DOUGLAS

23rd June 2017

If you say there's a problem with *de facto* blasphemy policing around Islam, in which open criticism of this one particular religion is—to understate enormously—frowned upon, you might be chastised by left-wingers, who will inform you dismissively that no such problem exists.

But there's a characteristic shared by all of these people who insist there's no issue around criticism of Islam: none of them ever criticize Islam.

In fact, it's worse than that. Many of them actively defend Islam from criticism. They obfuscate, draw false equivalences, and deny that there are any problems within the religion at all. They laugh at anyone who speaks out, and paint them as paranoid, or hateful, or having sinister, racist motives. In other words, by denying that there is a culture of censorship around Islam, and vindictively misrepresenting those who criticize the religion, they contribute to and reinforce that very culture of censorship.

It's like claiming that the Spanish Inquisition is enforcing Catholic orthodoxy, and then having the Spanish Inquisition deny that the Spanish Inquisition exists.

Of course, Catholic enforcers of the past used violence, while these new authoritarians use words, but nonetheless, the words have an effect.

Look at this tweet that was sent out by Matt Zarb-Cousin, the former media advisor to Jeremy Corbyn, and which was retweeted by left wing columnist/activist Owen Jones to his 615,000 followers:

"Douglas Murray is a hate preacher, pass it on"

It's only words, but just look at the toxic intent. It's a wretched slur. Rather than engaging with Douglas Murray's expansive analysis of how Islam is changing Europe for the worse, and demonstrating the purported flaws in his argument, it's simply intended to demonise Murray.

The strategy here is, being unable to counter the argument, delegitimise the source instead. Attack the speaker, hurl mud. These tactics are nothing new, and are as repugnant as ever, but the only thing they achieve in this case is to indicate that there's an undeniable truth in Murray's ideas. He's on to something, so his hapless attackers become pernicious.

By it's very nature the process of attempting to discredit him would, if successful, ruin Murray's reputation. And Zarb-Cousin and Jones are entirely comfortable with that. We should be thankful that such an outcome is beyond their limited capabilities, and that they instead come off looking like peculiarly Stalinesque children. What's starkly revealed though, is the callousness, spite, and lack of a moral compass which Zarb-Cousin and Jones display in pursuit of their aims. Unfortunately, this dysfunctional malice has become characteristic of the modern, regressive left.

Making what they did even worse, is that although they themselves don't use violence, they are unknowingly allied with more savage forces. Zarb-Cousin, Jones, and others in and around the regressive left are useful idiots. They send out tweets and pen columns discrediting critics of Islam, generating slurs, hurling false accusations of bigotry, and all the while provide cover for something deeply sinister.

Dutch filmmaker Theo Van Gogh was murdered in the street for making a short movie about the treatment of women in Islamic societies. Activist Ayaan Hirsi Ali, who was his collaborator at the time, lives under constant threat of death because of her condemnation of Islamic practices. The staff of Charlie Hebdo were massacred in Paris for drawing cartoons of Muhammad. Anyone who offers robust criticism of Islam from a big enough public platform becomes a target for lethal jihadi violence. And liberal commentators who ignorantly police this criticism, mislabeling it as Islamophobia, are doing a favour to the jihadis.

Zarb-Cousins, Jones, and others like them make the target a little bigger, a little brighter. They would never explicitly endorse violence, but they put out a message to their audience that those who don't kowtow to Islamic sensitivities are doing something wrong. They legitimise the idea that we must tread carefully around Islam, when in fact, if we believe in liberal, secular democracy, we have no obligation to do anything of the sort. Regressive leftists are the know-nothing propaganda wing of Islamic fundamentalism. Perversely, the more loudly they proclaim to oppose fascism, the more they assist in advancing the causes of a particularly insidious strain of theological tyranny.

These arrogant, self-righteous blasphemy police use pointed words such as racist, Islamophobe, and hate. Jihadis use real weapons: knives, guns, and explosives. But take a step back and as the longer trajectory is revealed their mutual bond becomes apparent: they are both working toward the same ends. They both further the cause of radical Islam. The difference between them is that one side is aware of the grand scheme, and the other isn't. And if, just hypothetically, the jihadi end game were ever achieved, there's one side which would waste no time at all in disposing most brutally of the other.

OUR SAVIOUR
JEREMY CORBYN

Some have questioned what drives Jeremy Corbyn's recent surge in popularity, but if you have to ask, you should be regarded with suspicion. Because Jeremy Corbyn is, simply, a *good* man. He hugs people. He cares and is empathetic, he will provide and protect. Forgiving and incorruptible, he nods, divines, and heals.

But don't question him, because his powers require devotion. Lend him your faith, unconditionally, and there will be no limit to what can be achieved. He is the conduit for the collective, and so collected we must be. Deviation threatens the greater good and besides, we've already established that we *are* good, so if you disagreed, what would that make you?

Might there be violence? Unfortunately, yes, but only in order to dispatch those who would stand in the way of progress. And just to make sure that you don't feel bad for those at the blunt end of our zeal, we'll organise a little chant, mob up, and dehumanize them so you can attack without restraint or regret. You see, they're not even people really. They're far-right *Tory scum* oppressors, who use vile tools of state tyranny such as freedom of speech and democratic elections to maintain their fairly decided, majority-endorsed right to govern.

Unlike the despotic elected government though, Corbyn can do all things. If you're from an ethnic minority, then he'll *unlock your talent.* Trust in this career Socialist, who has two A Levels at grade E, and no experience of work outside trade unions and Westminster, to guide you to success and show you how to better yourself.

"Only Labour can be trusted to unlock the talent of Black, Asian and Minority Ethnic people." He tweeted.

Furthermore, Corbyn is a repository of high grade compassion. Do you remember his profound words when asked whether Theresa May cared about the victims of the Grenfell disaster? Sagely, and with infinite restraint, he let it be known that, "everybody cares to an extent, some to a deeper extent".

Yes, Corbyn cares *more deeply.* His emotions are divine, untainted, perhaps not fully comprehensible to hate-filled Conservative monsters. When Corbyn embraces you, you might sense for a moment the bottomless reservoir of universal love that exists within him. And if he doesn't hug you, and leaves you for Owen Jones' frothing mob instead, you can be sure that the decision was taken in wisdom: for the many, not the few. Certainly not for you.

The Hezbollah-hugger's brilliance is so otherworldly, that he can even solve inequality where none exists. Speaking to the Glastonbury hive mind, he said he wanted all children "to have the right to write poetry, to paint, to make music".

Inshallah, those regressive, imaginary restrictions on children writing, painting, and making music will finally be lifted. Steel drums and marimbas will be distributed by the state, and the towns and cities of Britain will spontaneously erupt with radical left-wing street parties, in which ragged urchins bang out avant-garde minimal-Calypso renderings of

Rag'n'Bone Man and the Libertines.

At a rally last weekend, Labour's IRA-idolising iconoclast pointed out that he would reverse the trend preventing working class young people from attending university, even though there is no such trend, and more people from low income homes go to university now than ever before.

Is there any other leader with such miraculous abilities to fix injustice, whether it's there or not? And as for those foreign workers at Glastonbury on zero hours contracts, exploited by the event organisers in order to cut costs, while Corbyn himself appeared on stage to deliver his message of social justice? Ah sorry, no, they're not part of the narrative. They must be *the Few* too.

But don't think about that, just fall in line and let your consciousness dissolve. Our jihadi-genial vegetarian saviour is faultless, infallible, and backed by an entire musical genre. So let Russell Brand dribble lies about dead dictators into your ear, while Ruby Tandoh guards the door, muttering about what a prick you are. You needn't have original thoughts anymore, we'll provide those. Just grab a placard and give yourself up to the greater good.

You'll regret it if you don't.

ARE YOU A TRUE PROGRESSIVE?

13ᵗʰ July 2017

Young people are getting involved in politics, and a significant number have been corralled over to the left. I can understand that. There are all these bearded, wisecracking chaps over there, beckoning and leering for your attention. The likes of Ricky Gervais and Nick Frost are lusting for virgin flesh, and an irresistible siren call has been put out. In the words of lefty philosopher queen Caitlin Moran, **"voting for Labour = not being a c**t"**. Who could resist such melodious logic?

No-one wants to be picked on, so why not just agree with the famous people? Don't ask whether saying they want Labour in power is just a way for them to ease their weak-minded liberal guilt. Whether they're so rich and out-of-touch that politics to them is merely an academic exercise. Whether they're co-cooned and unaffected whatever happens.

You don't really have to do much at all. Retweet a few jabs at the Tories. Blame everything on the Capitalist freedoms which safeguard your right to erroneously blame Capitalist freedoms. Maybe cry a bit because bad man Nigel Farage stole your future.

It's all so easy, but then again, perhaps you're a stickler who likes to check the terrain before crashing forward. In that case, hold on a second. Before you are subsumed into the flabbily grasping lefty melange, it might be worth doing a final check on the alignment of your political compass.

Here's a short questionnaire, to make absolutely certain that your progressive credentials are in order.

1. Are you in favour of racial segregation?

This is a core belief among the most radically progressive social justice drones. At Evergreen College in the US, on-site civil war erupted when a Jewish professor objected politely to being requested to leave the campus, due to his race, on a no-whites day. He found himself hounded by zealots, advised by the police to stay away from college as his safety couldn't be guaranteed, forced to teach lessons in a public park, and branded, incredibly, *as a racist.*

In the UK too, left wing thinking has embraced racism in it's battle against racism. Robert Peston's ITV politics show advertised for an intern, but stipulated that white people are prohibited from applying. It's unclear whether or not Peston will be using Nuremberg Laws classifications as a template for determining racial purity—how many white grandparents equate to media-ineligible offspring? If you're of the left you won't question this brazenly grotesque discrimination though. Pointing out racists is racist.

2. Do you think LGBT people should be forced to be left wing?

At the recent **Pride in London** festival, a celebration to promote **solidarity** for the LGBT community, there was an unexpected introduction of *shame* and *isolation,* as Conservative LGBT attendees were booed and treated with hostility. It's not difficult to extrapolate the thinking here. Your politics are assigned from above by the dominant class according to factors beyond your control, such as sexuality and race, and refusing to conform will result in abuse and marginalization. Now, you might think that structure sounds like what the left was supposed to be fighting *against,* but that's the beauty of progressivism—it could end up progressing toward anything, including intolerance and totalitarianism.

3. **Do you believe that religious laws should be enforced on non-believers?**

Over in utopian, open borders Germany, Salzburg kindergartens have decided that all the children in their care must follow Islamic law with regard to what they eat, regardless of whether or not they're Muslims. Political correctness is now informed by Sharia, and if a problem is encountered which isn't yet covered by the PC doctrine, then Sharia should be used as the precedent guideline. So why stop at children's meals? Do you object to banning the burka? Easily solved: let's make all women wear burkas. They can't penalize everyone, and in addition to thwarting Islamophobia, there'll be an significant increase in chaste devotion.

Please note that deference to religion only applies to Islam, to which you might even want to consider converting, boosting your identity politics credentials and saving yourself some future jizya.

4. **Are you relaxed about children being murdered?**

In the wake of a terrorist atrocity such as that in Manchester, there are two golden rules which must be followed:

Tell everyone to shut up and stop being racist.

Pretend everything's fine.

On no account must you allow people to speak openly, or ever concede that there may be something of a problem. But don't forget, as with religious compliance, this only applies to Islamic terror attacks. Any non-Islamic violence should be greeted with furious swipes at Tommy Robinson, the Daily Mail, and any other mouthy kafir who we don't like.

5. **Have you read Harry Potter?**

Everything that happens, anywhere, at any time, must be compared to events in the Harry Potter canon. You can try something else—Lord of the Rings, Peppa Pig, the Epic of Gilgamesh—but it won't really cut it. If you can't be arsed with Rowling's highbrow political game changer, just learn what the goodies and baddies are called, and divide the real world accordingly.

If you answered yes to all of the above then congratulations, you're a member of the progressive left, of Lineker-grade moral purity. If you answered no to even one, then you're not welcome, and should be profoundly ashamed of your bigoted selfishness.

What's that you say? It's seems harsh to be condemned just for disagreeing on one or two points? That's a problematic attitude, heretic. Conform absolutely or show yourself out.

A WEEK IN
IDENTITY POLITICS

20ᵗʰ July 2017

If someone were to ask, "what's the best way to divide society, make everyone hate each other, and bring the whole thing to a state of collapse from the inside?" I might answer with just two words: "identity politics".

It's difficult to imagine a more regressive approach to life than that endorsed by this horrible philosophy. As a quick reminder, the ideology is simple. Just take society and divide it into competing categories by assigning everyone to a group based on an immutable biological trait—race, sex, sexuality. There are also categories based on non biological factors. Being Muslim is a separate demarcation, and with the creation of infinite gender identifications, endlessly modifiable and capable of changing from day to day, an element of random confusion has been thrown into the mix.

Having been assigned to a category, your individual motivations become secondary, and you will be treated as little more than a worker ant in your particular collective. The supposed motivations of the collective itself are applied with a broad brush by those who oversee the identity politics framework—corrupt social justice tyrants who rely on crude stereotyping, and who are driven by an urge to reallocate power. To themselves. Some identity groups are given unquestioned privilege, while others are treated like a plague ridden corpse.

Identity politics acolytes share ground with Marxists, but replace class struggle with conflict between identity categories who've been set against one another. They don't want equality, they want an inversion of the hierarchy of oppression to which they subscribe, regardless of the extent to which it actually exists. And they are deeply bigoted, seeing everyone and everything in superficial identity terms.

They've been putting the hours in this week, so let's have a look at what they've been up to.

The most critical component of a functioning, modern civilisation is Doctor Who. It was announced by the BBC on Sunday that for the first time ever the Doctor will be a woman, to be played by **Jodie Whittaker. Is this a big deal? It depends on your perspective. There have been** plenty of female science fiction and fantasy leads up to now, from Ellen Ripley and Buffy, to Aeon Flux and Red Sonja. These are all original characters, created without a great political fuss, and it's indicative of the powerplay element of identity politics that converting the gender of an existing character should be presented as cause for celebration, while decades' worth of original, hugely popular female leads pass without comment.

Some people are very happy with the casting decision. Although it's nothing new in the science fiction genre as a whole, it's a departure for Doctor Who specifically, and it's interesting to try something new and see where it leads.

And some people accept it but wouldn't have made that

choice themselves. Not everyone wants to see their favourite character suddenly change gender, particularly if they've been a fan since 1963. That's an artistic consideration, or perhaps reflects the sentimental nuances of a longstanding fan relationship.

And then there are a small number of extremists on either side. There are some unreconstructed sexists who don't like the casting for misogynistic reasons. And facing off against them is an element of the intersectional left-wing set, who depict the casting of Whittaker as some kind of major blow to the *patriarchy* as they set about restructuring society.

Both sides are mildly comical, trading emotional blows over an alien who travels through time fighting monsters, and both sides are in many ways the same: prejudiced, stoking conflict, and grasping fearfully at Pyrrhic security and an illusory reflection of power.

Meanwhile, over at King's College London, a cowardly dean at the Institute of Psychiatry, Psychology and Neuroscience gave in to the social justice mob and promised to take down portraits and busts of the faculty's founding fathers because they're—brace yourself—white men. They'll be replaced with portraits of people who are not white men. And also not the founding fathers of the institute.

But perhaps the angry cultists are right and we should all be desperately ashamed that prominent figures in 1924 didn't meet the diversity targets that would be set by political correctness ideologues almost a century later. Yes, British demographics were entirely different in the 1920s, but that's no excuse for the lack of intersectional feminist slam poetry in the literature of the age.

And for a further idea of just how controlling and censorious the identity politics movement is, take a look at the Advertising Standards Authority. This week they ruled that **advertisers are prohibited from making commercials which depict stereotypical gender roles.** Or in other words, advertisers *must* portray fictional men and women in the gender roles the moral judges at the ASA dictate. These creepy jobsworths do so according to their own postmodernism-inflected views, and are to be kowtowed to by an entire nation, whether we like it or not.

Two years ago, in a fit of Victorian pique, the ASA ruled that an advertisement on the London Underground featuring a model wearing a bikini "can't appear again in its current form". That was an astonishingly illiberal step to have taken, but now they're going further. With a reckless disregard for freedom of thought and expression, they'll use legal authority to enforce a set of personal moral codes around something as undefined, variable, and subjective as gender roles.

Church and state might be separated, but the commandment-issuing high priests of identity politics are not to be dissented from. So cover up, don't look at pictures of white people, and above all, keep well away from hazardous gender stereotypes.

BEYOND CRITICISM

27th July 2017

Earlier this week it was announced that the Conservative government is planning to make changes to gender identity rules, allowing people to change their birth certificate so that it records them as the sex of their choice, or even just assign themselves a biologically impossible X in place of boy or girl, all without consulting a doctor. Currently it's necessary to have a diagnosis of gender dysphoria, and to have been in transition for at least two years, in order to record a change of sex. Under the new rules these requirements would be thrown out, redefining gender assignment as a non-medical personal choice.

This is sure to go down well with Conservative voters, who vote for the Conservatives because they believe in conservatism and want to conserve things. Things, perhaps, like science, women's safety, and not pretending there are more than two genders because Miley Cyrus once declared herself pansexual.

But what are you going to do, start a petition? As it goes, a woman named Caroline Campbell did just that, on the 38 Degrees website, but within a day it was removed. Here are the website's reasons for taking it down:

"Dear Caroline, I'm afraid your petition is inappropriate for this website. The 38 Degrees team have reviewed the petition and whilst we absolutely understand the need to create safe spaces for all genders, we believe that this petition plays a lot on fear and discriminates against trans women and therefore breaks our terms and conditions. Obviously we all hope that the government gives full consideration to any new laws brought in, but we believe this petition attempts to play off the rights of one vulnerable minority group against the rights of another group. As such we are not happy to host this petition. 38 Degrees is independent of all political parties, and upholds values of freedom, democracy, peace, human rights, community, equality, fairness and sustainability. We reserve the right to remove any campaigns or comments that do not share these principles. We reserve the right to remove any petition which we judge to promote illegal acts, hatred, violence, discrimination or stereotypes based on race, gender, ethnicity, sexuality, disability, nationality or religion."

Is Campbell an LGBT-discriminating hate monger? It certainly doesn't look like it, if the entirely fair and relevant rationale she gave for the petition are anything to go by:

"Allowing anyone to self identify as a woman and abolishing the need for a gender recognition certificate, has dangerous implications for the safety of women and girls. It means that anyone who says they identify as female will be able to access women's shelters, hospital wards, toilets, changing rooms and will be able to compete against women in sport, occupy positions designated for women on boards, and take scholarships intended for women."

Campbell later put up a new petition at change.org, where it is, at the time of writing, still accessible. But what does it say that 38 Degrees refused to carry it? It seems that anything prefixed with 'trans' or brightened up with a rainbow flag is beyond criticism. Because criticism has been recast as discrimination, labelled transphobic, and put in a box marked *hate speech*. It's an authoritarian tactic which prevents open debate, policed by jobsworths who don't know better, or who are afraid of being labelled as *something*-phobic themselves. You'll see the same dynamic at play around discussions of Islam, where charges of hatefulness are levelled without restraint at even the most respected thinkers.

And what about the science behind transgender ideas, are the principles the movement wishes to enforce evidence backed? It doesn't look like it. Humans are a sexually dimorphic species. Around 1% are born intersex, meaning they have an objectively recognisable combination of male and female physical characteristics. And an estimated 0.3% of the US population are transsexual. These are people who might undergo medical procedures to transition to the opposite sex, although genetics and reproductive abilities can never be altered.

The modern transgender movement's reasoning is different, in that it isn't concerned with medical or biological definitions, asserts that gender is merely a social construct, and proposes an ever increasing list of fantastically named gender categories. The assertion is that what they call *gender identity*—what you say you are—is distinct from and unrelated to biological sex, and that your gender identity trumps all else. At the same time, they've pushed the concept that gender is fluid, unfixed, and can fluctuate. You might be completely without gender, or perhaps you're prone to switch unexpectedly, taking your pronouns with you. They insist that there are a multitude of genders, although there's no agreement on how many. New York City has opted to legally recognise 31 different gender identities, which seems an entirely arbitrary number. How did they reach that consensus? Will they add more? What the hell does any of it mean?

We have YouTube activists like Riley J Dennis—who has constructed her very own science-free alternative universe—telling people it's discriminatory if a straight man doesn't want to have sex with a female-identifying man (which means, physically, a man). Biological imperatives don't matter to Riley, since although the female-identifying man might appear a bit blokish, they say they're a woman, so they are a woman, so they have a woman's cock and balls. Incredibly, Dennis has no qualms about deploying accusations of transphobia to coerce straight people into having gay sex.

This dystopian corridor, in which turning down sex is a thought crime, is several million miles away from the original intent of the gay rights movement, which was about legal equality, liberation, and sexual freedom. That we should all be able to form whatever kinds of relations we like, with whomever we consensually choose, and that nobody should have the authority to interfere with that. It's a noble, liberal cause which has greatly changed society for the better. But elements of the T now seem to have co-opted the LGB in order to bring about something altogether different.

Activists like Dennis might seem like cranks on the fringes, but the government's proposed changes operate in complete agreement with their ideas. Deep rabbit holes of postmodern thinking, characterised by mind-wrenching absurdity, are being mainstreamed. Just think about some of the logical extrapolations of the government's proposals.

Male athletes will be able to compete in women's sports. This is actually already happening in some places. A biological male won a women's cycling contest in Arizona. Teenage girls in Alaska were beaten in competition by a male sprinter. Weightlifting has seen a similar story unfold. What reason is there to think that as objective gender categories are dissolved and unverifiable self-identifications become law, this won't spread to all women's sports, at every level? We'd then have nothing but male competition, while female athletes would be forced out of their own contests. It might not happen, but it absolutely could, and the logic of the changes proposed encourages it.

Or let's imagine a man with criminal intentions, but who doesn't like the idea of spending time behind bars if he gets caught. Given the choice, a women's prison might seem like an easier option. Simple then, before embarking on any criminal endeavour, just fill in the necessary paperwork, choose to be female, or perhaps an enigmatic X, and should our progressively-minded con happen to get sent down, it will be to a women's nick.

And who else might benefit? How about sex offenders? Women's changing rooms, toilets, showers at the gym, saunas, all are immediately accessible to the man who has become—through the power of a single, unchecked announcement and nothing more—a woman. But of course, still, there's nothing for women to worry about here. As Riley J Dennis and her allies will explain, those aren't just any hairy bollocks, they're a woman's hairy bollocks.

Or is it all bollocks? Is it the uniquely puerile, irrational bollocks that only postmodernism can gestate and discharge, sparkling with glitter and rainbows, into a culture browbeaten into submission by a lifetime of progressive dogma?

You'll probable notice something about the scenarios given above. While illustrating the precariousness of the entire transgender edifice they also show that on a practical level, dishonest men stand to benefit the most from the government's proposals, and would do so at the expense of women. If these changes go through, then it's women who get thrown under the bus, holding on to their fellow sacrifices, reason and reality.

ON THE BUS WITH AN SJW AND A NEO-NAZI

17th August 2017

I was on the bus the other day, and to my surprise a conservatively attired neo-Nazi and a blue-haired social justice warrior got on and sat together in front of me. I was waiting for the sparks to fly, but incredibly, they got on like a house on fire. The conversation was fascinating, so I sneaked out my notebook and started discreetly scribbling down their chat.

Social Justice Warrior: You know what, I really believe that black and minority ethnic people should be given their own safe spaces, free from white oppression.

Neo-Nazi: I couldn't agree more, the races should be separated.

SJW: Did you hear that at the University of Michigan, they're so progressive, student activists demanded segregated areas for students of colour?

NN: This is exactly as it should be—the races are distinct and should stay that way. We must all strive to keep our unique practices intact. Honestly, it sickens me to see whites shamelessly adopting the customs of other cultures.

SJW: Me too. I got so angry the other day when I saw a white man wearing his hair in dreadlocks. It's cultural appropriation, and you know what? I'm not ashamed to say that I punched him. He was erasing marginalized histories, which is a form of violence, so my actions were justified.

NN: Quite right, blue-haired one, violence is, in fact, very often the most appropriate course of action. It is a means to an end, no?

SJW: It is, and I'm coming round to your short back and sides. The fact of the matter is, we're battling from within an oppressive and immoral social structure in order to free ourselves into a better way of life—sometimes physical force is the only option.

NN: Yes, you're correct. The degenerates who grasp on to power now will be made to submit. Our doctrine is correct, but demands loyalty. Listen, learn, and adhere to the message.

SJW: You're really speaking my language now. But you know what gets me, is the way that my community is misrepresented by dishonest journalists.

NN: For sure. It's the libertarian types who are the worst, with their self-serving so-called freedoms.

SJW: They always talk about freedom of speech, but that's just part of their system. We're working hard to shut down anyone who challenges our lived experiences.

NN: Oh yes?

SJW: Yes, basically, we intimidate and publicly shame them, defame their reputation, try to get their funding cut, just throw anything at them. They don't deserve a platform. They're harmful.

NN: Any violence..?

SJW: Sure, sometimes. And if that all fails, then we'll appeal to a higher authority—administrators, their employers, the police—anyone who can crack down on them.

NN: They must respect authority.

SJW: They must obey!

NN: All must obey!

SJW: And by controlling the media, the message, the *language...*

NN: Then we control thought.

SJW: Mwa haha!

NN: Ha ha haa!

SJW: I despise those hate speech peddlers in the media...

NN: The vile Lugenpresse...

SJW: Our philosophy, basically, is that we value safety and inclusion above all else.

NN: Again, you are correct. Security is of paramount importance, and we march together as one. There is no room for selfish urges.

SJW: The needs of the collective take precedence over individual freedoms.

NN: I'm also deeply troubled by the many degenerate works of art in existence.

SJW: Oh, I agree. Actually I'm campaigning at the moment to have several problematic statues and historical portraits destroyed. They simply shouldn't be allowed to threaten our well-being.

NN: Destroyed? That's a coincidence, we just burned a huge pile of books last weekend. They were very subversive, you know. Quite unacceptable.

SJW: I understand completely. It's essential to ensure that no counter-revolutionary art or literature threatens our glorious purpose.

NN: Purity is everything. When you're on the correct path, it's vital not to let immorality corrode the movement.

SJW: Exactly, like, why bother debating people if you know they're wrong?

NN: Precisely. There is nothing to win or lose by participating in such distractions. Simply stop the debate from taking place.

SJW: Shut it down.

NN: SHUT THEM ALL DOWN.

The bus slowed and pulled over.

SJW: Well, this is my stop.

NN: Me too... Are you going on the march?

SJW: Counter march.

NN: Of course.

IN THE DARK HEART OF REMAIN BRITAIN

24ᵗʰ August 2017

A pragmatic decision was made by the people of the United Kingdom last year, to jump the listing European Union tanker and make a bid for freedom. Following the referendum, relieved and optimistic voters around Britain have been looking forward to a future which is both global and sovereign.

There have manifested though, pockets of the country in which the door has been slammed shut, the curtains drawn, and upon which a fog of impenetrable gloom has descended. In these bunkers of despondency, inhabitants see no future, for themselves, their families, or their country, and spend their days weeping over postcards of Tuscany, slurping Merlot from the bottle, and desperately hammering out Facebook missives on the perils of isolationism.

This is Remain Britain, and it's a bleak landscape. I decided to take a trip around the maudlin, Brussels-fetishizing enclaves, and speak to the people who can't move on. The 4.8%.

My first stop was Cambridge, where I met Rupert, a diversity training and green sustainability officer. He was in the corner of a quiet pub poring over a copy of the New European, and sniffing at a thin glass of gluten-free craft IPA. I asked him what he foresaw for the country.

"I'm very well educated. I know things. All this will be gone soon, like tears in rain."

I pushed him for details.

"As an open-minded Liberal Democrat of no political bias, I've assessed that it was lies, all lies, and they didn't know what they were voting for, except for the lies, which they liked very much."

I tried to elicit more.

"It was the message... on the bus. They implicitly trust buses and anything written on them. Why didn't we get a bus too?"

Cutting the conversation short, I made my excuses and moved on. The next interviewee was Jemima, an artisan patissier. I asked her why she thought the majority had opted for Leave.

"They didn't." She replied, "it wasn't 52%, it was far fewer. About half a percent or something, taking into account the whole population."

Was she including babies and children in this reckoning?
"God yes, obviously, my children live and breathe the EU."

And everyone else's?

"Yes, mine do. Mine. Me. And besides, most of the people who voted Leave are dead now anyway, from old age or stupidity or something. But I'm not dead am I? Me, here, me, am I? Am I dead? Am I?"

I started to speak, but was cut off.

"Me. Mine. I. Me."

Jemima started twitching, and I realised she wasn't looking at me. Her eyes were glassy and unfocused, drawn to some indeterminate point behind my head.

"Me, me, me…"

Her whole body was stiff and jerking convulsively, and I noticed her fists were clenched by her sides. Her fingernails, which were painted in the blue and yellow of the EU flag, were digging sharply into her palms. She was rocking slightly, brow furrowed, and her voice had become rasping.

"Meeeeee…" she grated mechanically, still staring dead ahead, as I slowly edged around her and backed out of the shop.

Feeling unsettled, I drove on to my next stop, an appointment with a renowned professor at the university. Sinking into a well worn armchair in his office, I asked him how the country could move forward together, and if the schisms could be healed.

"We will fight this, we will resist, I will not be cowed."

But with Article 50 having been triggered and negotiations entered into, I queried whether it wasn't time to be more conciliatory.

"It hasn't been triggered! I mean, it has, but it means nothing, we're not leaving. And even if we leave, we won't leave. It means nothing whether they *say* we're in the EU or not, I will never accept that we're not in the EU. We're in the EU."

I was a little taken aback, but explained that it was now inevitable that we were leaving.

"We're in the EU. We're not leaving."

I wanted to change the line of conversation, but hesitated upon noticing a tremor shiver through the professor's frame, which had become noticeably rigid. I took a breath and opened my mouth to shape another question.

"We're not leaving," he repeated before I could ask anything. His words were ejected staccato, accompanied by a shuddering bodily spasm. His left shoulder started to jerk back and forth, and he droned, again, "We're. In. The EeeeYu."

I shifted my body to the side of my chair, keeping my gaze fixed on him, but his eyes continued to stare straight forward at the space I had vacated.

"Brussels. Strasbourg. Juncker. Brandy. Brussels. Strasbourg. Juncker. Brandy."

He was shaking constantly now, shoulders jerking, bushy grey-topped head trembling violently. His voice was completely monotone, but increasing steadily in volume.

"WE'RE NOT LEAVING. WE'RE NOT LEAVING..."

Dropping my cup of tea I made a dash for the door, slamming it shut behind me and moving at speed down the corridor, the professor's looped proclamation fading as I stumbled down a staircase and out into the bright afternoon sunlight.

As I jumped into my car and sped away, a swelling urge to get out of Cambridge overwhelmed me completely. Not until I was well past the city's edges and heading south did the tension subside. I took a deep breath and let the nervousness fully dissolve, leaving me with a listless sense of drained puzzlement.

I was calm but it wasn't to last, as with each mile of road consumed a sense of imposing dread grew within me.

There was no escaping the fact that I was going to Brighton.

CHANNEL 4 CHAN

31ˢᵗ August 2017

Having fought for years for gay and lesbian rights, having stood up in defiance of the religious right for the liberty to ridicule the church, having rejected thin-skinned theological calls for special treatment, having championed individual liberties and freedom of thought and expression, the progressive left has now decided to give all that up and convert to Islam. Allahu Akbar.

Channel 4 News operates an openly pro-left, painfully right-on bias at all times, confirmed when their senior Brussels obsessive Jon Snow was caught chanting "*f**k the Tories*" at Glastonbury.

But being a progressive champion now also means supporting radical Islam, so Channel 4 put out a video hosted by Assed Baig—known previously for expressing all manner of unpleasant bigotry—the purpose of which was to promote "Muslim women fighting back by rejecting stereotypes".

Except that one of them, Nadia Chan, literally introduced herself as an Islamist. In fact, not just an Islamist, but an 'anti-colonialist Islamist'. This is quite a feat when you consider that core to Islamism is a belief in *khilafa*: the establishment of Islamic states, leading to a global, pan-Islamic new caliphate. Which sounds more than a little *colonialist*. Also central to Islamism (or to put it another way, aggressively expansionist, overtly political Islam) are sharia and jihad.

A look at Chan's Twitter history revealed that she wasn't just putting it on for the cameras, but is a full-time racist and a dangerous extremist. For a taste of her insanity, have a look at these highlights from her account:

"Listen honkie, your kind are murderous and genocidal maniacs. All whites are the police"

"Muslims clean themselves 5 times a day, unlike u dirty white cave parasites, muslims gave ya'll soap remember"

"the parasitic entity known as Israel MUST cease to exist. Furthermore, every single Israeli is a parasite"

Regarding Katie Hopkins entering hospital: *"May God put her to sleep, permanently"*

She quoted Robert Mugabe: *"The only white man you can trust is a dead white man"*

She's championed Palestinian use of *"everyday items to resist, whether it's knives, cars, just everyday items to strike the fear in hearts of their oppressors"*

Bizarrely, she even supported the North Korean nuclear weapons programme, and called mixed martial arts champion Conor McGregor an *"arrogant, white Irish parasite"* who *"needs to be silenced and his career finished"*.

So, thanks for clearing up those stereotypes then, Channel 4. There are close to 3 million Muslims in Britain, and you found a violence-promoting, radicalized lunatic, and interviewed her in a windowless boxing gym. I'm sure everyone's really at ease with Islam now.

Then along came the story of a 5-year-old girl from a Christian family being put into the care of two different conservative Muslim foster households in the space of six months, by the authorities in Tower Hamlets.

Reports stated that one of her carers wore a burka, and another the full face veil. That the girl's crucifix necklace was confiscated. That she was told *"European women are stupid and alcoholic"*, and that *"Christmas and Easter are stupid"*.

The girl herself was described by a social worker as being "very distressed", and is reported to have sobbed and begged not to be returned to her foster carers, saying "they don't speak English".

In response to this, ideological tribalist Rupert Myers, a lawyer shackled to the doctrine of progressivism, and as a result damned to be buried in whatever illiberal intellectual pit his political bedfellows might excavate, tweeted the following:

"Seems to me you could only have a problem with a Muslim family raising a Christian child if you had a problem with mainstream Islam."

So to be clear, in his claim that the foster carers represent 'mainstream Islam', Rupert's defence involves the thoughtless drenching of all moderate (mainstream) Muslims with the regressive characteristics of, in fact, an ultra-conservative form of Islam. He creates a false association between moderate Muslims, and the extremism represented by the burka, insults directed at European women, and contempt for Christian customs. He's also tying moderates up, whether they like it or not, with a terrible decision which made a young girl desperately unhappy.

Way to go, Rupert. You're the valorous spokesman that 'mainstream Islam' has been waiting for.

When anti-Muslim bigots put the boot in, one of the things they do is create a false impression that the worst excesses of the most brutally hardline Islamic denominations are representative of all Muslims. Evidently, this is something which Rupert is also unwittingly adept at. His application for BNP membership is in the post.

This parallel between liberal progressives and racists—a shared tendency to treat minorities as homogeneous identity blocks—also manifests in the callous disregard progressives show toward the individuals harmed by their counter-intuitive posturing.

Rupert and his allies are oblivious to the blindingly obvious, which requires no analysis or intellectual wrangling for anyone who has a greater range of emotional understanding than Data from Star Trek: a child is being traumatised.

It's mind-blowing sometimes how the progressive sect will make claims of moral superiority, and of being fundamentally more caring than their opponents, yet are at the same time perfectly willing to throw under the bus, for example, a vulnerable child. Are they doing this simply to avoid questioning the awful cultural relativism they self-defeatingly hold to be axiomatic? Is it for some utopian greater good, which lies just around the corner? Are they somehow not even aware of the discrepancy?

And it wouldn't be the first time that children have been sacrificed at the altar of illogical leftism. How can I put this...

Rotherham.

Grooming gangs have been allowed to operate, around Britain, because of a fear of speaking out, facing the facts, and investigating thoroughly, because to do so would contravene the scriptures hallowed by the church of political correctness.

And still it goes on. Sarah Champion was this month pressured to resign from the Labour shadow cabinet for telling the truth about grooming gangs, and Amina Lone was deselected by the Labour council in Manchester, allegedly for speaking out on the same topic. On the left, this stifling of realistic debate shows no sign of abating.

Finally, just to reinforce their commitment to misplaced outrage, and the protection of Islam above all other religions, some progressives decided to condemn a post-Barcelona illustration on the cover of French satirical magazine Charlie Hebdo, which depicted dead bodies run over by a van, and the words, "Islam, religion of eternal peace".

Mass murder in the streets? Whatever. Part and parcel.

Forthright cartoon by a magazine which actually had 12 staff slaughtered in their Paris offices by slavering jihadists just two years ago?

Sorry, we can't allow that.

Notes

Channel 4 has subsequently pulled the controversial segment from its website, without explanation or apology. Assed Baig no longer works for Channel 4, having intended to leave since before the broadcast went out.

The girl who was with the Muslim foster family has now been placed in her grandmother's care. Judge Khatun Sapnara, herself a Muslim, ruled that the child's needs "in terms of ethnicity, culture and religion" would be best met in this way.

PREGRESSIVES

14th September 2017

Social justice progressives are like a sack of rocks tied round your waist when you're trying to run a marathon. It's not that they're bad people, they're just so far behind what's really going on. They're sitting at the back of the class, wiping gunk from their eyes and babbling nonsensically, while the rest of the school sighs heavily and waits for them to calm down and catch up.

The biggest hindrance to progress we have right now is progressives.

Look at the whole sad debacle around Antifa, Communism, punching Nazis, and all the rest of it. The first thing to say is that this is a wholly infantile topic. That the level of debate should have been reduced to Nazis vs Communists is miserable, but there you have it. Progressives drag us all down.

The social justice line goes something like this:

Nazis are really bad. It's our civic duty to do everything in our capability to stop Nazis—just like the Allied forces in World War 2, or Indiana Jones in Indiana Jones—and all other moral considerations can be set aside for this purpose. Suspected Nazis can be assaulted at will. Can they be put in a coma, or murdered? That hasn't been clarified. Related to this, the totalitarian thugs known as Antifa are actually heroic, and should be supported unquestioningly in their battle against fascists, even though they behave like fascists.

But Antifa are the good fascists, because their name means anti-fascist, reminiscent of how the Democratic People's Republic of Korea is a bastion of fair governance.

Antifa is the black clad, masked up, sucker punching, ten-on-one, car burning, window smashing, free speech hating, flag immolating, veteran abusing, piss throwing, brain dead, shit head, Guardian eulogised, progressive terrorist militia wing. But if you point out they're an anti-democratic mob that beats people in the street then you're also fair game for attack: verbal, digital, who knows, maybe even some Mace in your eyes and a pole to the skull.

Progressives though, in their state of worked up excitement, frantically blathering on about the far right, don't quite understanding something of considerable importance: *we all know Nazis are bad.*

Everyone on the entire majestic planet is utterly cognizant of that fact. Even Nazis know Nazis are bad.

So activists, Antifa, those at the back carving hammers and sickles into the desk, you really, genuinely don't need to keep going on about the Third Reich.

And this is where it becomes so apparent how far behind the curve progressives are. The credible threats our society faces don't actually come from fascists at all. This isn't to say we should be complacent about the far-right. Rather, it's to be aware that we're inherently defensive against such a threat—it's part of our societal DNA. Essentially, we're set up to see off fascism without a second thought, and everyone—left, right, and centre—is culturally configured to despise Nazism, completely and without caveat.

By contrast, we are not at all prepared for the new threats which are of the most pressing danger to our way of life. That means Islamism, and the postmodernism-soaked, Sharia-sympathetic, regressive and neo-Marxist militant left. We've not been wired to hear alarm bells when a mutant strain of theocratic authoritarianism begins to solidify on the left. But many people can identify it nonetheless. Counter-intuitively, it falls to the conservative right to conserve the very liberties that the progressive left once fought for, while suffering a barrage of abuse from that very same formerly progressive left.

Meanwhile, those who call themselves progressive, but who are now nothing of the sort, are so slow and ambling that they can't recognise where the contemporary threat comes from at all, or that in fact—through their own misplaced activism and obstructive tactics—they may even have become a part of it.

Staggering, dragging knuckles, they weaponize their own ignorance and use it as a rhetorical club, battering their opponents about the head in a state of triple insulated vacuity. They are twitchily fearful of free expression, and strangle attempts to criticize the liberal agenda, particularly if the subject of debate relates to Islam, which they fetishize perversely. They operate enveloped in the deluded belief that in a black and white fantasy world of their own creation they're playing the good guys. The politically obedient, utopia hatching, wrongthink purging *anti*-fascists.

Intolerable, incessant, they lecture us interminably on things we *already know* ("really, you don't like *Nazis*? What a principled stance"), they obstruct *en masse* the means of both preservation and progress, and they inflame the culture wars.

Except, increasingly, this culture war doesn't resemble a war at all. It seems more like a library full of normal people reading up and making plans, into which bursts a gnashing swarm of absurd, histrionic goons, intent on setting fire to all the books.

DOWN WITH
FREE SPEECH

20th September 2017

The cry from the left is unmistakable now: free speech is dangerous, and to support it marks you out as a suspicious individual. Naturally, you wouldn't want to be added to any hit lists of people who favour free expression, so best just to grab a pitchfork and hope the mob doesn't intuit your thought crimes.

A particular favourite of vapid hipster conformists is to implicitly support the de facto reinstatement of blasphemy laws. You have to be very careful with this one though. Stick up for the wrong religion and you'll be thrown to the wolves. Crucially, to be part of this odd crowd, you must be fearfully respectful only of Izlam and the Prophet MacHamed, while showing utter contempt for the stupid bloody Christians and their church fetes.

The choice way to broadcast your subscription to the fashionably authoritarian new-left mindset is to wait for the next jihadi terror attack to occur, and then express no criticism whatsoever of the terrorists. Do not connect jihadi terror attacks with Izlam. In fact, if possible you should avoid mentioning the terror attack at all, and instead declare an all-consuming, visceral loathing toward former stockbroker Nigel Farage, who now represents the 'far right'.

Please note that the calling cards of the contemporary English far right are the enjoyment of fishing trips, being photographed holding pints of beer, and wearing blazers. What absolute future-stealing b'stards.

If you're concerned that you might be dangerously far-right yourself, then answer this question: Do you think Nigel Farage should be sentenced to thirty years hard labour for wrongthink? If your answer is no, then I'm sorry to say that you're a fashisht.

Back to the blasphemy though. As a good progressive, should you become aware of right wing infidels disrespecting the Holy Kerran'g, violating sharia, or expressing the slightest concern about any aspect of Izlam—even trivial non-issues like throwing gay people off tall buildings—then you must immediately call them out as bigots and racists. Everyone who breaks your rules is either a bigot or a racist, and letting them know about it will signal unequivocally that you are a devout liberal believer, while causing intellectual disorientation in the target of your politically halal verbal stoning.

On the subject of stonings, taking ideological transgressors and executing them to death is unfortunately not currently allowed in the UK, because of all the ignorant kafir in charge of shit. But don't worry, useful-until-such-time-as-they-shall-be-disposed-of social pressure group Hope Not Hate are campaigning to revise the bureaucracy around beheadings, public lashings, and all that Allahu Akbar stuff, so just hold on for a while.

If you're torn on the idea of punishing unbelievers, then don't worry, you needn't be. It's difficult to keep up, but the latest progressive updates iterate clearly that Western democratic freedoms are fashisht, and that in the interests of diversity and togetherness a Happy-Salafi approach to community organisation will be strived toward. Anyone opposed to the Saudi way of doing business is a Kipper and a wrong'un, and will be lashed in the public square when the Worker's Caliphate gets properly set up.

Until then though, just stick with name calling, defamation, and rapidly deleted online death threats. If you call someone a bigot and they appear indifferent, then you can beef up the calibre of your rhetorical weaponry by prefixing the b-word with 'right-wing', 'Tory', or similar.

As in, "you don't want to burn copies of the Sun and punch people? You bus influenced, Daily Mail reading, monocle wearing, literally alt-right, despicable Nazi bigot."

The message we need to get out there is simple and irresistible: Join our progressive movement! For inclusivity, state censorship, and a global caliphate.

THE RUSSELL SQUARE REFORMATION

22nd September 2017

Forgive my transgression but I am about to commit a terrible sin and speak badly of Maajid Nawaz. His counter extremism organisation Quilliam, based in Russell Square, is a difficult group to figure out. On the one hand Nawaz speaks a lot of sense. He draws attention to grooming gangs, has advised Muslim women against wearing the veil, called out left-wing violence, and talks directly about terrorism and radicalisation. But then...

There was the dishonest Guardian hit piece on Tommy Robinson authored by a Quilliam staff member. And there are inane, regressive-left statements from Quilliam's executive director, Adam Deen.

"If the Prophet came back today, first people he would condemn would be #ISIS & terrorists. Then the #Islamists, then the Puritans then others."

There are deeper, less immediately tangible problems too. Nawaz is one of the only vocal critics of Islam that a certain type of Guardian subscribing left-liberal will listen to. Tommy Robinson sends such people into convulsions. They're unlikely to accept Anne Marie Waters, or anyone else connected with Ukip. Non-left-wing street demonstrations cause them to faint.

But Maajid Nawaz, they can stomach. If you see everything through the lens of identity politics, and are saturated in progressive media hysteria about far-right extremism, then Nawaz's minority status and left leaning politics make him a safe bet. Basically, he ticks the right boxes if you're a brainwashed metropolitan leftist. Which is not to talk down his credentials, it's to say that brainwashed metropolitan leftists don't think in terms of credentials, they think in terms of identity.

This scenario, in which so-called liberals entrust Quilliam with the task of confronting Islam, seems increasingly reckless. The sense I get is that in Quilliam's constant counter warnings about far-right extremism, coupled with explicit animosity toward Tommy Robinson, they're intentionally manipulating public perceptions.

Sure, they seem to be implying, you could support Anne Marie Waters. You could engage with Robinson's message. You can look into what the Football Lads Alliance are doing and attend a demonstration. But mightn't that all be a bit *right-wing..?* Wouldn't it be much safer to let those respectably left-of-centre, Guardian-approved chaps at Quilliam sort it all out instead?

I mean, haven't you heard? After 1400 years of totalitarian carnage, it turns out all it takes to reform Islam is a nicely located office full of smartly dressed London liberals.

And there lies another key point. The core message pushed out by Quilliam is that of reform. But is reform likely, or even possible? Have you seen anything to indicate—after a solid decade of Quilliam working full-time on it—that this reform is coming?

A sign that reform is possible would be that after ten years of working on it, the situation had improved. Well let's see. This year in Britain, there have been four Islamic terror attacks, killing 36, and injuring 377, along with the Finsbury Park Mosque attack, which killed one and injured ten. It's unprecedented. The situation has become not better, but considerably worse.

And besides which, who agreed that the elusive Islamic reformation—with its raped English girls, and its murdered English children, and its ripped up English buses—should take place in Britain? How much longer do we keep pretending there will be a breakthrough? Another decade? A hundred years? One more millennium and a half?

On his LBC radio show last Saturday, Nawaz explained to a caller from Manchester that stoning people to death isn't a good idea, and the clip was then widely shared on social media by his approving fans.

But wait a minute. We're cheering because a former extremist explained to a dark ages zealot that *stoning people to death is bad?* Is this what it's come to, in Britain, in the twenty-first century? And I'm supposed to… what exactly? Applaud? Put away the stones? Rejoice that the reformation is proceeding, one retard at a time?

Tellingly, he also managed to drag in an underhand comparison to Tommy Robinson and Donald Trump while condemning the caller's beliefs. He said that what the caller advocates is worse than what either Robinson or Trump believe in, but this is no compliment. It's a subtle means of undermining his opponents' reputations by surreptitiously placing them on a spectrum of extremism with homicidal religious fanatics. Regardless of whether you support or oppose them, neither Robinson nor Trump deserve to be mentioned in the same breath as people who believe in stoning adulterers to death.

In the end, a man on the radio pointing out to fanatics that their beliefs are sickening doesn't strike me as a glorious achievement, it seems more like a hideous regression. Hearing people openly air such grotesque ideas simply underlines what a dreadful situation the country has allowed to develop.

Let's not get tricked into thinking that any of this is normal. It's tragic that such thinking is present in modern Britain, and it's only because of the endless tolerance and civility of the British people that there hasn't been a great backlash against Islam.

Such restraint is admirable, but we must also be careful not to send out the message that religious idiocy will be tolerated in the long term. Britain is not Islamic, and Islam is not relevant to any aspect of our society. We owe precisely nothing to this foreign faith, and have no obligation to tolerate it for a second longer, should we choose not to. The rules should be clear: foreign religions can operate, but only as long as they make not a single imposition into non-believer's lives, integrate with British values, and never break the law.

But Islam, of course, is not following these rules.

And it's concerning that a constant barrage of culturally relativistic pro-Islam hectoring from the Guardian, the Independent, and other left-wing media is conditioning the younger generation to believe that it's normal to have pockets of barbaric thinking—such as that expressed by Nawaz's *LBC* caller —in our midst.

Or to think we must have sympathy and patience with violent theocratic fascists. Or that everything will be fine if we just let Maajid Nawaz get to work at Quilliam. And that we can't really hope to understand the problem anyway, because if you haven't studied the ridiculous Islamic texts you care nothing about, then you've no place in the discussion. The discussion about *your own secular country*, and the safety and liberties of everyone you know.

Britain has had its reformations already. It's a country which has battled for and won gay rights, women's rights, racial equality, and freedom from the tyranny of organised religion. Are we really going to do it all over again, with *another* religion? And all the while divert our attention—with candles and sing-alongs—from mutilated bodies, and bombs on trains, and throats slit open by the River Thames?

We don't know whether or not Islam can be reformed, it looks close to impossible in an acceptable time frame. And considering the stakes, it's barely worth considering as a realistic solution.

AGENDAS &
APOLOGIA

25th September 2017

It's not a backlash against Islam that Britain needs to fear, it's the opposite. That the country is too restrained, too tolerant, and too fundamentally decent, still, to react to its changed circumstances. But decency means knowing when to defend yourself and your values. Decency means knowing the difference between when to remain passive, and when to stand up to a bully.

After the Manchester Arena Islamic terror attack, the story was moved along with bewildering efficiency, from carnage to tribute concert in the space of just two weeks, despite another jihadi attack occurring on London Bridge between the two. And then we were all moved on, by people who'd rather not dwell on the difference between a country in which there's very little Islam, and a country with slightly more.
Maybe the difference between our liberal denialists and those who can't ignore reality, no matter how relentlessly we're encouraged to do so, is in what makes us each feel better. Directionless sentimentality and textureless platitudes work

for some people, affording a quick cure to get them past the horror and the dissonance. But if all you want to do is make yourself feel better and move on, then you're fundamentally selfish. You've got your fix, but what about the *next* set of victims? Do your thoughts not turn to ways of ensuring that there are no more victims? And if not, why not, doesn't that seem heartless?

Attacks from the left on anyone who demands more robust action on all aspects of Islamic incursion into secular democracy are frustrating, and obstruct progress. As a matter of course, those who address the facts honestly will be accused of pushing a callous, perhaps racist agenda.

But don't these accusations actually describe well the mindset of the oblivious tealight adherents?

If you're content to carry on as normal (which is actually the far from normal *new normal*), knowing that more people will suffer, simply because such a course of action is established, uncontroversial, and means you don't have to rethink your politics, what are you if not callous?

And isn't it that peculiar brand of bigotry so common on the modern left—the soft bigotry of low expectations—which leads to Muslims being treated as particularly vulnerable and prone to making bad decisions? From which leftists cry foul when Islam is placed under increased scrutiny, when of course —in light of the constant terror threat across Europe—Islamic institutions absolutely *should* be under increased scrutiny.

As for pushing an agenda, yes, that's true. Here's the agenda: stop people from dying and being abused. Protect children. Safeguard liberal values. Stand up to misogynistic, homophobic, religious ultra-conservatives, who at their fringes utilize extreme violence and cause suffering around the world.

And do the aloof progressives offering up our safety and freedoms in sacrifice to a uniquely PC brand of religious tyranny not have their own agenda? One that involves open borders, and a servile devotion to multiculturalism at all costs? Or are they so immersed in their agenda that they can't see there's even an agenda to be immersed in?

The modern progressive-left is incapable of discussing national identity, as it provokes in them some weird, conditioned sensation of otherness and revulsion. They don't care about history other than as a stick with which to beat the West. They appear to hold Britain in contempt, and they'll make a self-conscious performance of how little they care about the liberties they've inherited.

They're fashionable and disinterested. And also censorious, intolerant, and morally disorientated. They've been knocked out of whack by years of indoctrination and spin. Deconstructed and reconstituted, they sip sloppy coffee with purpose, and tetchily instruct the world to do nothing. They'll posture cynicism while embodying conformity, and tell you haughtily to stop making a fuss. This is just the way it is now, they'll inform you.

But it isn't. It's just the way *they* are now.

And if you try to engage, and counter their fatalism with some concrete suggestions—about Islam, terrorism, immigration —well, that will get you nowhere. You'll be boxed off as a populist, or a reactionary, or an alt-right crypto-fascist, using the threat of a theocratic darkness they deny the existence of, in order to bring about a variety of fascist darkness which actually presents zero credible threat in modern Britain. Their reasoning is perfectly circular, and excludes any possibility of non-leftism.

Nonsensical, negative and self absorbed, the progressive-left in its current state should be out of the political fight, but in a state of submission to Islam and political correctness, it's somehow hanging on. That mightn't be so bad, but in an unknowing slave condition it's working as the apologia-and-normalization bureau for Islamic extremism, and threatening to drag the rest of us down with it.

Around an enemy which would kill us—which *is* killing us—is a sentient protective wall, and it reads the Guardian.

THE LABOUR PARTY CAR CRASH 2017

28th September 2017

The Labour Party Conference 2017, taking place in Brighton, has been a horror show from start to finish. Here's how chilling, off-the-rails, and utterly devoid of self-awareness the Corbyn freak-out has become.

It's reported that at a fringe meeting called Free Speech on Israel, there were calls for two Jewish organisations, the Jewish Labour Movement, and Labour Friends of Israel, to be removed from the party.

One attendee is said to have told the room that Israelis should be treated the same as Nazis, while Israel itself was referred to by some speakers not by its name, but as 'the Zionist state'.

In an interview with the BBC, amber encased leftist film maker Ken Loach claimed that in all his time attending Labour and trade union events he had never heard a single anti-semitic remark. Then, in the very same interview, he was told about reports of holocaust denial at the Free Speech on Israel meeting, and was asked if he would condemn such behaviour, to which he replied the following:

"I think history is for us all to discuss."

The interviewer asked him to repeat himself. And he did.

Later, in an interview with Channel 4's Jon Snow, Jeremy Corbyn continued the theme of being shifty on the topics of brutality and state oppression. Pushed on the issue of Venezuela, he became strangely tetchy, and failed to offer direct, unequivocal condemnation of dictatorial leader Nicolas Maduro, whose government was recently accused by the UN Human Rights Council of "crushing democratic institutions and critical voices", amid calls for an investigation into possible crimes against humanity.

There's a game that interviewers can play with the Labour leader. Pick any violent left-winger and ask Corbyn to condemn them and their atrocities. And here's what he will do: not condemn them. That's because Jeremy Corbyn is ideologically aligned with a stomach churning list of dictators and dystopias.

Meanwhile, at a nearby Momentum event named, in the Utopian manner beloved of cults, The World Transformed, shadow chancellor John McDonnell speculated on the imagined consequences of a Labour victory at the next election. And it didn't sound pleasant.

"What if there is a run on the pound? What happens if there is this concept of capital flight? I don't think there will be but you never know so we've got to scenario-plan for that."

He spoke of "war game-type scenario-planning" and "detailed implementation manuals". He has a planning team headed by a character named Richard Barbrook, who runs an obscure political gaming site called Class Wargame. It's seems at least partly tongue-in-cheek, but nonetheless, here's a line from their manifesto to get a flavour of their character, about what the game does:

"Class wargame... trains the militants of the cybernetic communist revolution to come"

Agitated crank Paul Mason spoke alongside McDonnell, and also envisioned the beginnings of National Corbynism:

"We need everybody mobilised, in crisis mode... We might have to retreat the equivalent of 2,000km and, like in Stalingrad, be in a siege for six months. You might see the government make compromises and retreats. That's how you get victory. It's not very easy. But when you get it, my goodness, we will change the world."

These people are real, they reference Stalingrad, and their sixth form schemes run as far as changing the entire world.

Which brings us to famous racist Diane Abbott, who made it known that she favours segregationist policies. Her suggestion is that in constituencies with high levels of black and minority voters,

"We need to revisit the campaign for all-black shortlists"

Or to put it another way, she wants to create areas in which white people are prohibited from becoming Labour politicians, resulting in a nation carved up along racial lines. How very progressive.

A warning though, be careful about asking hard questions of Corbyn's Labour. At this year's conference, BBC political editor Laura Kuenssberg had to be accompanied by bodyguards, as a response to the threats and abuse she receives from Labour supporters. Yes, that's an actual security detail, at a Labour Party conference, to protect a journalist from the attendees.

Underlining the extremity of what has taken place at the conference, Warren Morgan, Brighton and Hove's Labour council leader, threatened to ban the Labour Party from holding future conferences in Brighton. In a letter to the Labour Party general secretary, he wrote,

"As the Labour leader of Brighton and Hove City Council, I will undoubtedly face questions as to why we allow any event where anti-Semitic views are freely expressed to happen in the city, particularly on council premises.

As a Labour Party member, I expect the inquiry announced today to take firm action; as leader I will need reassurances that there will be no repeat of the behaviour and actions we have seen this week before any further bookings from the party are taken."

He added,

"We are a city of sanctuary and I have to speak up against any form of racism as and when it is given a platform in the city."

This is not the BNP. It's not the EDL or Britain First, or any of the other far right fringe organisations we're continually informed to be on our guard against. This is the Labour Party, in 2017.

GENERATION Z CONSERVATISM

9th October 2017

Younger voters want change, and there's nothing wrong with that. Pushing on and looking to the future is how we get men on the moon, and carry smartphones that can change our photos so we look like cats. And what's wrong with shaking things up and pissing off stick-in-the-muds anyway? It's one of the pleasures of Brexit.

But in Britain, Corbynism has latched on to and taken advantage of that longing for change, like a scruffy leech. It's performed a con trick on those who want something to get excited about, and if the Conservative Party is to capture any young voters at all, it needs to counter the deceit being sold by Jeremy Corbyn's Labour.

The reality is that to adopt the socialism offered by Corbyn *would* be a change. That much is true. But it would be a substitution of political mechanism from one which embraces flexibility, to one which demands control. It's a radical alteration in course, but it would take us straight down a dead end street.

Corbynism has been painted as rebellious and anti-establishment, but underneath the endorsement from Stormzy and the party leader's appearance at Glastonbury (not that Glastonbury is pushing any boundaries) it's nothing of the sort. If the current Labour leadership's schemes were ushered in, they'd lead to constraint and conformity. And the *new* establishment would be authoritarian to a degree that its youthful supporters had not felt before.

There wouldn't be much of a celebratory mood in the air then, as it slowly became clear that all that rebelliousness was nothing more than a carefully-managed means to an end.

Conservatives should be highlighting all this, and at the same time pushing the message that a free market model provides the best possible mechanism by which for changes to occur organically. Crucially, that model is how we safeguard the *capacity* to change, but it isn't a change in itself.

If the Conservative Party were to realign around its libertarian element, then it might achieve resonance among younger voters, particularly those who come after the Millennial Red Army. Generation Z are shaping up to be open to a conservative message, and will surely react against the postmodern nonsense bought into by Millennials. Conservatives must be ready to meet them.

And the message should be simple: that the right-wing will safeguard classical liberal values and ditch victimhood-fetishizing identity politics. And it ought also to be made clear that socialism represents the polar opposite of all this: it's a half-fossilized ideology that would usher in micro-management, politically correct hectoring, and state imposition.

Conservatives needn't pay regard to the social justice diktats which have taken over left-liberal discourse and muffled people's rational capabilities. Simply by speaking directly and honestly, the politically correct narrative can be disrupted. And if that ruffles some left-wing feathers then all the better, let's refuse to apologise and then offend them some more. The *'facts don't care about your feelings'* trope may be a little clichéd in the arena of online culture wars, but it's as true as it ever was, and it hasn't been unleashed on the mainstream recently, so let the Tories be the ones to utilize it. I say *recently*, because in fact, the essence of that message is nothing new.

"*The facts of life are conservative.*"

So said Margaret Thatcher, and the Tories should cleave to her truism. There's no need to take on board anything offered up by the postmodern left, because they're no longer in touch with reality. Our only duty is to the facts of life.

Capitalists have history and statistics on their side. Graphs and charts like these need to be pushed out and brought to people's attention.

[Here were two charts, from Human Progress and the Cato Institute, illustrating the case for free trade and economic freedom.]

The Conservative Party ought to be rejecting SJW new-leftism unequivocally. Why not just state it clearly? If you value the sovereignty of the individual, if you want the freedom to say what you like, create what you want, and make of yourself what you will, then steer well clear of collectivist movements.

A serious party would throw out badly defined hate crime regulations, reject the CPS's garbage about policing what people say online, and get a grip on the police force so they stop tweeting photos of their trans-friendly, rainbow coloured cars.

There's a gap in the market right now as common sense, libertarian ideals go under-represented, and there's a Conservative Party that needs revitalising.

To win favour, and connect once more with voters, the Tories must get back to the facts of life.

PUNCHES, PRONOUNS & POWER

18th October 2017

The world of transgender activism is disorientating. Stare into it for too long, and it won't just stare back, it'll call you a TERF and punch you in the face. In the warped hinterlands of post-logic social justice, the ground slips easily from beneath your feet. There's no reason or consistency, and no truth to which you can anchor.

Draped over the entrance by way of demarcation or invitation are rainbow flags, but step inside and it's all kicking off. There are threats and slurs. And violence. Be aware that if you have the propensity to question what you're told, then you aren't simply curious or contrary, you're a bigot.

And the flags weren't really inviting at all, they were a declaration of identity political diplomatic immunity. Transgender activism has positioned itself as being categorically not up for debate. Contradict any of it at all and you'll be labelled transphobic. As stroppy alt-left propagandist Owen Jones put it,

"That's why transphobic attitudes must urgently be combated - not just on the hard right, but among self-described "centrists" and "liberals""

So that's pretty much everyone except Owen then.

But what is it that you are being compelled to accept? As I've written about previously, the plan is that gender becomes entirely self-determined, and we're all free to alter our birth certificates so that no official trace of our biological realities can be found. We will have rapists in women's prisons, and men shoving aside women in sporting competition. And all this is accompanied by an unquestionable mantra: *transwomen are real women*. But if those words are true, then what are we to call women who aren't transwomen? Do we need to make up a new word, because if not then how can we accurately describe these People Formerly Known As Women?

And can we then have sporting competitions, changing rooms, and prisons which are only open to People-Formerly-Known-As-Women, or would Transwomen-Are-Real-Women demand access to them too?

Here's another development that the modern transgender movement has brought about. Lesbians are harassed and called transphobic if they state that they're not attracted to men. Actually, that's not entirely accurate, let's be more precise. Lesbians are no longer allowed to state that they're not attracted to men, if the man has declared that he is, in fact, a woman. This is because, don't forget, transwomen are women, so to exclude them from sexual attention would be to doubt their self-declared womanhood.

Now, I don't deny that the man in question may well believe himself to be a woman, and really, I don't care. Everyone is free to live and present themselves however they choose. Change your name and wear a dress, a three piece suit, a kimono with wellington boots, it makes no odds to me. But are we seriously to accept that the evolved biological preferences of an entire species can be overridden by a social justice diktat?

There's a cock under that dress, and here's the thing: lesbians, by definition, *don't like cock.*

A matter of fact statement. But one which will lead to accusations of bigotry, prejudice, or some such horribly coercive nonsense. And the result is that, as in homophobic times gone by, lesbian and gay people are forced to watch what they say about their own sexual preferences, for fear of the reaction it might provoke. Not the reaction from the religious right, though, as used to be the case, but the reaction from the new transgender movement.

Here's another story. A man punches a woman in the face. The fact that it's a man punching a woman is important when describing that occurrence, right? If you were reading about it in a newspaper, you'd expect the reporter to put the words 'man' and 'woman', so you'd know what happened.

Now let's imagine the man has stated that he's actually a woman. Biologically, remember, it's the same person, nothing's changed. He still pulls back his male-length arm, and with his male muscles wrapped around his male bone density propels a man-sized fist into the side of a woman's face.

The only difference now is that he has made the subjective claim that he is a woman. Unlike the selectively caring postmodern left, let's *not* focus solely on our trans-bruiser and his feelings, but on clarity of expression, and the safety and understanding of everybody, and in particular the woman who's just been violently assaulted.

What do you want our onlooking reporter to do now? Do you want them to change the words to *woman hits woman*, so that

—in the absence of visual evidence—anyone who reads the story will take away the belief that a biological woman hit a biological woman?

If I wanted a faithful observation of what had actually happened, I would certainly like the reporter to write *man hits woman*. Because that's what happened. And yet there were influential voices arguing, when such an event actually occurred, that the violent man should be described as a woman.

[Linked here were tweets from American journalist Jesse Singal expressing his view that a transwoman—a biological man— shouldn't be 'misgendered'—referred to as a man—in an article describing said transwoman's assault on a woman.]

Let's just imagine that your only duty is to truthfully document the event, simply for your own records. And assume that it's absolutely vital you record the details accurately. If you wrote *woman hits woman*, and came back to it years later, when your memory of the event had faded, would that tell you what had really happened that day? If the answer is no, then *woman hits woman* is incorrect.

It might be dreadfully un-PC and liberal progressives of the modern variety won't like it at all, but I care more about accurately describing the real world than following arbitrary new speech codes which obscure the truth. And I care even less about the overwrought emotions of punch-happy political thugs, whatever their preferred pronouns.

DEAR SCUM

Dear Lowly Scum,

Here in the universities we've been distressed of late, as it seems some among you *think* (and we use that word loosely, it's more as if dull shapes wooze into existence at the bottom of your lizard brains) that there is some kind of left-wing, pro-EU bias in our institutions of study.

It pains us to have to explain this—not least because you're unlikely to have the intellectual capacity to process it—but *of course* we're all left-wing and pro-EU, for a very simple reason: those are clever people's opinions, and we're exceedingly clever.

We're not biased, we're correct.

Look, put down the pasties, leave the scratchcards alone, and think about it for a moment if you can. Intelligent people are left-wing, because left-wing people are intelligent.

Consider Brexit. What kind of deranged extremist would want to live in a completely independent, sovereign democracy? Who on earth would want their country to have full control of its own borders and laws, like almost every other country in the world? What halfwit would balk at the idea of a shared continental army? Who are these tin-foil loons pointing out that the EU is heading toward some dysfunctional approximation of federal integration, that it's demonstrably less democratic that its member states, and that its core values appear to be disingenuity, arrogance, and self-concern?

Who the hell cares about culture, heritage, and tradition? You want proof that the EU is a beacon of wonder, well here it is: *we like it*.

Then there's the mass immigration and multi-culturalism that you're always complaining about.

The chief of MI5 stated recently that the terror threat we face in the UK is the worst he's ever known and escalating rapidly. Well, so what? And why are you always going on about grooming gangs with–*yawn*–over 1400 child victims in Rotherham alone? Why bother highlighting that Britain has never had a single successful prosecution for FGM, despite there being over 5000 cases in England last year?

What terribly unsophisticated concerns you have. Facing up to reality is so... *right-wing*.

We must focus instead on saying things like *inclusivity*, *diversity*, and *the European project*. These are very progressive words, and make us feel comfortable.

And don't forget that we know best.

As Professor Francesca Stavrakopoulou put it:

> *"BREAKING: The Mail is appalled that 75% of those trained in independent thinking, analytical argument, and intellectual rigour voted Remain"*

And she's right. Who can withstand the powerful logic of our magnificent, continent-sized brains?

> *"In July 1932 Hitler won 37% of the vote, took power, and abolished democracy...sound familiar?"* AC Grayling

> *"Was Brexit your pathetic protest vote? Tempted to say you deserve what's coming to you. Alas you aren't the only one who'll pay the price."* Richard Dawkins

We'd also like to point out that by sending us one letter addressing a problem which definitely exists, you are engaging in a campaign of authoritarian state harassment.

Already, Britain's finest legal minds have been imprisoned and executed. How much longer do academics and left-wing comedians have left?

> *"First they came for the judges but I did not speak out, for I was not a judge.*
> *Then they came for the lecturers..."* David Schneider

But we stay strong. We'll never give up our academic freedoms. We'll give refuge to light entertainers and their disintegrating, tear-stained, left-liberal axioms. It's vital that we all keep repeating ourselves, day after day, month after month, until everyone feels a bit sick and even Graham Linehan calls it a day.

Nobody can stop us upholding progressive values, and if we must brainwash students, create an oppressive atmosphere opposed to dissenting opinion, and, all going well, undermine democracy and crush the fairly expressed will of 17.4 million people, then so be it. Liberalism doesn't come easy.

We hope your simpleton intellects can process the message here. We on the left are committed to ensuring that the voices of working class people are never heard, and that their political wishes are subverted and ignored. We pledge to sneer at and ridicule the people we desperately need to vote for the same political party as us. We promise that as long as we are the voice of the left, all who question our ideas will be out-grouped and disparaged, until they never trouble us again. Then you'll know how clever we are, as we scratch our heads and wonder how we lost another election*.

But maybe that's all too much for you to take in, so here's a summary:

You are scum and we hate you.

Sincerely,

Academia

(*It's the Daily Mail's fault.)

TORY BRITAIN, THE POSTMODERN VERSION

20ᵗʰ November 2017

Tory Britain, you have to love it. It's kind of a feckless experiment, like grenades-and-rape Sweden, or Justin Trudeau's identity-free-post-national Canada. Or is it more like France, where they're fashionably laissez-faire about external borders, but are constructing bulletproof walls around the Eiffel Tower? Or Germany, where mass sex attacks in the street are covered up, but a journalist gets a suspended sentence for publishing a historical photograph.

Conservatives conserve, or so you might think, but not in the case of Theresa May's party, which has decided to change everything instead. And not in a popular way. Or a logical way. Or in anything other than a change for change's sake way. Or a change to appease the left and its frothing SJWs. A capitulatory, cowardly, what-the-holy-f**k-are-they-doing-now kind of change.

Perhaps this is down to the reduced influence of Ukip since Britain chose to leave the EU, and Nigel Farage stepped down as the party's leader. Whatever your views on the Kipper contingent, there's no doubt that their presence on the right kept the Conservatives on their toes, whipping them into something resembling a right-wing party. Ukip were a reminder that it wasn't just the EU that was unpopular, it was also the soft liberal consensus and the erosion of libertarian values, in favour of Blairish nudges and social justice suffocation. And Ukip came up with policies, which could then be nicked by the Tories.

But with the popular, populist right-wing Kippers a mere shadow of their former selves, barely even worthy of harassment from leftist goons Hope Not Hate, the Conservatives have buckled and drifted, and are now cornering the market in not-quite-right-wing unpopulism.

So we have the distinct likelihood that *Equalities Minister* Justine Greening's proposed changes to the Gender Recognition Act will go through. That means that we can all choose our own gender, change our birth certificates, and not even have to bother consulting a doctor to confirm that we actually have gender dysphoria. In fact, you don't even need to have a gender at all. You can designate yourself a letter X instead. This, of course, is impossible. I mean, it's literally not possible (with the rare exception of those born intersex) to be neither male or female. It's not possible to switch overnight from one to the other, and then have that magical alteration ripple back in time causing the document that was filled in when you were born to become retrospectively inaccurate. But hey, who cares? It's what the kids on Tumblr are going nuts for, and the Tories now take cues from the mentally unstable SJWs who otherkin the desks at Teen Vogue.

And yes, if being addressed by the 'wrong' pronoun is enough to send someone into a fit of vengeful despair, then evidently they're mentally unstable, slightly undermining the argument that being confused about gender isn't a psychological condition.

At a secondary school in Oxfordshire though, maths teacher Joshua Sutcliffe is reportedly accused of the heinous crime of 'misgendering', having been suspended for addressing a girl who identifies as a boy as a girl, in addition to calling her by her name, rather than by her preferred male pronouns. So that's it then. This is the future the Tories have selected—you are compelled to change your language according to the subjective whims of your interlocutor, with no regard for staying true to the reality in front of you. Get it wrong (meaning right), and you can start clearing your desk.

Why would anyone want to go into teaching in this climate? Why put up with the stress and the bullshit of being pushed around by teenagers who need a framework of guidance and authority, but are instead told that everything they think and feel during the maelstrom of adolescence is unquestionably true, and that the whole world—schools, teachers and all—must melt and distort to adhere to their every fancy.

Who's in charge here? Oh yes, the Conservative Party (Postmodern Upgrade).

At least we can trust the Tories on matters of public safety and national security though, right? They'll know how to deal with the savage, psychopathic scum who left Britain to fight for ISIS—a world incorporating torture, rape, and genocide, in which they could inflict unthinkable horrors on men, women, and children, all in the name of a barbaric theocracy. The Tories won't show them any quarter, that's for cert... oh no, wait.

The government is considering giving them council houses.

They're not talking about killing the jihadis, or locking them up forever, or even just showing them around the inside of a courthouse, they're discussing *reintegrating* them. But here's a thought that occurs: if someone thinks leaving Britain, travelling to a war zone, and joining a military death cult seems like a good idea, *they probably weren't very integrated to start with.* And even if they once were… they're ISIS fighters now.

Reminder: the Tories, 2017 version, are in charge. Tough on biological determinism. Obligingly relaxed about genocide-complicit enemy combatants and their tendency to massacre infidels.

But you know, it's not all bad. Shifty theocratic nuthouse Iran might hang gays, but it has the world's second highest rate of sex change operations, the idea being that while homosexuality is *haram*, transitioning gets the doctrinal thumbs up. All going well, united in oppression and an acceptance of gender exploration, our pronoun-sensitive trans hardliners and the wayward Islamist butchers might just get along like a house on fire in Qaraqosh.

PROGRESSIVE LEFT INSTRUCTIONS FOR ALL YOU THICKOS

22nd November 2017

Hello, we are the progressive left, and as you're all a bit thick and racist, we've come up with a list of instructions for how you must change your behaviour. It's not your fault that you're thick, and you're racist mainly because you keep looking at the Daily Mail, which doesn't kneel before the majesty of Islam and endorse the dissolution of nation states as we do, but nonetheless, your ghastly knuckle-dragging ways must be corrected.

So do the following.

> 1. You must repeat this incantation, at least five times a day: TRANSWOMEN ARE WOMEN. If that's too difficult for you, then here's the Daily Expressified version, which might suit you better: WOMEN HAVE DICKS. Have you got that? Repeat it. Believe it. It's true and it's what we all think.

Everybody chant along now:

womenhavedickswomenhavedickswomenhavedicks.

2. ISIS fighters are a lovely bunch! They're just naive, didn't know what they were doing. What genocide? Was there some genocide? Anyway, they're all coming home now, and they'll be ever so hot and sandy, so let's be extranice to them and make sure they get settled back into their old routine of plotting to murder everyone. And come on, let's face it, us kafir deserve it really, with our oppressive freedoms and lack of modesty.

Welcome home ISIS jihadis!

3. Stop reading the wrong newspapers. You must not look at the Daily Mail, The Express, The Sun, or anything else like that. Don't listen to Katie Hopkins. Get off Twitter. Stop sharing Paul Joseph Watson videos. JUST BLOODY STOP IT.

Sorry, it's just... look... it's really important that you don't listen to anybody except us. The world is, it's... we're in charge, ok? Just nod if you understand.

Ok.

It's probably best if you stay inside with the curtains closed, and we'll drop you off a copy of Bella and some Kestrel. If there's an election we'll tell you who to choose, but you have to get it right next time, don't fuck it up like you did Brexit.

Hopefully soon we can get it sorted so you're not allowed to vote anyway. That would be best, just let us deal with things. Relax. Deep breaths. Women have dicks.

IN DEFENCE OF MANNING UP

23rd November 2017

Last Sunday was International Men's Day, an event which has objectives including, in the organisers' words, "a focus on men's and boy's health, improving gender relations, promoting gender equality, and highlighting positive male role models."

When you consider that 76% of suicides in the UK are male, the worth of such an occasion becomes clear.

And of course, it generates social media discourse. Here's a tweet that caught my eye, from YouTuber and at least partially reformed SJW, Laci Green:

"sending love today & always to guys who are told to "toughen up", to "deal with it", to "be a man" when they are in a dark place. we expect men to be fearless and to hide their pain. it's not a coincidence that men commit suicide 3.5x more than women."

Laci comes across as genuine and considerate, but her opinion—entirely well-intentioned though it no doubt is—didn't sit entirely comfortably with me.

It put me in mind of comments made by author Matt Haig. Matt tweets a lot, and I disagree with pretty much everything he espouses when he's talking politics, but let's leave his celeb-leftism aside. He also talks about his own struggles with mental health, and has strong opinions about how we should approach such issues, and that's fair enough. Here's an idea of where he's coming from:

"Never man up."

"Every dickhead who tells a depressed man to 'man up', or that a depressed woman is just being 'emotional', must be challenged."

"Men are three times more likely to kill themselves.
More likely to hide a mental health problem.
To be addicts.
To die young.
To be violent.
To be victims of violence.
To commit crime.
To end up homeless.
Or in prison.

Toxic masculine values poison inwards as well as outwards."

Like Laci, he's dismissive of the notion that men going through hard times should be tough and deal with problems stoically. As he puts it succinctly, and somewhat provocatively (I've been provoked at least), "never man up".

Let me be clear, I'm not dismissing this approach. I think it has its uses.

Sometimes.

Sometimes it's good to let it all out. Sometimes it's good to talk. Sometimes it's good to be emotional and honest.

But let me stress that word again: sometimes. And for some

people.

Because here's another thing. There's integrity in *not* revealing every thought, internal twitch, and emotional shift. There's honesty and contentment in knowing that some things need only be known by you and you alone. And there's a profound sense of empowerment to be found in, yes, dealing with it. Because when you've done that just once, you know that the personal capability exists to do it again.

And the funny thing is, that if you know you have the capability to deal with emotional distress, then you're less likely to feel emotional distress. I can think of few more valuable characteristics to instill than resilience.

But again, I don't mean to write off what Matt has to say on these issues. What works for him is what works for him, and will no doubt be effective for others too.

Where I would have stronger criticism though, is toward his line that "toxic masculine values poison inwards as well as outwards". In fact, I think this idea that masculine values are linked with toxicity is a very damaging one. Some people are more masculine, others are more feminine, and both are fine. Isn't the liberal ideal supposed to be that we let people be who they are, and express themselves as they wish?

And is it really helpful to call people *dickheads* because they tell people to man up? After all, we say man up for a reason. Manning up is shorthand, meaning to draw on all your inner resources, stand tall, and refuse to be beaten by circumstance. Doesn't that sound good? In moments of difficulty, wouldn't that be a great well from which to be able to draw?

It's seems to me that pushing this *toxic masculinity* idea on to boys and young men–saying, essentially, that their inherent nature is malign–is somewhat callous. And it's also untrue. What have traditionally been portrayed as masculine characteristics–bravery, independence, competitiveness–are clearly of great social value (and of course, are in absolutely no way limited to men, and nor do all men display them).

The other thing I'd stress is the necessity to treat anyone who needs support as an individual. It's stating the obvious, but while some people need a shoulder to cry on, others need a kick up the arse. And probably, a lot of people need both, delivered at timely moments. A shoulder offered in sympathy, but never sentimentality. A foot to the backside which registers, but is not cruel.

Compassion is good, but only when it's measured and rationed, and can be readily substituted for a strong word and a push in the right direction.

Here are the thoughts of Sir Alex Ferguson, an extraordinary leader who coached men and boys at Manchester United for 26 years, making it the most successful club in England. A man renowned for his acute ability to foster discipline, grit, and cohesion, and who could overclock players to the absolute peak of their capabilities.

> *"No one likes to be criticised. Few people get better with criticism; most respond to encouragement instead. So I tried to give encouragement when*
> *I could. For a player—for any human being—there is nothing better than hearing "Well done." Those are the two best words ever invented. You don't need to use superlatives.*
> *At the same time, in the dressing room, you need to point out mistakes when players don't meet expectations. That is when reprimands are important.*
> *I would do it right after the game. I wouldn't wait until Monday. I'd do it, and it was finished. I was on to the next match. There is no point in criticising a player forever."*

That might seem a little off topic, but I think his philosophy is applicable to many situations.

Encouragement, in straightforward terms. Criticism, where appropriate. And an ability to wrap up and package what has been worked through, and then look forward. It's incredibly constructive, and the sense I get from Ferguson's words is of momentum, balance, and focusing on the road ahead.

Here's one more quote from Sir Alex. Perhaps it seems even more off topic, but it communicates something relevant–that if you press out imperfections, you might also remove something valuable.

> *"One of my players has been sent off several times. He will do something if he gets the chance – even in training. Can I take it out of him? No. Would I want to take it out of him? No. If you take the aggression out of him, he is not himself. So you have to accept that there is a certain flaw that is counterbalanced by all the great things he can do."*

THE HATES AND
THE HATE LOTS

3ʳᵈ December 2017

Hate.

Are you a hater?

Perhaps a hate preacher of some variety?

I'm veritably overflowing with hatred. Perhaps, to some limited extent, I even strive to *spread hate.* I think I may be in the act of preparing to disseminate hatred right now, by typing these words in the hope that they'll be read, thereby furthering the corruptive agenda to which I have malevolently subscribed.

When I say *hate* though, I'm of course referring to the word's new definition. What it indicates now is *a different opinion.* And when I say *different*, that means taking the left-liberal cultural consensus to be the norm against which all other ways of thinking must be categorised.

And when I say *liberal*, I mean illiberal, intolerant, and censorious.

But when the left-illiberals hear *censorious* they understand it as *protective*, and so they're opposed to free speech.

Because free speech might lead to hate speech.

From hate preachers.

For haters who…

Hate.

And anyway, the chain of reasoning goes, who would want free expression, except people who want to express something deplorable? Why could we possibly need the freedom to say anything we like? If an opinion has been proscribed by the PC-left, then it's with good reason. It's because it's damaging. It might be far-right, lead to violence, and threaten the marginalised, who must be wrapped in cotton wool and treated like pets. The left requires those classed as marginalised to *stay* classed as marginalised, because if they (the marginalised) just get on with life—as they can—then they'll be lost as a form of identity political currency.

The illiberal-left needs its bargaining chips, which is why it lashes out so viciously at minorities who step out of line and refuse to align with nominally progressive parties.

At the same time as free speech is redefined as hateful, the police and the CPS push the concept of hate crimes. And it should be pretty clear where that leads. Free speech and non-progressive opinions are hateful, and hate might just be a police matter, so you'd better be careful. And perhaps you might start to doubt yourself a bit. It seemed like a reasonable opinion that I held, but is it really..?

They keep saying that men are women, and that any deviation from that line is unacceptable. I know it can't be true, but…

what's two plus two anyway? How many fingers are they holding up? How many lights are there?

And so hate, increasingly, just means anything the authoritarian-left disagrees with. And simultaneously, the idea that hatred is a criminal matter is drip, drip, dripped insidiously into the public consciousness.

Let's take the example of women's changing rooms being opened up to men, in the name of transgender rights. If you object to that, and take the (until very recently) uncontroversial view that changing rooms should be sex segregated, then you can be labelled transphobic. Transphobes are hateful, and somewhere in the background the CPS disseminates the notion that hatred is within their remit.

Now, I'm not suggesting plod will be kicking your door in because you said, "that's just a bloke in a dress." But we do have people thinking twice before expressing their true opinions. And it legitimises and emboldens the true bigots—leftist PC zealots—who will yell at and harangue anyone who doesn't toe the ever more intrusive line.

And don't forget we're talking about the stigmatising of completely normal statements. Things like:

A man doesn't become a woman just because he says he's a woman.
Mass immigration has downsides.

The more Islam we have, the greater the security threat becomes.

Are any of those things untrue? Are they even particularly right-wing? I see no reason why any of them couldn't sit comfortably in what used to be considered a fact-based, left-of-centre outlook.

It's an absurd, purge-happy world that the modern left is creating. And recently, I think the best way to negate their shaming tactics is to embrace the labels with pride.

If they redefine dissent as hatred, then let's take hatred as a badge of honour.

If you think women don't have balls and men can't get pregnant then they'll call you a transphobe or a TERF. Well, ok then. Transphobe and TERF mean scientific.

What about xenophobic? As far as I can see, that now just means you favour living in an independent country which controls its own laws and has normal border controls.

Islamophobic? Means critical and secular.

The negative side to this is that a very small number of actual bigots will find it easier to avoid being identified as such, but that's entirely the doing of the authoritarian left. They've taken important words and wrung out any last drop of their original meaning, and now we'll all have to live with the consequences.

So here's to being transphobic, a TERF, xenophobic, far-right, Islamophobic, and hate-filled. Or to put it another way, being someone who understands free speech, lives in the real world, and values common sense.

LIST MAKERS AND
LIT MATCHES

20th December 2017

The zealots of *Stop Funding Hate* and their supporters are utterly convinced they're doing the right thing, and that should give anyone pause for thought. Carrying out bad acts in the knowledge that they're bad is worrisome enough. Carrying out bad acts because you sincerely believe yourself to be in alignment with a higher, more virtuous endgame is the first step along the path to a contagious and resilient form of autocratic thinking.

Let's be honest about how unsavoury *Stop Funding Hate's* purpose is.
They want to censor the press, although they'll deny it, claiming they're just exercising their right to protest through capitalist mechanisms. This is only a half truth though. The reality is that they're exercising their right to protest through capitalist mechanisms **in order that writing they would disapprove of will be altered to please them, or will simply not be published at all**.

As Ray Bradbury once wrote,

> "There is more than one way to burn a book. And the world is full of people running about with lit matches."

If you cut off someone's funding to stop them publishing certain material, then you are censoring them, and *Stop Funding Hate* are campaigning to do precisely that. The clue is in their name.

Here's what people who *don't* want censorship will do, when they read something they disagree with: they might ignore it and move on. If they're aware the publication they read it in always runs that kind of material, then they'll avoid that publication. Or they might take issue with the content, and write something in response, explaining what's at fault with the offending propositions. They can beat the ideas presented with better ideas of their own. Or they might use ridicule, choosing to get on social media and take the piss.

The point is that if an idea is weak, then it will be easy to take apart and go to town with. There will be no need for censorship, because its flaws can be straightforwardly revealed for all to see. So when *Stop Funding Hate* move vehemently to have a line of thinking restricted, we should immediately wonder if there's something of interest in the ideas at risk of being declared off limits.

Stop Funding Hate and their supporters are so arrogant that they believe they ought to have the ultimate authority to decide what we, what *everybody*, should be allowed to read and publish. And let's extend that a little further. If it's verboten to read and write certain things, then it must also be socially unacceptable to say those things. What, then, should we do with the thoughts that we are forbidden from expressing?

If *Stop Funding Hate* think the views expressed in the *Daily Mail, the Sun*, and the *Daily Express* are so utterly heinous that companies should grovel in humiliation for having advertised next to them, then what are their views on the *millions* of their fellow citizens who align with those newspapers' editorial positions? Is everyone who intuits a degree of sense in the robust outlook presented by conservative tabloids also to be shunned, shamed, and have their income streams disrupted? Should they be sacked? Forced to recant? Where would such dissenters from the progressive rule book fit in *Stop Funding Hate's* heavy-handed left-wing promised land?

And underpinning all of this is a simple, wholly unacceptable fact: that a small group of people is trying to put themselves in the position of filtering what we can read, having installed themselves as our moral and intellectual superiors. They believe we can't be trusted with the freedom to make up our own minds, and so they will do it for us.

Anyone who has the least shred of personal dignity should object wholeheartedly to the jobsworth list makers at *Stop Funding Hate*, and all the brainwashed drones who embarrass themselves by siding with them. We must have space to read and write whatever we like, to present and consider the widest possible range of viewpoints, and to engage without fear in the marketplace of ideas. Those who back *Stop Funding Hate* might call themselves progressive, but in fact, they aim to hinder and restrict the very mechanisms by which a society makes progress. They're charlatans and vandals, assaulting priceless freedoms they don't understand.

Just imagine a world where everyone, of all political persuasions, behaved like the tinpot tyrants at *Stop Funding Hate*, and managed to achieve their aims. There'd be no public expression of opinion. The *Daily Mail*, *The Sun* and *The Express* would be gone. An anti-SJW mob would have made sure the *Guardian* and the *Independent* were completely destroyed. *The Times* and the *Telegraph* would get it in the neck from some group or other of ideological hardliners, for being trans-critical and pro-Brexit, respectively.

You might see arguments that *Stop Funding Hate* aren't opposed to the right-wing in general, evidenced by their not targeting the above mentioned *Times* and *Telegraph*, but this is a dishonest assertion. Because they only want to control *three* conservative newspapers and zero liberal ones, rather than *five* conservative newspapers and zero liberal ones, that should put our minds at ease? Am I supposed to doff my cap and be grateful they'll allow me to view any thread of conservative thought at all?

And make no mistake, the fact that they're only going after three newspapers right now means absolutely nothing. A censor lays his boundaries arbitrarily, and will re-lay them again, and again, and again, until nothing which weakens his position is allowed to pass. There's a reason why we resist this kind of restriction of our freedoms from the very start—it's because it doesn't stand still, and it never ends.

Give them a sniff of power, and they'll be back for more.

2018, WHEN ALL OUR DREAMS COME TRUE

21ˢᵗ December 2017

Progressive types have been pissing and moaning their way through 2017, constantly on the verge of either breaking a cup or checking in to a psych ward, but good news is round the corner. A vision was revealed to me and I can let it be known that 2018 is the year when all the metro-leftist dreams come true and society is remade in their image. Here's what to look forward to.

Allahu Akbar!

Yes, God is greater. Which god? Why, Allah of course! And he's greater than all the other gods, who don't even exist anyway. 2018 is going to a big one for Islam, and for that you should be grateful, because Islam is the best religion. It's easy to know it's the best one, because it has its own legal system, takes control of entire societies, dictates the minutiae of everyday existence, and kills people who won't join in. You must admit, that's value for money. And as they say, it's the religion of peace—after all, how can there be conflict in the Caliphate when disagreement is prohibited? Get on board!

You'll know Islam has come to town when Christmas markets look like fortified military compounds, the police carry assault rifles, Jews live in fear, gay people are assaulted in the street, women must cover themselves before going out in public, and you're not allowed to say anything bad about Islam, let alone draw a cartoon without being executed in a hail of bullets.

Yes, the religion of peace is gearing up to deliver a lot more of its very own stunning new interpretation of the word *peace*.

The Female Penis

As is well known, progressives hate men, especially straight, white ones, and think there should be more women ~~doing all the traditionally male dominated jobs like cleaning sewers and collecting the bins~~ doing all the good jobs. And they've found a magnificent way to sort that out: now *anyone* can be a woman. And not just a woman, but a transwoman, meaning they tick two oppression boxes. But they're not actually trans, because **transwomen are women** and there's no difference between the two. But they're also trans people who need protection from transphobes, so they're both transwomen and actual women, but certainly not men. Although they have penises. But female penises.

Listen, it might sound confusing, but here's the bottom line: although there will be men dominating women's sports, men in women's changing rooms, men taking women's professional positions, and dangerous men in women's prisons, there are actually no men doing any of those things because— and here's the clever part—*transwomen are women!*

Oh, and if you have a boy who likes dolls or a girl who plays with toy trucks, then get them to a gender clinic immediately.

Sex stereotypes must be strictly enforced, and your child will be dosed full of puberty blockers in preparation for irreversible surgery and a lifetime of medication. No, it's not a horror movie, it's what the left now calls progress, so give it a rest with being such a cishet stick-in-the-mud, and abandon reality like the rest of us. Seriously. That's an order and we'll tell your employer if you don't.

Stop Saying Things

One of the worst aspects of fascist Brexit Britain is that people are free to say and write anything they like. This, clearly, is very oppressive, but don't worry, 2018 will emancipate you from the tyranny of free expression, and ensure that you only encounter good, wholesome left-wing material.

Stop Funding Hate is currently hard at work shaming companies for advertising in perfectly normal, popular newspapers, but that's just the start of it. Once these widely enjoyed national publications are purged, we can move on to the people who read them. Please, embrace this process. If you are being shamed, it's because you have the *wrong opinion.* This is easily rectified though. Simply join Twitter and follow Gary Lineker, JK Rowling, Lily Allen, David Baddiel, and you can take your pick between John Simpson or Jon Snow. They will issue the correct opinions. Copy them. Repeat what they say. Think as they do. When you have been properly adjusted, you will be free to express yourself correctly.

Praise Corbyn

You don't have to kneel before Jeremy. You might not dream nightly of his gentle caress. Perhaps you haven't been the victim of a national tragedy, waiting, pallid and clammy, for Jeremy to arrive, with some photographers, whereupon he will cocoon you in his arms. But now is the time to open your heart to his holy Socialist compassion. Jeremy's profound affection knows no bounds, extending even as far as the IRA, Hamas, and Hezbollah.

It extends to the many.

But not *the Few*.

And we know who you are, Few. We know you are many, Few, but we will find each and every one of you, and crush you all. We are ~~Britain First~~ Momentum, and we pledge to thuggishly harass people, act like children who've suffered a knock to the head, and wrench the national political tone down to the level of an old, broken sewer, where it will stay for the foreseeable future.

So it's out with the old and in with the trans-tastic, totally halal, book burning, dissent purging, Tory hating new. Strap in and pray to god that Bitcoin will save the world, or at least continue to facilitate the purchasing of hard drugs and firearms. Raise a glass, try not to get booted off Twitter, and if we do end up shivering through the nights together in a diversity training correctional facility, then remember, we'll always have Brexit.

PART THREE

2018:
INTRODUCTION

From the constant, highly engaged output of 2017, to 2018, when there are only five articles of a political nature. One is related to East Asia, as I felt I had insight into how people felt in Japan, where I am resident.

One was, I believe, still important, about Boris Johnson and the right to blaspheme.

Of the others, though, there is a change in tone and topic. Although I wasn't regularly putting out articles, I was still completely addicted to Twitter, commenting and arguing constantly, and I was still ideologically locked in and insanely partisan.

But, by this stage, I was thinking also about the medium itself, rather than only the content, often considering that the medium and the content are, in fact, indivisible.

One other development was that my addiction to Twitter, and the news churn, and the endless online conflict, was interrupted by increasingly more numerous moments of clarity.

Although still far from clearing, the fog was not constantly thick.

DEREGULATE
AND CREATE

1ˢᵗ February 2018

The inherent leftiness of the arts and music scene is relentlessly stifling, the creative industries having become intractably connected with so-called progressive politics. Those in the industry articulate, of course, a belief in artistic freedom, but it's a false one, as the strict confines of the like-minded collective invisibly demarcate actual artistic practice.

There's a rejection of capitalism, while working in ways which would be literally impossible if not living in a society set free by capitalism. A herd-like embrace of all things 'progressive', while never asking what is being progressed toward, and if it actually lies at the front of a treadmill of nonsense. The avoidance of positive conflict and libertarian recklessness, in favour of milk-slop coffee, walled systems, and beardy-weirdy, nonthreatening acquiescence.

There's a rejection of patriotism and the nation state, failing to understand that there are external, objectively bad nation states which don't value artistic expression at all, rather, they torture and imprison it. There's a rejection of the nation state in favour—in the case of anti-Brexit sentiment—of being subsumed into a larger, more bureaucratic, and demonstrably less democratic entity, failing to notice that the larger entity simply wishes to become a new kind of state in place of those it swallows. Failing to recognise that those who voted to leave the EU engaged in an authentic moment of anti-establishment rebellion.

There is guided, template-formatted, safely uncreative creativity, slowing down and congealing over time, and threatening nothing of consequence as it quietly thuds off soft, pre-approved targets. Blathering on about the environment, as if it were a religion, and not a technological quandary. Po-faced, school ma'am disapproval of anything laddish, infra-dig, or fun. Stewing motionless in the same on-message newspapers, the same on-message blogs, the same on-message satire, the same on-message message as everyone else in the insular, on-message community.

Currently, if anything notable or unexpected happens in the celebrity world, it's because somebody gives not two shits about left-wing dogma. I sigh and tune out when Hollywood or the Grammys fawn *oh-so-earnestly* over Hillary Clinton. By contrast, the very best moments occur because key players are blissfully unconcerned, or unaware, that the mob dogma matters or even exists, at which point the spell is broken and we can operate, for a while at least, in total freedom, emancipated from the grey, leftist glue that sticks stiffly around everyone, restricting movement and thought. There are few established artists who are capable of such liberated autonomy, but Morrissey, John Lydon, and the now sadly deceased Mark E Smith come to mind; men who would be past caring, were it not for the fact that they never cared in the first place.

Formidable rap star Jay Z has shown support for the far-left, including Black Lives Matter and the Cuban regime, but dominant swathes of rap and hip hop—including Jay Z's own work—are voraciously capital focused. The political philosophy which Jay-Z actually embodies and showcases through his own prominent success is (whether he admits it or not) boot-strapped aspirational capitalism.

He aligns himself with the far-left, while abiding by nothing whatsoever that it preaches. And that hints at a problem with the now mainstream left-wing activist mentality. It coerces artists and everyone else into voicing support, or at least not voicing opposition. This is done both explicitly and as part of an unconscious creep, by which the corridor of acceptable opinion narrows inch by inch until everyone is the same; unquestioning of the movement's tenets, as their cortices submit to intellectual rigor mortis. This process is poisonously antithetical to creative freedom. Marxism doesn't work. But as Jay-Z lives and breathes even while signalling the opposite, free markets do. Just don't say it out loud. That grey glue really is sticky.

Jay-Z's sometime collaborator Kanye West is an artist less confined by orthodox political scripture, and actually went as far as to pay a visit to then-president-elect Donald Trump in Trump Tower, a move for which, inevitably, he took heavy criticism from the left. Perhaps Kanye intuited the potential value in a Trump term of office—amateur, chaotic and, because of these things, tantalisingly loaded with variation and opportunity. Or perhaps he just doesn't care, and will do as he chooses. But surely, in a musician, either of these possibilities is preferable to mindless conformity.

There is inherent risk in a venture such as the Trump presidency, and it seems now that there is reputational risk if any prominent artist refuses to condemn it, or even—*take a deep breath*—expresses support. But when did we start expecting artists to play a conservative game? What great creative achievements have been pulled together while secured to a harness, wobbling above a safety net? What more gloriously compelling performance is there than to say fuck it, go all in, and snatch an unlikely victory, or crash and burn with panache?

And what would be the alternative to the Trump spectacle? Predictable, pedestrian, tested. Politically correct and restricted. The worst possible formula, stagnant and grey, in which for artistic expression to evolve.

It's informative to look back at the UK rave scene of the late 80s and early 90s. They've been called apolitical, but from an ideological perspective, the movers and architects of that musical era took the economic liberalism of the Thatcher years and pushed it to Ecstacy-augmented, loved-up extremes. Wild-west anti-statism aims to eschew governance completely, and the rave scene embodied that spirit. It was big-bang, free of red tape, and at liberty to expand as it pleased.

It was hedonistic, naive, idealistic, and simultaneously a hyper-maximal extension of the free-market philosophy. It unilaterally deregulated the nightlife scene, disseminated its product without industry oversight through self-assembling pirate radio stations, and made ruthless land grabs in the Essex countryside. And by doing so, it upgraded the cultural landscape first in the UK, and then–in myriad offshoot forms– around the entire planet.

Can we possibly, in the near future, catch another such wave? Can a similarly open-ended, starry-eyed, money-making, boundary-pushing, on-one creative mindset emerge from our current state of politically correct stupor? If we reject the joy-less priests of establishment leftism and their monotonous browbeatings, if we *decentralise,* then we might have a shot.

GOOD INTENTIONS

28ᵗʰ April 2018

"Robert Oppenheimer, a little while before he died, said that it's perfectly obvious the whole world is going to hell. The only possible chance that it might not is that we do not attempt to prevent it from doing so. Because you see, all the troubles going on in the world now are being supervised by people with very good intentions. There are attempts to keep things in order, to clean things up, to forbid this and prevent that, possible horrendous damage. And the more we try, you see, to put everything to rights, the more we make fantastic messes, and it gets worse, and maybe that's the way it's got to be. Maybe I shouldn't say anything at all about the folly of trying to put things to right, but simply on the principle of Blake, let the fool persist in his folly so that he will become wise."

That's from a talk by the masterly Alan Watts, a compelling philosopher and Bodhisattva. I don't know when the talk was given, but Alan died in 1973, and it's striking that what he says here seems so operative and resonant, given the decades that have passed since he articulated such ideas.

Is it better, then, not to do good? Certainly, that phrase, a *do-gooder* makes me shudder a little. No-one wants to be a do-gooder, and not a goody-two-shoes either. Where would be the fun in that?

And at an institutional level, it becomes not just tiresome and graceless, but impositional, restrictive, and ultimately dangerous. Institutions have power. The authorities have clout. When they decide that a certain behaviour is *good*, it means other ways of conducting oneself might be *bad*, which means they may not let you do them for much longer.

Or in this age of self-censorship, you may not let yourself do them.
And it might then follow that English author TH White's words become unfortunately relevant.

"Everything which is not forbidden is compulsory."

So how do we avoid such a future?

Let's turn to a contemporary figure, who has generated an astonishing level of media heat for nothing more than supporting Donald Trump, and sending short communications promoting free thought, tolerance, and diversity of opinion.

He got to the essential core of how best to proceed from here in a single word:

"decentralize"

But since we're on the topic of Yeezy, and I can't help but detect a certain mysticism in the air at the moment, let's work with this too:

"spread love. Put more love into the universe."

HOPE AND CHANGE IN SINGAPORE?

14ᵗʰ June 2018

What to make of Tuesday's meeting in Singapore between US president Donald Trump and North Korean leader Kim Jong-un?

As is to be expected when Trump does anything at all, two camps immediately spring into action. On the Trump train, his every gesture is indicative of a coming golden age, in which we'll all play golf, wear red hats, and listen to Kanye West.

And in the world according to CNN and the BBC, we lurch one more step toward Armageddon, hunkering down for the apocalypse and praying for American economic disaster, families suffering in poverty being a small price to pay for hauling DJT out of office and replacing him with *anyone-you-like-it-doesn't-matter*.

At any given moment either of these camps might hit on something and be worth paying attention to. Or they could be peddling fakery. Or they might just be shouting at each other.

I was Trump-skeptic, but never considered him to be a harbinger of the end-times, so I hope I can be objective, and in that case I'd say that while Trump ultra-fanatics are not living in the real world, the anti-Trump liberal contingent has gone completely off the deep end, and can't be trusted to report on his actions in anything resembling good faith.

And so almost everything that occurred at the historic summit can be spun two ways.

The optics were magnificent, US and North Korean Flags sharing colours and representing to the entire world the beginning of a new era of peace and cooperation.

Or alternatively, it was glitz, smoke and mirrors. A photo-op for a pair of narcissists (one a fully qualified murderous tyrant) to claim historic glory and win favour with their respective domestic audiences.

The terms of their agreement were non-specific and open-ended, allowing space for discussion that didn't previously exist. A first step toward something profound.

Or, if you were the other way inclined, the agreement was vague and insubstantial. Just part of the spectacle that looked good but solidified nothing.
Trump's praise for Kim was realpolitik in action. The necessary diplomatic buttering up required to bring a recalcitrant and unpredictable despot to the table.

Or, perhaps, it was an act of normalisation that failed to address the grotesque human rights abuses occurring right now in North Korea under Kim's regime, allowing him to present himself as a respectable leader.

Where does the reality lie? Take your pick.

What's certainly true though, is that while North Korea is fresh ground, none of the factors involved are new or unique to Trump. He's not the first American president to put on a show, or to flatter a tyrant. And he's not the first American president to strike deals.

Does he do it more ostentatiously than others? Sure.

Does he do it better? We'll have to wait and see.

Just anecdotally, I got an idea of the general feeling here in Tokyo about the summit. Japan is well used to North Korea's belligerence and violations. Across the water from the rogue state, Pyongyang's test missiles have crashed over Hokkaido and into the ocean, and citizens have been abducted from Japanese soil and held captive by the dishonest and aggressive regime.

The sense I get from residents in the Japanese capital is one of restrained skepticism. That more detail and substance were necessary from the start, because while Trump may be new to dealing with Pyongyang, its neighbours in Asia certainly aren't. And that North Korea cannot be trusted for a second, and might change direction or do something contrary to good relations without warning.

There is, in particular, disappointment that no mention was made of the Japanese abductees. This is a major issue here, and a quietly burning sense of injustice and sadness sometimes becomes perceptible when the subject is raised. Certainly, Japanese people are not going to smilingly embrace the hand-shaking, Rodman-friendly version of North Korea being presented before the cameras, when the abduction of Japanese people, snatched from their families, remains unresolved.

At the same time though, there's a pragmatic recognition that anything is better than nothing. That tensions have certainly deescalated from just a few months ago, when the national broadcaster, NHK, actually sent out an incoming missile warning, thinking it could have been real.

The common recognition is that while Trump might not be particularly liked (or particularly disliked, for that matter), nonetheless, what's happening now is a significant improvement on the situation under Barack Obama. Many Japanese are of the opinion that Obama handled North Korea badly. That he was too passive, lacked ideas or interest, and did nothing in particular, allowing the situation to worsen.

While Obama promised hope and change, Trump has positioned himself as the man to deliver it. Whether or not that's going to happen depends on who you ask.

DELETE YOUR ACCOUNT

21ˢᵗ June 2018

Twitter is toxic, delete your account.

I will, of course, be sharing this on Twitter as soon as I hit the publish button.

And there's the problem. Is it possible to be engaged with current affairs without engaging on social media?

I don't know. And let's be fair, Twitter does has some positives.
It enables ideas not represented by the mainstream media to disseminate. By the time regular journalists pluck up the courage to deal with an issue, it will already have picked up momentum and been thrashed to pieces on social media and in the blogosphere. At which point, mainstream commentators will note that there's enough support for a previously off-limits position that they can cautiously begin to advocate for it.

The clearest recent example of this is the debate in the UK around transgender activism and gender self-identification. Online, a sprawling coalition of radical feminists, conservatives, contrarians, and—to put it simply—people who deal in common sense, weathered threats and name-calling, and questioned (with logic and good intent) whether the new tenets of the trans activist movement were fit to be implemented.

Eventually, people in the mainstream media took notice, or put aside their cowardice, and started dealing with the issue, and it seems like finally the bubble will burst and trans issues can be discussed more critically.

So, Twitter helped enable that, providing a medium by which to break down politically correct stonewalling.

Twitter can affiliate people who wouldn't otherwise be able to organise, and it can provide a means by which to challenge the dominant media message, acting as an outlet and exchange for subversive and unorthodox thinking.

But, for my money, these benefits are greatly outweighed by the negatives.

During a recent conversation on The Rubin Report, neuroscientist and public intellectual Sam Harris put it like this,

> *"It's a kind of hallucination machine, where you begin to think you need to pay attention to certain voices that in the real world you would never see"*

Referring to controversial engagements he's had on Twitter, he states,

> *"The net result has always been that you're getting back to zero if you're lucky"*

And he also remarks,

> *"You become what you meditate on, you become what you*

pay attention to"

Offer it too much of your mind, and Twitter has the power to distort you, along with all the rest of its component protagonists.

In his newest book, Ten Arguments for Deleting your Social Media Accounts Right Now, philosophical computer scientist Jaron Lanier says the following of his early experiences on social media in the 1970s,

> *"I just stopped using the stuff because I didn't like who I was becoming. You know the adage that you should choose a partner on the basis of who you become when you're around the person? That's a good way to choose technologies, too."*

He goes on to explain,

> *"Some have compared social media to the tobacco industry, but I will not. The better analogy is paint that contains lead. When it became undeniable that lead was harmful, no one declared that houses should never be painted again. Instead, after pressure and legislation, lead-free paints became the new standard. Smart people simply waited to buy paint until there was a safe version on sale. Similarly, smart people should delete their accounts until non-toxic varieties are available."*

And in my opinion, not only is social media heavy with lead, it also doesn't emancipate, improve, or expand your thinking. Instead, it boxes and reshapes it, as you are forced to operate within the restrictions of its non-human, sometimes claustrophobic formats.

After all, what kind of a way to communicate are skeletal 280 character statements, stark of nuance, caveat, or context?

They volley between anonymous entities, picking up dangling tails of spite and psychic bilge as replies are attached, while good faith is stripped away and burned.

Who talks to strangers that way? Well, it turns out that anyone might if they spend enough time in the tweet dungeons. If you're smug, arrogant, dismissive, shitty and neurotic in real life you won't get far. On Twitter, you'll pick up a few thousand followers.

And remember, again: you are that on which you meditate.

But there are several versions of you now. There's the real one, and there are the ones in the machine. Those creased facsimiles: glitchy impostors approximated in grainy, fading ink.

Twitter is a version of high school so treacherous and unpleasant it should have a warning sign at the entrance. There are bullies and cliques; snobs, snitches and show offs; cowardice, conformity, and cackling mobs putting the boot into whoever's turn it is to get dragged and humiliated, perhaps for fear that the boot will be turned back on them if they don't laugh long enough.

There are no grey areas, just low resolution black and white, within which howling, infantile conflict can whip and flare forever, there being neither means nor desire to seek resolution. Twitter is an endless game with no prizes, only psychological loops that keep you trapped in its infinite descending corridors.

In reality, I confess, I haven't deleted my account. But I'm aware that what utility Twitter has is very limited, that it's an enormous waste of time, that it's addictive and bad for emotional well-being, and that it entrenches division more than it brings people together.

So if you care about yourself, delete yourself.

STRANGE REVOLUTION

11th August 2018

Have you ever thought you knew a place, looked away for a moment, and when you look back it's changed?

Have you ever had that happen for an entire country?

I hadn't–not for a whole nation–until just now, when I looked at Britain and saw the most bizarre of infernos taking hold.

It appears that Britain has been laid with tinder, and Member of Parliament Boris Johnson, with the very tiniest of sparks, has set the whole place ablaze.

As a recap, Boris (one of those rare political figures who is known by his first name alone) wrote a newspaper article defending the right of Muslim women to wear niqabs and burkas. It was not a dry legal analysis, but an opinion piece, and he included in it some jokes. His point was a liberal one, that Denmark had made a mistake in banning the wearing of face coverings in public. While defending the right to wear the burka, he made it clear that he had no affection for it, calling it "oppressive and ridiculous" and comparing the appearance of its wearers to "bank robbers" and "letter boxes".

So, one defence of the burka, two jokes, and a media/political meltdown.

Boris was, as is par for the course nowadays, labelled a racist and an Islamophobe, accused of stirring up hatred, and generally set upon by the mob.

The situation has dominated the news and social media.

And let's just reiterate: one defence of the burka, and two jokes.
A lot of people scratched their heads in bewilderment, but the maelstrom raged on, and you could have been forgiven for doubting your own sanity. The burka is, quite clearly, oppressive and ridiculous. And not only that, it represents a thoroughly illiberal and extreme faction of Islamic thought. It most definitely does not represent mainstream, moderate Islam.

In Iran, women are exhibiting the most incredible courage in order to be liberated from theocratic control, as they did forty years ago.

"100,000 Iranian women march against forced veiling in 1979, Islamist men shouted threats, several women were stabbed" Rita Panahi

But back in Britain, people are looking around and asking themselves, didn't poking fun at and criticising religious fundamentalists used to be perfectly acceptable?

Well, thankfully Twitter came to the rescue, and reminded us that yes, not five minutes ago it was completely normal, *across the political spectrum.*

> *"If Boris Johnson is guilty of anything. It's nicking gags from Stephen Fry and the Have I Got News For You team."* *@MrAlfredGarnett* [And the tweet included a video from Have I Got News For You in which some of the panellists joked about a photograph a a woman wearing a full burka.]

[@MediaGuido tweeted a quote from a 2001 Guardian article by Polly Toynbee: "Something horrible flits across the background in scenes from Afghanistan, scuttling out of sight. There it is, a brief blue or black flash, a grotesque Scream 1, 2 and 3 personified - a woman. The top-to-toe burka, with its sinister, airless little grille, is more than an instrument of persecution, it is a public tarring and feathering of female sexuality. It transforms any woman into an object of defilement too untouchably disgusting to be seen. It is a garment of lurid sexual suggestiveness: what rampant desire and desirability lurks and leers beneath its dark mysteries? In its objectifying of women, it turns them into cowering creatures demanding and expecting violence and victimisation. Forget cultural sensibilities."]

"So Warsi is attacking @BorisJohnson but made these comments. Bit bigoted to try and put your morals into other people. The hypocrisy is astounding." @ChiefEditorMG [Included a link to a 2017 article headlined "Muslims should help full face veil disappear from UK within 20 years, says Baroness Warsi"]

And just for good measure, here's the now painfully right-on and regressive Independent weighing in on the debate. Although I should mention this is them weighing in on the debate five years ago, before whatever the hell has happened, happened.

[Here was a screenshot of headline and lede:

"Let's face it – the niqab is ridiculous, and the ideology behind it weird

Why everyone is being so polite? Religious expression is not an absolute right, and should be limited if it affects the rights of others]

A few days after Boris' article, actor and comedian Rowan Atkinson decided to intervene, in the form of a short letter to The Times, which then also became a major talking point. It's notable that when Atkinson gets involved in politics, people listen, perhaps because he so rarely does comment on politics. Additionally, he's non-partisan and consistent in his defences of free speech and the right to blaspheme.

"Sir, As a lifelong beneficiary of the freedom to make jokes about religion, I do think that Boris Johnson's joke about wearers of the burka resembling letterboxes is a pretty good one. An almost perfect visual simile and a joke that, whether Mr Johnson apologises for it or not, will stay in the public conciousness for some time to come. All jokes about religion cause offence, so it's pointless apologising for them. You should only really apologise for a bad joke. On the basis, no apology is required."

We were also treated to the news that one hundred burka and niqab wearing women, along with Conservative peer Mohamed Sheikh, were demanding Boris be ~~publicly whipped~~ removed of the party whip. To which the only sane response can be: no, sorry, we don't punish blasphemy.

And there were strong statements in support of Boris from

Imam Taj Hargey, and Qanta Ahmed, writing in the Spectator.

Over on Twitter, the nominally liberal mob were furious with Rowan Atkinson for holding the same authentically liberal opinions he has always held, but he had outsmarted them by not being on Twitter. Presumably there will soon be demands that he be forced to sign up to the hellish social media platform in order to that he may be properly shouted at.

And there was a remarkable pronouncement by Guardian columnist Jonathan Freedland, who stated, with reference to "the Tories" and Ahmed's Spectator piece:

"Doubtless, they could find a handful of unrepresentative Muslims on the fringes who will tell them that Johnson actually made a rather good point."

So that's a highly privileged, non-Muslim, left-wing man ruling that the opinions of Muslim women–on a matter that directly affects Muslim women, and which is specifically concerned with female oppression, theological intolerance, and actual patriarchy (not the third wave/Laurie Penny kind of patriarchy)–are to be disregarded without consideration, because they happen not to align with *his* political leanings.

[And here a tweet from Amina Lone in reponse to Freedland: *"This is beyond offensive and supports the notion that #Muslims practice a monoculture. It's also normalising ultra regressive Islamic practices. The new Muslim orientalism."*]

There was also a peculiar, second phase contortion to the Boris bashing, which attempted to condemn him for blasphemy while maintaining for oneself the right to blaspheme.

"Cards on the table. I make the most horrendous jokes with my friends. Because every single one of them knows where I stand on

those issues and wouldn't be encouraged to be racist, sexist etc because of my joke. I don't put those jokes in national newspapers! Boris Johnson isn't known for his progressive views and inclusive narrative. Publishing his comments in the Telegraph just gives licence to other people who don't care about social inclusion to hurl abuse, rather than actually discuss the topic with respect." Femi Oluwole

In other words, we're Good People, and therefore when we make jokes, they are simply that: jokes. But Boris is a Bad Person–a Conservative, a Brexiteer, a schemer– so when he makes jokes, well, that's a different matter.

Besides the childish double standards, damning someone for the intentions behind a joke (as ascribed by the accuser, with zero evidence) is, in the end, exactly the same as just damning them for the joke itself. The only difference along the way is that you reveal yourself as being comfortable with finding people guilty of thought crimes.

And speaking of crime, if all this wasn't dizzying enough, there was the following statement from Met Police Commissioner Cressida Dick,
"I spoke last night to my very experienced officers who deal with hate crime and, although we have not yet received any allegation of such a crime, I can tell you that my preliminary view having spoken to them is that what Mr Johnson said would not reach the bar for a criminal offence."

That this should even require saying, and that there was an exchange between senior police officers to discuss the matter, should set off alarms about what kind of a state the UK is becoming.

Britain, what happened?
Are people, particularly those on the left, really prepared to

trash freedom of speech and conscience, in order to make short-term party political gains?

Is it acceptable that hate crime regulations are steering the country toward outlawing blasphemy by a different name?

And how did this strange revolution occur so quickly? Because make no mistake that it's real: behaviours, speech, and thoughts that were perfectly normal just moments ago are now being categorized as some variety of moral crime, and perhaps even as a police matter.

There has been talk of sending Boris Johnson for diversity training, which makes me wonder, does such training program people not to say the burka is oppressive and ridiculous, or not to think the burka is oppressive and ridiculous, and which would be worse?

[And a tweet from Sonam Mahajan, containing a video of Iranian women dancing in the streets: "*After publicly tearing off their hijabs, Iranian women are now on the roads, dancing like there is no tomorrow. This is illegal as per the Islamic laws, prevalent in Iran but who cares! Retweet if you love their moves.*"]

PART FOUR

2019:
INTRODUCTION

By this stage, I'm still banging the drum, but infrequently. Still wasting hours on Twitter, although now likely to become exasperated not with other people, but with myself for getting sucked in, despite the pointlessness of it. And I'm often deleting everything I've tweeted, hoping not to tweet any more.

The two articles here that best represent the direction in which I was moving are *Hallucinations* and *Rough Sleeper*, both of which are concerned with the process of switching off from politics. *Rough Sleeper* remains up on my blog.

Political Shifts is fairly prescient, in describing the mainstream backlash against the cultural left that was to come, and also in hinting that the right was itself likely to go further off the deep end.

I remember an enjoyable coincidence when writing *Hallucinations*. The article contains a descriptive passage that refers to Pacman. I was reading Haruki Murakami's *Dance Dance Dance* around that time, and shortly after publishing Hallucinations, I came to a similar passage in the novel, referring to Pacman, and noted the similarity.

Why, exactly, I don't know, but it struck me as a good omen.

DRESS DOWN
AND SHUT UP

30th March 2019

Curiously, society is being propelled in two contradictory dir-
ections at the same time. On the one hand, we are compelled
to loosen up and let everyone just do whatever the hell they
want. But simultaneously, we are henpecked by uptight cultural authoritarians over the most minor of newly-confected,
sometimes barely comprehensible faux-pas.

We are being Googlized and Mary Whitehoused at the same
time. Take your shoes and socks off, but for God's sake watch
what you say.
So chill out, mate, no need to put on a suit. No need to dress
like an adult at all, slip into a pair of shorts and a Thundercats
T-shirt. Rock up on a Raleigh Grifter eating a packet of Space
Raiders. Doesn't matter, whatever.

Forget about capital letters and punctuation too, that's some
outdated, boomer shit. In fact, don't even bother with words,
we have emoji now.

Jesus, what do you want separate men's and women's toilets
for? What are you, alt-right? Just piss anywhere. Piss out the

window if you want. Transphobe.

Borders? Immigration checks? Passports? Are you canvassing for Ukip or something? Let's just go wherever we want. Everyone. All the time. And vote when you get there, like citizens of the world or something. Who even votes anyway?

Great, glad we agree. I mean, you did agree, didn't you? Because if you didn't, that might be problematic. Career threateningly so.
By the way, did you just say a word not to my liking? A pronoun, did you use a pronoun I haven't formally approved of? Use the one I demand, exactly as I say, and check every morning that I'm still using the same one.

And that hairstyle, change it. That's cultural appropriation and you're the wrong race. Get your hair cut exactly as I tell you.

And if you *are* going to vote then don't vote that way. You must vote the way you've been told. Vote the same as me. No, you can't have an independent country, you must be in the EU. Yes, you can have free speech, but you mustn't say any of these things on this list, they're prohibited because they spread intolerance.

Look, basically, we believe in progress and open-mindedness. To prove it here's an illustrated chart of things you must never do, say, or think, and please make sure to read this short booklet explaining your new opinions to you so you can express them correctly.

Get any of this wrong and there will be severe repercussions.

And now, let's all relax, shall we? We're very relaxed here.

HALLUCINATIONS

I don't know that there's much point following the news, current affairs, that kind of thing. You can skip it a bit, and it makes no difference. A day. A week. Doesn't affect you, doesn't affect anyone else. Actually, that's not true, it will affect you in that you'll start getting stuff done and enjoying the day to day a bit more.

Maybe this willingness to drop out (and consequentially back in, to the things that matter) is brought on by the fact that the discussion going on in the mainstream seems now to be, in significant part, conducted by aliens.

Seriously, it often means nothing to me. People with some degree of intelligence and a decent job are treating the most normal and familiar of opinions as if they've been issued by a visiting malevolent phantasm.

Look at this, from an interview in the Guardian with Bret Easton Ellis about his new non-fiction book, titled *White*.

> *"the book is a provocation – and it's up to you, the reader, to choose to what degree you are prepared to allow yourself to be riled."*

Oh wow, so what does he say that is so fucked up and incendiary?

> "It attacks what he regards as the narcissism of the young, roundly dismisses the rush to offence and the cult of victimisation, and chases down the self-dramatising of those liberal Americans who must be passed the smelling salts at the mere mention of Donald Trump. Although he thinks the #MeToo movement had real meaning when it began, Ellis dislikes the way it has since extended to include, most recently, such supposed crimes as what some might call the overfriendliness of the former US vice-president Joe Biden. He is largely dismissive of identity politics, and despises the way that people can now be "cancelled" (erased from public life) over some relatively small but dumb thing they may have said in the past."

Oh, so just some totally normal things that absolutely loads of people think. Things you might or might not agree with, but nothing that any reasonable person could possibly find riling or provocative. Or so you'd think.

Care for a drink?

Have whisky, a protein shake, anything that steers you away from the wretched nonsense being mercilessly slopped up by the media/academic shitehawk zombie set.

What can you do, rather than choke down their gruel?

Anything else, anything at all.

Is there any point in getting on your stupid social media account on your stupid phone that you stare at stupidly all the time abandoning all norms of politeness, interaction, and life in the present moment?

You can try yelling at people that they've gone weird, and might be in the grip of some form of mass hysteria or abused-becomes-abuser brainwashing cycle, but all they'll do is yell back, and then you'll be yelling at people and getting yelled at, and a day from now no-one will even know or care.

Even if you're famous: no-one cares. Even if you're famous for yelling at people, no-one will remember *what* you yelled, they'll just remember *that you yell*. And that you totally owned that theatre critic. Or was it a famous chef? Or a deeply earnest pop stunner turned cultural ghoul? Whatever. Some variety of freakish, Twitter-verified human commodity with a gruesome personality disorder. And you really got them good. Or maybe they got you. Or perhaps you just wrestled in the mud like pigs.

I guess it depends on which side you're rooting for. Or whether you're simply in it for the blood.

Which is not for a moment to suggest that this is all about tribalism. That would be too flattering a proposition. After all, tribes built things. Tribes went to war and made sacrifices. There is value in that which tribes eked out, established, and passed on.

This isn't tribalism, this is Pacman. But you can't play as Pacman. In fact, you can't even be a ghost.

You're a dot. You're getting eaten.

You're a piece of fruit at best, but don't bank on it, and you're still getting eaten.

You might not even be a dot, come to think of it, maybe you're the coin slot, or the bloke who empties the ashtrays. Maybe you're the ash.

Well, so, you see what I mean, maybe. You could bother with all this. With the news, and the people who tell you things about the news, and the people who tell you things about the people who tell you things about the news.

You could do all that, carry right on.

Or you could shut down the hallucination. Have a drink. Look out the window.

POLITICAL SHIFTS

21st June 2019

I'm feeling some movements in the aether, strange energies, my teeth are numb and the cat looked at me funny, so I had a look in the tea leaves to see what's on the way. Two lapsang souchongs and a fig roll down and I can tell you, the political sands are shifting like my bowels.

Have you noticed that intolerant leftist grip over everything? On politics, culture, comedy, whether or not it's acceptable to listen to Morrissey? Well, the patterns at the bottom of my china tell me that while that politically correct, new left orthodoxy is layered over everything, *it's paper thin*. So thin it might start to tear. So thin you can almost see through it, and there's something moving under there.

I had another cup and asked to see what was going on with the right-wing, and here's what was revealed: Despite being battered relentlessly in the 'culture wars', and caving and capitulating and conforming at every critical moment, the right—along with those who aren't quite on the right but certainly aren't on side with wokism—still keeps doing something of far greater significance than, for example, dictating what jokes it is and isn't acceptable to laugh at. Specifically: the right and its allies keep winning elections. Even now, with the woke left at its zenith, and with hardly a true conservative in sight (and those that there are subject to abuse and smears), still, the right can take majorities of votes.

And that's not all. The right tends to outwit new-left arguments online, while the left resorts to censorship. The right deals in what are regarded as common sense perceptions, while the new-left believes the world to be populated by genderless blank slates. And while the left unites behind a rainbow flag on a Budweiser cup, the right convenes behind the somewhat more commanding flag of the nation state itself.

The tea has run out, so I have a can of Fanta and cast Taiwanese divination blocks on my wooden floor.

There's something else about the state of the right, they tell me. Something very important: the right is currently harbouring an enormous sense of grievance.

Is the sense of grievance justified?

That doesn't matter. All that is of consequence is that it exists, and it's a driving, slow-burning, accumulating force.

And there's something else the right has too, something underpinning all of this: a numerical advantage.

A couple of weeks ago Naval Ravikant appeared on the Joe Rogan Experience, and during his interview said the following (attributing it as originally someone else's words, although he didn't say whose):

> "The left won the culture war and now they're just driving round picking off survivors."

It's a great line and a striking image, and at the time I thought it was accurate, but actually, I've changed my mind now. For a start, leftists can't drive or operate firearms, but there's more to it than that.

Rather than being dead or dying, the right has effectively been in hiding, or, in some pockets, in what resembles a mirthless, drugged state.

Zombified. Sleepwalking. Anonymous.

But present, nonetheless, and in numbers. And now that the new Maoist left's antics have reached such a provocative, puffed up, smug and intolerable pitch, it's starting to look like the right can't help but wake up and react. As in, not just a fringe, but with purpose. It's been a long time coming, but the drugs are wearing off and the fortress door creaks open.

We have movement!

The left is currently so emboldened and wrapped up in itself that not only are milkshakes thrown at right-wingers in the street, but this is then cheered on by mainstream commentators and—get this—fast food chains.

> *"Dear people of Scotland.*
> *We're selling milkshakes all weekend.*
> *Have fun.*
> *Love BK #justsaying" @BurgerKingUK*

And at the same time as leftists revel in the throwing of milkshake, indicating that they approve of this strategy, and so will presumably apply it further, they become indignant when a right-wing MP intervenes to prevent a trespassing activist from doing whatever it is trespassing activists do after marching through a room they don't have permission to enter.

[Tweet from Talk Radio, with a video clip of the incident: "Foreign office minister and Tory MP Mark Field has apologised for manhandling this climate change protester and escorting her from a dinner in London last night. Was he in the wrong?"]

There is an argument to be had over whether Mr Field used reasonable force, or was excessive, but on a more fundamental note, what do left-wing trespassers expect–to be waved through? Handed a dairy product to chuck around? Bought a pint?

I throw the divination blocks in the tea cup, shake the whole lot around, and perceive a final message.

The left hasn't been picking off survivors at all, it's been prodding people with sticks. And prodding them some more. And sharpening the sticks. And prodding. And following that up with some sharpening and prodding.

Noam Chomsky said this about left-wing aggression, in 2017, while criticising Antifa:

> *"When confrontation shifts to the arena of violence, it's the toughest and most brutal who win–and we know who that is."*

The right isn't about to embrace mindless violence, but the principle underlying Chomsky's words applies to current left-wing tactics in general. When a critical mass of non-leftists switches, and concludes they have had enough of what the left has been up to, and that there is nothing to lose, and that– *what the hell*–let's play by the left's rules, let's throw it all back at them, then there will be—for better or worse—enormous shifts.

For better, because the current situation, the left-wing cultural hegemony, is unsustainable, unhealthy, and stifling. Too many people have had as much of it as they can take. Too many people want to see the back of the liberal priesthood.

And for worse? Who knows exactly. But my horoscope this morning said that when a faction gets in the habit of playing dirty and aggressive, the habit can be difficult to break.
But the visions are fading now... reality aligns... that was some strong lapsang souchong.

ROUGH SLEEPER

22ⁿᵈ August 2019

Are you politically homeless?

Then breathe a sigh of relief, and be thankful.

If you feel regretful and lament that you have been rendered homeless, then snap out of it, quickly. You may have exiled yourself from your former camp because you didn't like the direction it had taken. Or perhaps they exiled you for not keeping up. You may take this as a sign that you are not a tribal person, and pat yourself on the back for your ability to walk away or be willingly cast out.

You're not one for blind loyalty, you tell yourself. You are an independent thinker. But if you tell yourself these things while declaring that you're *politically homeless*, then you're deluded, because to say that you are homeless indicates a sense of tribal loss. You feel that you *should* have a political home, and resent not being able to find one. You are a tribalist without a tribe, mistakenly taking the sense of isolation that reveals your tribalism as an indicator of a lack of tribalism.

The reality is that it would be very strange for a political faction to represent accurately your desires and drives. It would be misguided even to feel at all that politics, of all things, should offer any kind of a home or a shelter. That would be a sign of misplaced longing, and over-engagement in the news, and of looking for the wrong things, in the wrong places, for the wrong reasons.

If you do want to vote, or to participate in other party political ways, all you can do is select the group that comes closest to your current views, knowing that none will ever come close enough, and that in fact, even the closest may still be far away.

If none of the party options reflect a single thing that you believe in, or if all contain so much that you dislike that you can't stomach any of them, then you can simply choose the one that personally benefits you the most at this moment, or that benefits someone you care about, or that benefits a group or cause that you wish to help.

Or, you can sit this phase out, and come back later. This is likely the best option. You have given it your fullest thought and drawn a blank. Good news! Now go away and do something else. There will be more elections and more events, but there will be nothing new, because it's all been done before, just dressed up differently.

It never ends, and so it doesn't matter if you sit out one day or one decade or the rest of your life. Things will happen without you, just as they happened with you. The exact same things, either way. And if that's wrong, and things were different for your absence, well, so what? They might have turned out better, but then again, they might have turned out worse. You might, after all, be wrong about everything and have terrible judgment. You might be destined to sit out the next ten years for the good of all mankind.

What unfolds, unfolds, and whether or not you or anyone else runs through the motions of participation is just part of the unfolding.

And so *now*, you are politically homeless. Really, authentically politically homeless. And you can really, substantially enjoy it. You're a rough sleeper, far away from the machine-like din, but not unaware of its presence, softly audible but incomprehensible in the distant blackness.

And despite its constancy and its mass, the edifice has no pull on you. Being homeless, you have no attachments and remain in motion. If you choose to go with a particular group for now, you are not in any way bound to it, and you can choose again differently later.

You are free from commodification, and acquire flexibility and perspective, allowing you to move around the political landscape as you see fit, or to exit altogether if you'd prefer.

In fact, it becomes clear: you never had a home in the first place, and you never will.

CHALLENGING MAINSTREAM REPORTING

2ⁿᵈ September 2019

I have grave doubts about social media, and Twitter in particular. The idea that it can trap people in bubbles, leading to feedback loops, extremism, and the othering of those with whom one disagrees, seems to be playing out. It might be rewiring people I previously thought were balanced and worth paying attention to. Entertainers, authors, musicians, all seem to be particularly susceptible. Some of them appear to have been driven mad. Some give the impression that they aggressively hate the majority of the people in their own country.

And it's addictive. Twitter is bad news, I thought, as I sat staring at Twitter.

However, a couple of conversations I had recently (in real life, not online) with people who are not obsessive about politics, led me to partially reconsider. This is purely anecdotal, but to summarize:

The first person I spoke to follows the news by relying on what is still referred to as the liberal media. That is, outlets such as the Guardian, the BBC, and CNN. Organisations that are mainstream and on the left. He doesn't use social media to follow news or politics, and in his eyes, Brexit is simply a very bad thing. Trump is a barely concealed dictator. Climate change will end the world. You know how it is. The package.

The second person I spoke to dislikes Trump, but doesn't for a second believe him to be a dictator. She has no position on Brexit, but is aware of the arguments on both sides, and thinks it will likely work out fine. She's not currently going into prepper mode in anticipation of a Koch-funded carbon apocalypse (although to be fair, neither are the climate fretters, whose dread about the end of civilisation isn't quite severe enough for them to actually alter their lifestyles).

And the other, crucial, difference between my two interlocutors? While the second one reads the same mainstream liberal media as the first, she also then goes on Twitter and reads the reactions and replies to the stories that the mainstream liberal media is constantly pumping out.

And when she does so, she finds rebuttals, and reasoned disagreement. She finds that the liberal media is selective in its reporting. That it runs with this but not that, because this is convenient but that isn't. She finds all its flaws and biases being exposed, every day, by pesky anonymous accounts who very often happen to have background knowledge, time on their hands, and an intense dislike of misleading journalism.

Twitter provides instant pushback against suspect reporting.

It might well spread fake news from disreputable alternative sources, but it also flags up misleading stories from the supposedly respectable mainstream sources. And it does this every day, all the time, because the misleading stories just keep on coming, while the curmudgeons in the replies—sticklers for detail, contrary, never doing as they've been told—aren't budging an inch.

So I'm torn. As I've written elsewhere, there is much about Twitter that is damaging and unpleasant. But, on the other hand, it's currently providing the opportunity for an unprecedented challenge to the top-down, narrative-controlling authority of the mainstream media. Whether on the left or the right, journalists, ideology-hawking celebs, and politicians themselves, simply cannot get away with being dishonest or badly informed.

Or rather, they can, but only as long as no-one goes on Twitter and checks the replies. And my sense is that a growing number of people are realising that if you don't go online and look for the voices answering back, if you don't listen to the dissenters, then you aren't really hearing the news at all.

Towards the end of my time as a Guardian reader, I barely even bothered with the articles anymore, and would simply skip down to reader comments, where I was sure that some more balanced, rounded, and propaganda-free views could be found. The Guardian isn't so keen on comment sections anymore, and I doubt if they're that keen on Twitter either.

But they can't moderate Twitter. They can't close social media.

Out there online, where everything is disseminated, they're

not in control.

JEREMY CORBYN'S SHAMEFUL LABOUR PARTY

26 September 2019

You have to hand it to the Labour Party under Jeremy Corbyn, they are utterly unfazed by things like public opinion, winning general elections, or even, for that matter, holding general elections.

Certainly, it struck many as odd that they chose to prevent Boris Johnson from going to the polls in October, making Corbyn—who had been demanding an election since he lost out at the last one—the first ever opposition leader to have blocked a general election.

But then, as the Beastie Boys once asserted, "don't play no game that I can't win", and when you look at what Labour have revealed about themselves at this year's party conference, their decision not to allow a nationwide test of their suitability for government seems sage-like in its wisdom.

One stand-out from their crackpot meet-up, besides the now

requisite Palestinian flags?

A cosy old socialist punt: let's sacrifice to a faulty ideology most of the country's best schools and ensure that the state has close control of your children's edu-indoctrination.

Perhaps indoctrination is a strong word to use, but I can't help noticing that even as conservative fears about brainwashing in the classroom are dismissed as paranoia, we then watch children being given a day off school to march the streets with climate activists who include in their movement explicit socialist messaging.

Back to the party conference, though. In summary, Labour want to abolish private schools, absorbing all such existing institutions into the state schooling system. A move which includes, in a sassy despotic flourish, the government taking possession of and redistributing the seized schools' assets.

It takes a special sort of mind to look at a system with two components, and conclude that one thing works better than the other, so let's get rid of the one that works better and there you go, equality. It takes a leftist mind, specifically. The same kind of mind that is at ease with the state appropriating private property on a whim.

When I read about this policy belch, I was reminded of Peter Cook in character as potential England football manager, Alan Latchley, in a 1993 interview with Clive Anderson. Expounding on the strategic workings of his time at Manchester City, he explains how he dealt with discrepancies in the aptitude levels of his players, through his concept of "equal playing facilities":

"...if you had skillful people on your team, that was no excuse for them playing better than the others... my tactic was to get them all down to exactly the same level."

Finally, as an added un-populist bonus, what's the latest Labour message on Brexit? As in, how do they view that thing that the majority of voters opted for three years ago, which happens to be the biggest mandate in British political history, and is, as it goes, supported by huge numbers in the traditional Labour heartlands?

Well, in addition to wanting to negotiate an exit deal they would then campaign against after having cancelled the valid existing referendum in order to force an anti-democratic second one... in addition to that... to some in the Labour Party, Brexit is, inevitably,—like seemingly everything else this current incarnation of the left opposes— "a far-right project" *[quote from a Labour Party conference delegate]*.

What a way to speak to the country.

THE SIXTH-FORM REMAINER LEFT

9th October 2019

British politics, a place of stirring oratory, robust cut and thrust, and an effectively adversarial tradition, between politicians, parties, and the public they serve.

Or at least, that was British politics until about five minutes ago.

Suddenly though, the political arena is highly strung and in a state of permanent, gasping outrage. Anything that comes out of a Tory or a Brexiteer's mouth is at risk of being branded beyond the pale, or likely to incite violence, or a coded message to some orc-like, racist fringe, lurking in the shadows, enamoured with Priti Patel.

And anyone who has a full-bodied pop at the political class is a thug, and should be kept a close eye on, but that's if, and only if, they're positioned right-of-centre.

So, as was well rinsed on Twitter, when Boris Johnson said humbug, it was cause to fall over in shock. He had said it in response to the suggestion that his language stirs up trouble, and reference was made by his accuser to the late Jo Cox, but, with all due respect, what difference does that make? Is the man not allowed to disagree? Can he not refuse to go along with, in this case, a false and opportunistic suggestion? Or does the mere mention of the name Jo Cox mean that the listener must nod and acquiesce, even as a defamatory accusation is hurled in their direction?

I don't think it would be fair to demand such obedience, and I think of all the possible ways to reject the premise being advanced, humbug is second only to poppycock in its mildness.

Let's not forget, also, that the initial language that led to Boris being barracked was surrender, as in, his calling the Benn Act a Surrender Act. I mean, come on. If you can't cope with the word surrender then it's this simple: get out of politics.

This then leads to Priti Patel's speech at the Tory Party Conference, in which she used the phrase 'North London metropolitan elite'. Now, I don't know precisely the areas of London in which the metropolitan elite live, but I suspect the north is a heartland, and if not, then the stereotype is strong enough that we all know what she's talking about: the holier-than-though, politically correct, prole-hating Guardian readers who have been forcefully weeping and demanding an end to democracy ever since the tail-end of June, 2016.

But the metropolitan elite doesn't like people criticising the metroplitan elite, and so on Twitter they ruled with a bewildering level of self-righteous pomposity that Patel's words were, in fact, an antisemitic dogwhistle.

Yes, this is the same Priti Patel who was famously in trouble for having secret meetings with Israeli government officials. That is, the same Priti Patel the hard-left hate for being too close to Israel. The same Priti Patel who has never, in her entire career, done a single thing to suggest even the slightest hint of antisemitism or any other kind of racism.

In fact, due to her own race, her career success would, were she on the left, be hailed as a victory for diversity. Conservatives tend not to do this, preferring to concentrate on character and policy. I personally think focusing in on someone's race, sex, or sexuality is crass and small-minded. But the point is that the left would behave that way, were it not for the fact that Patel disagrees with them, leading them instead to actually smear her as a racist, for the crime of... no, come to think of it, for no crime at all. For absolutely nothing.

And that's the great thing about labelling something a dog-whistle. You can take whatever you like and claim that it's a coded message, and your accusation, no matter how absurd, is unfalsifiable. In fact, denying that it's a coded message is exactly what someone defending a coded message would do, so, checkmate, whistlers.

Passing mention must also go to the story of Nigel Farage being reported to the police and bawled about on Twitter, for using the phrase, "take the knife to" with relation to Whitehall bureaucrats. Do we really need to explain that he's using a figure of speech? Is that the level at which we're now operating?

This war on metaphor, and on recognisable ways of describing intolerant London 'liberals', and on Boris Johnson having a personality, is becoming tiresome.

It's as if the entire left wing has degenerated into the most obnoxious and irritating sixth form socialist you can imagine. And this regression is affecting very mainstream, relatively famous voices, who like to domineer Twitter and soak up the adulation of their weak-minded flunkies.

The resulting clown show is increasingly off-putting for those who have an interest in politics, but now have to wade through so much pointless sludge, while having fascist yelled at them by some millionaire light entertainer in his fifties, due to having done the unthinkable and voiced dissent.

Something else struck me when I looked at another story. It was about Lady Hale, she of the Supreme Court's deeply controversial decision to rule unlawful Boris Johnson's prorogation of Parliament. In direct reference to Boris' recent jibe at David Cameron, when he called the former prime minister a 'girly swot', Hale, speaking to the Association of State Girls' Schools, reflected that she herself had once been a girly swot, used the phrase, "let's hear it for the girly swots", and stood in front of an image of herself on which was the quoted headline, "Spider woman takes down Hulk: viewers transfixed by judge's brooch as ruling crushes PM". This is a triumphant description of the Supreme Court decision, referencing a spider brooch Lady Hale wore, and a line referring to The Incredible Hulk that Boris Johnson had used.

As absurd as some of the details in that passage might sound, Hale's performance points to what Brexit supporters have strongly suspected to be the case all along: political prejudice at the highest level, and attempts at an establishment stitch-up.

As I read about this, I could still remember that the natural left-wing response to such events would once have been justified indignation, and a robust challenge to institutional power and its misuse.

But that is no longer the case.

Nowadays, if you express your contempt for this new aristocratic class—not the elite, but an elite—lording it over you and messing about with your vote, then the left will have you escorted from the premises, while an MP sobs aggressively in your direction.

What's happened is that the left quite like elitism now. They like their elite, at any rate, but whatever you do, you mustn't mention the existence of such an elite. These sixth form aristocrats don't like that at all.

PATTERNS OF AUTHORITY

15th October 2019

I look at the so-called culture wars, and the political polarizations taking place around the world, and in the end they boil down to a single issue: authoritarianism.

On Twitter, I click on a clip from ITV's Good Morning Britain. The host, bullish and belligerent Piers Morgan, is asserting his right not to believe that there are one hundred genders. His opponent, journalist and commentator, Benjamin Butterworth, suggests that Morgan must comply. Things take a turn to the absurd (which is good, absurdity is the great revealer) when Morgan asserts that the new rules are one-sided, as Butterworth won't respect his identification as a "two-spirit penguin". Butterworth counters, naturally, "being a penguin isn't a gender, that's not on the gender spectrum".

This seems remiss. To create ninety-eight new genders and yet no penguins? In that case, why not make one more, and keep Piers happy?

Butterworth throws out a mini-tale about growing up gay, but the discussion isn't about being gay, it's about transgender beliefs, and the right to dissent. This is how some people operate, though: falsely conflating issues, and appealing to emotion. After all, you're not homophobic, and you support gay rights, so how come you don't think there are one hundred genders, and no penguins.

Ultimately, Morgan is correct when he claims to be resisting "control freakery". Of course there aren't a hundred genders. Why would it be such a round number, for a start? And there's no such thing as a gender spectrum, either. There are feminine men, and masculine women, and there are men who live as though they're women, and vice versa, but none of this is anything new, and it doesn't require that we suddenly change our language, and allow men to claim medals in women's sports, or record male criminals as female, or stop saying 'ladies and gentlemen', or fire Piers Morgan, as is the most recent demand.

The claims and demands being made by the trans movement sound supernatural, and have the tone and character of religious fundamentalism. Gender identity is invisible, nebulous, and cannot be falsified. If you're a man whose gender suddenly shifts, on your word only, to somewhere between male and female, then you must immediately be given access to women's facilities, and be addressed as a woman, but only until it shifts back, and actual women who don't much like this will be bullied and silenced.

And this absolutely must be confirmed and acquiesced to by anyone of whom the demand is made. Do you believe this person is both/neither male and/or female? Only one answer is permitted. Do you believe in the existence of x number of genders? Only one answer is permitted. Do you think there are only two sexes, male and female, and that the ordering of society around this biological reality works and should be protected?

You're fired.

The trans movement may as well be demanding sackings of people who don't believe in ghosts, or seances, or Bigfoot. In another era they would be part of a religious inquisition, collaring heretics, or they'd be ducking witches, or sniffing round Hollywood, smoking out Marxists.

What's the common thread? Authority and control.

It happens now to be left-wing, but that's nothing new. It's corporate-backed, but corporations have never had ethics, they just play dress-up with the signifiers of what are currently paraded as ethics, as fashion and margins demand. And it's adorned in rainbow flags, but what does that matter? The colours might change, but the mindset is the same. This instinct runs deep.

And all the while, imposing just around the curve of the Earth, there is China. Beating protesters in Hong Kong. Setting up networks of total surveillance, and social credit schemes. Demanding that the world not recognize Taiwan as an independent state. Detaining and abusing Uighur Muslims. Repressing freedoms in Tibet.

And on top of all that: eliciting compliance from US corporations, and from the National Basketball Association and its players.

On the one hand, the NBA, in 2017, pulled a game from being played in North Carolina due to what it regarded as transphobic bathroom laws. A stand for social justice. But now, NBA players are publicly apologizing because a tweet had been sent by a team's general manager expressing support for the Hong Kong protesters. You know, the protesters sometimes seen waving British and American flags, and opposed to authoritarian rule. So that's the NBA now taking, what, a stand against liberty?

At first glance these appear to be strangely contradictory positions, but easily explained: money. China pays, so get in line. Supporting transgender demands may or may not pay—there are a great number of fans who don't want sport to become a political vehicle—but it certainly follows a current trend, and so might seem financially safe.

But then, even putting the profit-motive to one side, perhaps there is no contradiction. China clearly has a viciously authoritarian ruling class, and the demands made by social justice activists are of an authoritarian nature: there are the rules set down by the transgender movement, as flaunted by Piers Morgan, and there is, in general, an attitude of opposition to free speech, and an embrace of censorship, in the name of safety and combating hateful attitudes. (Who defines what is hateful? Not you.)

Perhaps it's not so much of a stretch to imagine that someone of an authoritarian nature could make themselves comfortable with both social justice and the Chinese regime. Particularly when it pays enough to remove you completely from the demands of a regular life.

And this isn't a one-off. You can find recent high profile cases of similar pandering and obedience to the Chinese government from the likes of Marriott International and Activision Blizzard.

Apple has just partially dropped the Taiwanese flag emoji, hiding it from users in Hong Kong and Macau. The corporation previously removed Hong Kong singers who are pro-democracy activists from its Apple Music China service.

That's the same Apple whose CEO, Tim Cook, said last December, while talking about banning people from its platforms:

"I believe the most sacred thing that each of us is given is our judgment, our morality, our own innate desire to separate right from wrong... Choosing to set that responsibility aside at a moment of trial is a sin."

And in Europe? Well, the French authorities have been assaulting gilets jaunes protesters every weekend since last November, and in Spain, nine Catalan independence leaders have just been jailed for sedition.

Such authoritarian instincts may not seem immediately to overlap, but they all feed into, legitimize, and strengthen one another. They operate on multiple levels, the micro and the macro, and everything in between.

On a micro level, it is demanded that an individual, in violation of their conscience and all that they know to be true, refer to a male athlete as 'she', and clap in celebration as that man beats his female opponents in a women's athletics event.

On a macro level, China monitors and controls the behaviour of its citizens.

Somewhere in the middle, you buy an iPhone from which Apple has removed the Taiwanese flag, and read about a famous basketball player who is vocal about social justice activism while distancing himself from criticism of the Chinese regime.

And at the same time, something else happens, something odd. There are large-scale, successful movements which, while too broad to be categorized as only one thing, most definitely contain factions who are opposed to bureaucratic control. But these movements—coherent, recognizable reactions against authoritarianism—are written off by some sections of the commentariat as being themselves authoritarian.

Delve into Brexit chatter, not in the mainstream media, but in the blogosphere and on Twitter, and you'll find it permeated by classical liberals, who regard the EU as an overbearing and illiberal organ of centralized, top-down control.

Investigate what makes Trump supporters tick, and you'll uncover all manner of beliefs, some good, some bad, most of them buried by liberal media, and covering a broad spectrum of ideologies. But I guarantee that you'll come across a great many strongly spoken libertarians, and ardent defenders of the American constitution. They are advocates of freedom, in its most robust, arms-bearing sense.

Look at footage of the gilets jaunes protests in France, and you'll see French citizens being savagely beaten by armoured and masked agents of the French state. You can bet that if this was happening under a Marine Le Pen government, there would be daily media uproar about fascism expanding. But as it's happening under Guardian-friendly EU-phile Emmanuel Macron's administration, it barely warrants any media coverage at all, and if you do see any liberal commentary, it's likely to cast the gilets jaunes themselves—the ones on the ground being truncheoned bloody—as a suspiciously populist rabble.

Through a particular kind of media lens, the world gets flipped upside down.

And what can be done about all this?

Take a step back and observe. Take note of what's happening. Be aware of authoritarianism in all its forms, on every layer and level, and of the ways in which they feed one another. Notice how closely each resembles the other, how their forms and structures are similar, no matter on what scale they manifest.

And from that, identify when something is labelled as authoritarian, but actually has a completely different form to the events you know to be authoritarian. Notice then who is doing that inaccurate labelling, and ask why they do so. Is it just a mistake, or is it intentional? Be charitable. Don't assume the worst.

And above all, I think, act on a personal scale. That is, individually choose a non-authoritarian path, and live accordingly, because the micro is the macro, and the macro is the micro.

As within, so without.

DONE THE
RIGHT THING

Britain just dodged a bullet.

What did Jeremy Corbyn and his closest allies represent at the polls?
Marxism, authoritarian leanings, expansion of the state, economic vandalism, a history of support for terrorists, military incompetence, the undermining of domestic security, national self-hatred, extreme and divisive identity politics, dragging out Brexit indefinitely, with all the instability and conflict that would prolong, mob politics, spite, hatred, abuse, and, perhaps most shamefully of all, antisemitism.

Enter the working class, who, seeing what was at stake, seeing an open threat to Britain's Jewish community, and to the country as a whole, and to the Brexit vote too, set aside tribal considerations and did the only thing that could avert the catastrophe of allowing a racist movement to govern, lending their support to the Conservative Party.

And so I don't think it's an exaggeration to say that the working class, in the face of constant wrong-headed condescension from arrogant celebrities and biased commentators telling them not to vote Tory, just saved Britain by not voting Labour.

Or rather, by not voting for the party that calls itself Labour, but is in fact a hijacked vehicle.

To do the right thing is admirable. To do the right thing, while going against enormous pressure to do the wrong thing, and weathering abuse and insults for your efforts, is magnificent. And to steer a country from the brink of disaster, through pillory and defamation, is noble.

And so there it was, when the results came in. That sense of relief. Of tranquility after the storm, for a while at least. No route to Remain remaining, and a stable, Conservative government.

And as for the Corbynites? They're still there, on Twitter, screeching and railing, and calling the entire country racist, and here's the thing, the wonderful thing: *it doesn't matter.* Nothing they say is of any consequence anymore, it's just noise. Juvenile, temper tantrum noise. You can ignore it, or you can watch the spectacle, if you like. Try to identify the personality disorders. It's funny, and disturbed, and ridiculous. And one thing is for sure: if someone's response to not being elected is to become very angry with the electorate– *with you*–for not electing them, then you can be absolutely certain that your judgement was sound.

> *"I hate the public so much. If only they'd elect me, I'd make 'em pay."*
> Homer Simpson

But even as you tune them out, don't forget who they are, the cheerleaders for this hard-left sewer that has toxified British politics. Don't forget Owen Jones, Ash Sarkar, Aaron Bastani, and the rest of them, covering for extremism and intimidation.

[Tweet from Israel Advocacy Movement, with an accompanying video: *"Watch in horror as a group of anti-racist Jewish activists are subject to a torrent of antisemitic abuse at Jeremy Corbyn's closing party. A kinder, gentler politics. #NeverCorbyn"*]

[Tweet from Conservative Party member and school governor Charlotte Salomon, containing screenshots of extremely gratuitous verbal abuse directed at her from Labour supporters.]

Don't ever forget that Guardian editorial. The one that, with these shameful lines, "The pain and hurt within the Jewish community, and the damage to Labour, are undeniable and shaming. Yet Labour remains indispensable to progressive politics", explicitly urged its readers to vote for an antisemitic party, because, well, because what? The ends justify the means? Is that how they operate? Is that what that word, 'progressive', now conveys?

I don't even want to know. It's too dark to contemplate, but when I read that passage, it felt like something–liberalism, or the progressive left, or perhaps just Corbynism and the Guardian itself–had died.

For all that though, I'm strangely glad to have witnessed the takeover of the Labour Party and its subsequent descent. It did us the favour of dragging left-wing racism and terror-support into the full light of day, and clarified that there is a poisonous channel running through the far-left that's every bit as dangerous as that which can be found on the far-right.

Those who supported Corbyn have to learn from this, as starkly as society as a whole has learned how to quarantine and repel right-wing extremism.

And there are lessons for the media too. It has become over-run with people who *feel* rather than those who *think*.

"BBC reporter: "How did you feel voting Conservative for the first time?"
Man from the North East: "I didn't feel anything. I thought it was the right thing to do."
This man's marvellous statement is the antithesis of the BBC's political coverage." Ben Irvine

There is, of course, a place for those who operate primarily according to their feelings. We're simply talking about different personality types. But when there are *only* those types of personalities, then you will run into trouble, as would be the case if you had nothing but those who shun emotion in favour of logic. This shouldn't really need explaining, but here we are. You need both in order to follow the centre path.

And therein is another problem: What's the point in a commentary class who don't fully understand what they're commenting on, because they're a part of what needs commenting on? I don't know the solution to that one, other than what seems a little too obvious: expand out of the bubble, and ensure diversity of opinion and thought.

Britain can do better now. Politics can re-calibrate. The media can steer away from partisanship and what looks like activism over journalism. And I'd hazard that many people have had enough, in all areas of society, of having every decision and discussion steered according to vague feelings and identity politics, while those who by their nature don't operate according to such drives are sidelined or vilified, despite being, it would appear, in the majority and with much to offer.

There has been a perfect storm, taking in Brexit, the refusal by influential Remainers to honour the result, identity politics spun out of control, and the hard left takeover of the Labour Party, that escalated Britain to a cultural breaking point.

Now, perhaps, the country is out the other side and ready to move forward afresh.

It feels like a time to discard labels. Suddenly, Leaver and Remainer are outdated and pointless. Left vs right doesn't adequately describe the position in which many voters now find themselves, with so many former Labour communities having lent their support to the Tories. Identity political categories feel regressive and narrow-minded.
But in the end, I like this lack of meaningful categories. After all, who wants to be boxed in?

I've argued before that tribalism is restrictive and unfulfilling, and this election has seen the mass removal of political loyalties in order to forcefully reject one of the worst tribes Britain has seen for some time.

Maybe now it would be for the best to simply forget the old labels, respect the democratic process that has always served Britain so well, and move forward with a much missed sense of composure.

OUTRO

Well then, did it happen? The composure, the calm, the new era? The rejection of tribalism, and the abandoning of labels?

Haha. Yeah right.

It was inevitable, once Brexit was done—once Britain had officially left the EU, anyway, although negotiations roll on quietly at the time of writing—that those who supported it would revert back to their long-standing political tribes, or at least reject any new ones into which we had temporarily become assimilated (or even helped to create).

Brexiteer was a temporary alliance only. *Woke* and *anti-woke* are two sides of the same coin. Perhaps we all learned something from one another, and perhaps we didn't.

Perhaps I don't care either way, and I hope you feel the same.

But I'm glad for all I have seen. Most valuable of all, I'm glad to have learned not to care.

Thanks for your support, and thank you for reading.

What a ride.

ABOUT THE AUTHOR

Sam White

Sam is a writer and photographer from the UK, currently resident in Japan. More of his work can be found by visiting www.upallnight.tokyo.

Printed in Great Britain
by Amazon